YARDENING

OTHER BOOKS BY JEFF AND LIZ BALL

The Flower Garden Problem Solver

The Landscape Problem Solver

The Garden Problem Solver

Jeff Ball's 60-Minute Flower Garden

The Self-Sufficient Suburban Garden

The 60-Minute Vegetable Garden

YARDENING

Jeff and Liz Ball

Macmillan Publishing Company · New York   Maxwell Macmillan Canada · Toronto
Maxwell Macmillan International · New York · Oxford · Singapore · Sydney

Macmillan Publishing Company
866 Third Avenue
New York, NY 10022

Maxwell Macmillan Canada, Inc.
1200 Eglinton Avenue East
Suite 200
Don Mills, Ontario, M3C 3N1

Macmillan Publishing Company is part of the Maxwell Communication Group of Companies.

Library of Congress Cataloging-in-Publication Data

Ball, Jeff.
Yardening / by Jeff and Liz Ball.
p. cm.
Includes index.
ISBN 0-02-506431-2
1. Gardening. 2. Organic gardening. I. Ball, Liz. II. Title.
SB453.B335 1991
635—dc20   91-17002
CIP

Book design by Jennifer Dossin.

10 9 8 7 6 5 4 3 2

Printed in the United States of America

This book is dedicated to Edward C. Ball, who has contributed to it in many important ways.

Acknowledgments

A book such as this represents the coming together of hundreds of informal conversations, experiences, and events. It is the culmination of years of listening and learning. It is not so long ago that we were yardeners ourselves, struggling with yard care, attempting to grow some flowers and vegetables and searching the garden center for the proper supplies and equipment. We are enormously grateful to all our new friends in horticulture who have helped us make the transition from yardeners to gardeners over the last ten years. We are also in debt to our garden-writing colleagues whose books and articles provided references, and our editors and publishers over the years who have helped us become effective communicators.

For this book we are particularly indebted to Pam Hoenig at Macmillan for her gentle guidance and to Bob Scanzaroli for keeping our garden going while we sat in front of computers all summer. Our special thanks, too, go to our friends Joan, Tina, our neighbor across the street, and all the other yardeners in our lives whose questions and concerns helped us to understand what yardeners want and need to know these days. We are very grateful to Michell Muldoon for her wonderful line drawings.

Finally, we want to thank Jeff's dad, Ed Ball, for being there for us. His helping hand and advice were invaluable. Whether testing shredders and lawn mowers, keeping the wood stove going, or installing irrigation timers, he has been a constant support for us in our work.

Contents

Introducing Yardening to America

This book is written for people who own plants but do not consider themselves gardeners or regard gardening as one of their hobbies. These folks still do a fair amount of yard care and are concerned about the plants on their property, so we call them "yardeners." We have written this book expressly for the yardener.

There are over 30 million American homeowners who fall into this category. Yardeners willingly care for their lawns, trees, and shrubs because they are part of the landscape around their home and enhance its appearance and value. They often have some flowers around the yard and possibly a couple of tomato plants out back, just because they appreciate the taste of fresh vegetables. However, they are not "into" gardening. And for that reason they are not interested in consulting gardening books and other traditional sources of information about gardening, even though they feel the need for information about taking care of plants and how to use the products and equipment they see in the garden center. Environmentally aware, they are alert to the problems in water, soil, and air quality in this country. Yardeners want to know how to make wise, safe choices and how to perform yard tasks efficiently so that they can spend their leisure time on the activities they prefer. This is what this book provides. It is a yardening book, not a gardening book.

Yardeners are not indifferent to plants—they care a lot about how their property looks. Yardeners have high standards when it comes to taking care of their property, whether they do the work themselves or hire it done. They are not simply lazy gardeners. Consequently, the yardening information in this book is not about shortcuts and lower standards. It is about efficiency, pragmatism, and simplicity. It recognizes that yardeners have goals different from those of gardeners. Yard care for them is a means to an end, not an end in itself.

Design of the landscape. Both the yardener and the gardener want attractive landscapes. While gardeners may choose to develop fairly elaborate landscapes featuring a diversity of plants and complexity of design that requires more maintenance, yardeners are more likely to have fairly traditional landscapes. Theirs are also aesthetically pleasing, but they revolve around convenience, not plants. They are less complex and so require less maintenance.

Plant selection. Both the yardener and the gardener want their plants to be healthy and to look attractive. While gardeners will more likely choose plants that are a challenge to grow and are willing to devote the time to their culture, yardeners value reliable plants that are attractive and easy to care for.

Health and quality of plants. Both the yardener and the gardener want all the plants on their property to be healthy and to live as long as possible. While gardeners want the biggest or most unusual zinnias with the brightest colors, the yardener is happy with some colorful zinnias at the corner of the house. While the gardener tries to achieve a lawn with the densest turf and the most brilliant greens, the yardener wants the lawn to be green and healthy, but a few weeds are okay as long as they don't detract from its appearance from the street. The gardener will be more likely to use more complex fertilizing, watering, pruning, and general maintenance techniques to get the very maximum performance from each plant in the landscape, whereas yardeners are satisfied with more general maintenance techniques as long as they extract satisfactory performance from the grass, trees, shrubs, and flowers in the yard.

Time. Gardeners get so much pleasure and joy from being out in the yard and fooling around with plants that time is not a major concern for them. Taking care of plants is fun, no matter how long it takes or how much effort and sweat it requires. Yardeners want to do a good job with their plants too, but they want to do it in as short a period of time as is feasible. For them, taking care of the yard is basically work, while playing golf or taking the kids to the zoo is fun.

YARDENING—THE WHOLISTIC VIEW

Consequently, yardeners look at landscape care from a different frame of reference than gardeners do. Where gardeners tend to see their landscapes as the sum of their collections of individual plants, artistically arranged, yardeners tend to perceive their landscapes as "yards," single entities. From conversations with friends, neighbors, and colleagues from our former lives and from letters we've received from people who've seen us on television, we know that yardeners need a book that speaks to their concerns for the yard in general. So we are writing this book specifically to address the yardener's perspective on yard care. It offers straightforward, practical, current information and advice on maintaining the yard as a whole. By design it presents the research, the insights, and the experience gleaned from the horticultural community tailored for the use of the average nongardening homeowner.

Because many gardeners are also yardeners, they will find this book useful as well. It is not an uncommon phenomenon that people who are dedicated rosarians or obsessive vegetable gardeners may share the attitudes of yardeners toward the rest of the yard. They keep the lawn mowed and think about pruning the shrubs, but their enthusiasm for these activities does not match their interest in roses or vegetables. In fact, the rose gardener may know no more than a yardening neighbor about bagworms in the cedar trees and how to deal with them.

Basic encyclopedia-type gardening books routinely categorize information on plant care into familiar topics, such as lawns, trees, shrubs, flowers, and vegetables. You will notice that, of logical necessity, this book is divided in just about the same fashion. However, there is a significant difference. This book takes a wholistic approach to these individual topics, discussing them as part of the total system that is the yard. Even though they are covered in separate chapters, we see lawns, trees, pests, and flowers as integrated into a whole. Our recommendations on fertilizing, watering, treating pest problems, and protecting plants are based on this integrated approach. Gardening books usually give specialized fertilizing schedules, one for lawns, another for

flowers, and yet a third for the vegetables. This kind of information does not serve busy homeowners who are not gardeners. In this book, you will find help with the big picture. There is advice for overall care of the yard and the plants in it.

Two of the seven chapters deal with special plant groups, flowers and vegetables, that many yardeners are not interested in. Other special topics, such as pest control and landscape ideas, may also be of limited interest to many readers. Because we expect that readers will skip certain chapters, we repeat some of the basic information so that it is available to all readers. Our main thesis is that the basic principles of caring for a yard are the same, whether it is lawn grass, trees, flowers, or vegetables that are the beneficiaries. In part or as a whole, it is hoped that this book will serve as an informative guide to yardeners who want nice yards with healthy attractive plants, with a minimum investment of time and energy.

This is not a plant book. Its main focus is on yard care concepts and techniques, not individual plants. However, we have included in it lists of plants to accompany these discussions to serve as examples and resources for readers who wish to purchase plants. These lists are not by any means comprehensive. They cite only the most common, familiar, or dependable plant species for the issue under discussion. Also, for the most part, they represent plants that are suited for northern regions of the country. Southern and western homeowners are well aware that they live in climates that require specialized information, which we hope to provide in a subsequent book designed for these regions.

Although, understandably, yardeners have little interest in or mastery of the Latin names that gardeners use, we have provided them for all of the listed plants except the vegetables to assure that there is no confusion about specific recommended trees, shrubs, or flowers. Often the same common name is given to several different plants, so it is difficult to be sure that the one listed in the catalog or offered at the garden center is, in fact, the one listed if its formal Latin name is not used. There is no need to worry about pronouncing the words; just show them to your landscaper or nurseryman.

For those yardeners who are interested in taking the next step beyond the general scope of this book and delving into the care of individual plants, we have provided a catalog of plant-care tip sheets at the back of this volume. We have written these four- to six-page information sheets for homeowners who are considering the purchase of a particular plant and would like to know more about it or who would like to assemble a book on the care of the existing plants on their property. These tip sheets are written especially for nongardeners. They provide specific information on individual plants and, collected in a looseleaf binder, represent a customized plant book that makes an ideal companion to this general volume.

CHAPTER 1

LAWN CARE

Lawns are a luxury. Historically, having one's own plot of grass rather than sharing a common "green" with the neighbors symbolized certain economic and social status in the community. Even today, a lovely green lawn automatically enhances the value of a home. Of course, most modern homeowners do not have servants to care for this labor-intensive landscape feature, so we undertake the maintenance ourselves. Lawn care has become virtually a national pastime in the regions of the country where lawn grass grows.

Now that we are doing all the work, we have discovered that we want lawns that need very little fertilizer, need little or no water, need mowing only once every two weeks or so, have no noticeable weeds, and look nice all year round. In addition, while we are wishing, many of us also want assurance that the lawn-care products we use are ecologically safe—for us, for our kids and pets, and for the environment in general. Does this sound like an impossible dream? Well, it's not. Right now it is possible to approach this level of convenience and safety in lawn care in many parts of our country. By combining modern lawn-care practices with new advanced products, homeowners can enjoy the luxury of a lawn that virtually takes care of itself.

Ironically, most of our present lawn-care practices are totally counterproductive to healthy, low-maintenance lawns. We fertilize much too much, we mow too closely, we frequently overwater, we seldom aerate, and we generally use a variety of grass seed inappropriate for a low-maintenance lawn. All these factors contribute to lawns that require enormous amounts of time and money for upkeep, yet never look quite as good as we expect them to. It is time to turn this situation around. With a little work, and a year or two of patience, it is possible to thoroughly renovate a lawn, building a new low-maintenance lawn from the soil up.

More than likely, you have a lawn now and

you would prefer not to start all over again from scratch. For that reason this chapter outlines the steps to take to improve the quality of your existing lawn, reduce the cost of its maintenance, and cut the amount of time it will take to care for it. First, we describe how to revitalize the soil in which your grass grows, a fundamental step. Next we suggest some changes in the type of grass you are growing. Once these steps are taken, the condition of your lawn will improve dramatically. Then we recommend routine care practices that will assure its vigor and beauty over the seasons. Finally, we offer some tips on solving the occasional problems that all lawns experience.

Our advice is appropriate for those parts of the country where the climate permits growing lawn grasses. This, of course, rules out arid or tropical regions in our South and Southwest. While some residents attempt to grow lawn grass in these areas, we feel that this is an inappropriate burden on the ecosystem, and, therefore, a very expensive, labor-intensive activity, and not to be encouraged.

One way to reduce the time and money spent on the lawn is, obviously, to reduce the size of the lawn. Is your lawn bigger than you really need? How big a lawn do you want? Most of us have lawns of a certain size because that is how the lawn was configured when we bought the house. But a few moments of thought might suggest that the existing lawn really is bigger than necessary, that some of the area might be more attractively planted in ground cover, or devoted to a garden bed or patio. After all, turfgrass not only involves a lot of work, it also requires an enormous amount of water, an important consideration these days. Limiting lawn areas saves water too.

Evaluate your landscape and determine if a lawn the size of yours is justified. Consider gradually reducing that large lawn area over the next year or two by replacing heavy traffic areas with paths. Those lawn areas that are always turning into dirt patches are prime candidates for woodchip or gravel paths. Stone and brick make attractive walkways as well, if available.

Try ground covers. In the minds of professional landscape designers, lawns function as connectors of the various aesthetic features in the landscape, linking them with a smooth, soothing emerald green sward. Lawn grass also provides a carpet on which to walk and play, so we definitely need it where the kids play. But do we need grass for that green connecting carpet at the front of the house? Not necessarily. Ground covers are not only green, but they offer a variety of textures in a low-maintenance environment. They can serve as effective visual links between a handsome grouping of shrubs, the front walk, and the facade of the house. Think about how to reduce the size of the lawn, especially the front lawn, with patches of ground covers. Similarly,

A yard consisting of nothing much more than grass can be made more attractive, with less grass to mow, by adding trees, shrubs, and ground covers.

would it make sense to cut down on lawn at the sides of the house? How about in the backyard?

Ground covers can also soften property boundaries and reduce weeds on undeveloped or remote areas on the property. Ajuga, vinca, pachysandra, and English ivy are attractive, usually evergreen, and virtually carefree. In addition, in most parts of the country they require little or no watering, a significant advantage over lawn grass. (See chapter seven for a list of ground covers.)

Mulch around trees. Another fine way to reduce the size of a lawn is to mulch the areas under large shade trees. A large circle of ground-cover mulch at the base of each shade tree not only reduces the lawn area in the landscape, but also substantially improves the health of the trees. Turfgrass steals food and water from trees. They die sooner and are not truly healthy while they are alive. There are many suitable mulches. Use shredded bark, wood nuggets, pine needles, woodchips, or even stone or decorative gravel. A large circle of mulched ground cover such as pachysandra planted around the tree trunk requires watering only during very serious droughts. Ground covers do not need the amount of food and water lawn grass requires, so they don't compete with trees for moisture and nutrients. This planting also eliminates that ugly "surface root" problem that messes up the appearance of so many properties where trees sit in the middle of turf.

IMPROVING THE LAWN SOIL

Once the area of property to be devoted to lawn is established, it is time to begin renovating the existing lawn by reinvigorating the soil in which the lawn grass plants are growing.

The key to an attractive, sturdy lawn is the soil beneath the turf. Conventionally, we take care of the grass, when we really should be taking care of the soil. If it is healthy, if it is able to carry out its natural biological processes, it will take care of the grass. This is the secret of a low-maintenance lawn. The "eco safe" low-maintenance lawn-care strategy we recommend is based on the fact, supported by extensive research, that grass can get most of the nutrients and water it needs from healthy, well-aerated soil. Such soil will contain sufficient organic matter to support a full range of active microorganisms. As these conditions are met, and the microorganisms get busy, the need for fertilizer and supplemental water is dramatically reduced.

It is relatively simple to improve soil.

1. Every year aerate the lawn once or twice to introduce oxygen into the turf.

2. Over the mowing season leave the grass clippings on the lawn to decay and return organic matter back to the soil.

3. To augment the organic matter already in the soil, add some organic material like composted municipal sludge, peat moss, or compost to improve its water retention.

4. An optional but valuable step is to add some microorganisms to reinforce the population already residing in the soil. Utilizing available oxygen and water they will, over time, take over the production of the nutrients that will feed the grass plants.

Following this program, after a few years it will be possible to reduce the amount of supplemental feeding to one application of a modest amount of a granular, slow-release fertilizer, applied in the spring. Lawn care will primarily involve aerating and adding organic matter through grass clippings.

Soil Compaction Is a Lawn's Enemy

People work at cross purposes with lawns. While grass grows well only if its roots do not live in compacted soil, people establish lawns to walk on, and walking compacts the soil. Even if we don't routinely walk on the front lawn, years and years of walking behind a lawn mower—or worse, driving a mower—every ten days or so has caused most lawns in this country to become compacted. It is extremely difficult to grow healthy grass in compacted soil. It stores little water and has little oxygen available for absorption by the grass roots, resulting in a very low level of microbiotic activity and low fertility. So, are we fighting a losing battle? Not at all. We need to do what the golf course and athletic field turf managers have been doing for decades: We need to aerate the lawn once or twice every year.

AERATING THE LAWN
Aerators are pronged tools that puncture the turf and draw out a plug of soil, leaving a little hole about one-half inch in diameter and about four inches deep. The soil plugs are deposited on the turf where they soon break down in rain. Power-driven aerating tools that will do two thousand square feet in an hour or two are available for rent. There is now a home-

This power aerator punches holes three inches deep or more into the lawn turf and deposits the soil cores onto the lawn. This permits the access of oxygen, water, and nutrients to the soil, necessary components to its health. It will thoroughly aerate an average lawn in less than an hour.

Small lawns can easily be aerated with this hand-held device. Step on the foot plate and press the four-inch hollow cores into the turf. It removes a plug of soil each time it is pulled up.

size version of a power lawn aerator as well as a hand aerating tool on the market.

What does aeration do? By creating a space in the soil through which oxygen can penetrate, aeration stimulates the activity of soil microorganisms and increases root development. Both the movement of the roots through the soil and the increased microbiotic activity significantly reduce the compaction problem.

Aeration also eliminates potential problems stemming from thatch buildup. Many homeowners believe, mistakenly, that thatch is a result of the accumulation of grass clippings left on the lawn and collect their grass clippings, thinking they can avoid thatch. The fact is that thatch is actually made up of the roots of grass plants growing above the ground, which is usually compacted. These grass roots accumulate other debris and create an environment that attracts pest insects and disease.

Many homeowners routinely dethatch their lawns with some kind of dethatching device to avoid this problem. If that is all they do, they will have thatch again next year. Thatch does not occur in lawns that are properly aerated. The bustling activity of the microorganisms causes lawn debris to decay rather than accumulate. Normally thatch buildup occurs in three to five year cycles, so aerating the lawn every year controls and prevents it from building up. In addition, because it increases the population of the microorganisms which produce soil nutrients for grass roots, aerating does away with the need for at least one application of fertilizer.

How often should I aerate? Lawns that have never been aerated will benefit from aeration twice a year for a few years. Do it in the spring and again in the fall. After two or three years of improvement, aeration once a year is sufficient. However, it will not do any harm to maintain the twice-a-year routine, as it will always do good things for the grass and the soil it grows in.

USING HUMIC ACID

In some cases, especially in badly compacted clay soils, it may be advisable to supplement aeration with an application of humic acid for a few years. It contains absolutely safe chemicals and enzymes that loosen the soil, allowing the grass roots to penetrate more easily. For badly compacted clay turf, use this product during the aeration process. Otherwise, spray it on the grass twice a year, with or without the aeration step. Within two years it will loosen hard, compacted clay and substantially reduce compaction problems. If the soil is particularly vulnerable to compaction, then add a humic acid product routinely once a year along with one or two aerations.

SPIKING THE SOIL

Managers of turfgrass in commercial operations such as "pitch and putt" facilities have learned that in addition to a semiannual aeration, turf under very heavy foot traffic benefits from a spiking process throughout the season. Spiking makes little holes in the soil without pulling out a plug of soil, as is done by the aerating tools. A yard subjected to heavy activity by children will benefit greatly from periodic spiking. Spiking tools are not widely available to homeowners yet, but are expected to become so in a year or two. There are some spiking attachments that fit on regular shoes available by mail order. Strap them on and walk/spike around the yard, especially the heavy traffic areas. Unfortunately, walking around in golf shoes will not do the job. The spikes are not long enough.

Alternatively, consider using a power tool (Mantis makes one) that cuts slices into the turf, rather than puncturing it. It, too, is designed to improve oxygen availability to plant roots and to enhance the water-holding capacity of the soil. While this slicing tool achieves the same objective as the spiking tool, it does cause more damage to the turf. It might take a few weeks for it to return to its normal appearance. However, like spiking, it does not replace the need for aeration; it just supplements that step.

Adding Organic Material

The more organic matter (or humus) incorporated into soil, the greater its capacity to hold water and air, and, thus, its ability to deliver nutrients to plants. While it is easy to add valuable organic matter to flower gardens and vegetable gardens, it is more difficult with established lawns.

LEAVE THE GRASS CLIPPINGS. There are a number of ways to augment the organic content of the soil under existing lawn turf. The easiest way is to allow grass clippings to fall on the lawn as it is mowed. On an average lawn, these green clippings make available over two hundred pounds of nitrogen-rich organic material for every one thousand square feet. Homeowners customarily collect the clippings because most lawn mowers, their collection bags removed, tend to deposit them in clumps on top of the newly mowed turf. This looks unsightly and sloppy, whereas collecting the clippings makes the lawn look neater, more groomed. However, the lawn is then deprived of a valuable source of nitrogen and the collected clippings create a yard waste problem. This is a no-win situation.

The lawn mower industry is now responding to this situation and is producing "mulching mowers" designed to chop grass clippings into very small particles that fall down to the soil between the grass blades. With these new mowers, a newly mowed lawn looks neat and groomed as well as enjoys the benefit of the added nitrogen. Also, no yard waste is produced.

Homeowners without mulching mowers should still leave grass clippings. To overcome the clumping problem, mow more frequently so that the clippings are not overlong. If they are short they will fall more easily down among the grass blades. Encourage any remaining clumps of clippings to find their way to the soil with a grass rake turned upside down or with a broom. Do *not* allow the clumps to remain on top of the grass. They will prevent sun, water, and oxygen from penetrating. It really is worth the effort to keep the clippings on the lawn. Not only do they add organic matter to the soil as they decompose, they also eliminate the need for at least one application of lawn fertilizer.

ADD ORGANIC MATERIAL. In addition to leaving grass clippings, add organic material to all turf areas every year or two for major benefit to the soil and the turf. Spread a layer (one-eighth to one-quarter inch) of material such as composted municipal sludge, compost, or Canadian sphagnum peat moss over the entire lawn. A layer this thin quickly falls down between the blades of grass and doesn't even

Top Dresser is ideal for spreading a thin layer of organic material on the lawn annually. Use Canadian sphagnum peat moss, municipal sludge, or compost to add humus to the soil.

show after the first rain or watering. The big question is where to get these products.

Peat moss. Canadian sphagnum peat moss is the most widely available product, but also the most expensive. A four-cubic-foot bale of peat moss costs about nine dollars and will cover anywhere from two hundred to five hundred square feet of lawn, depending on how thickly it is spread.

Compost. Commercial compost sold in garden centers is generally too expensive to even consider for this job, but more and more communities are making compost out of the leaves they collect. Many municipalities make it available to residents free or very cheaply.

Municipal sludge. The sewage disposal plants in over one hundred cities across the nation are producing sludge. More properly called *composted municipal sludge*, this product is available in enormous amounts for use in municipal and residential landscapes. It offers rich, dark, coarsely textured organic material that nourishes and conditions the soil. Early technical problems related to the presence of heavy metals in sludge have been overcome, making it ideal for lawns and other ornamental uses. Sludge is inexpensive enough to make annual applications to the lawn feasible.

Spread organic material on the lawn in either the fall or early spring. There are special spreaders for compost or peat moss on the market. If one is not available, use a shovel to spread the material, then follow up with a grass rake to scatter the thicker piles and make a layer uniformly thin. Soil organisms, especially earthworms, will move this organic material out of sight down into the soil. By the first spring mowing, most of this topdressing will already be incorporated into the soil. This is also a prime time to overseed the lawn to help thicken up the turf. It is good to introduce some of the modern grass varieties into existing turf periodically to insure its vigor and drought resistance. (See the discussion of overseeding on pages 16–18.)

Live Microorganisms Enrich Soil

Now here is new step for most homeowners —introducing microorganisms into the lawn soil. This is not at all as complicated as it sounds. Aerating and spreading an organic topdressing on the lawn provides a good opportunity to add some biological magic. Available by mail order and in garden centers, these new products are specifically designed to help tired, damaged lawn soil. They are packaged live microorganisms (about a billion per tablespoon) in the form of dry powder. Spread on top of the lawn by hand or with a fertilizer spreader, these microbugs will enter the soil

By adding microorganisms to your lawn's soil, you increase its ability to fight disease and pest insects while simultaneously improving the soil's ability to provide needed nutrients to the grass plants.

and serve as welcome reinforcements for those microorganisms that have been struggling in the stressed soil. Whether you do this in the fall or in the spring (they winter over), it boosts the biological activity in the soil in the spring as the soil warms up, giving the lawn a jump start on the season.

These microorganisms handle the organic matter you have added to the soil, gradually breaking it down into nutrients for the grass plants throughout the entire season. They are typically packaged as "biological catalysts" under several different brands. Expect a rapid green-up of the grass in the spring soon after adding these biological soil builders. However, unlike the fleeting flush of green that follows a dose of quick-acting nitrogen fertilizer, this healthy glow remains.

It is a good idea to combine the application of microorganisms with the annual application of a slow-release type fertilizer. Some companies have even combined the two into a single product to make this easier. Look for more specific information about fertilizing lawns later in this chapter.

Maintaining Proper Soil pH

The degree of soil acidity or alkalinity is expressed on a continuum from 1 to 14, and is referred to as the "pH" of the soil in gardening and lawn-care books. A perfectly neutral soil registers a pH of 7. The lower the pH number below 7, the more acid the soil. The higher

Measure the level of acidity in your soil with this pH meter. Insert the sensitive probe into the soil and check the needle on the meter for your pH reading.

above 7, the more alkaline. Like all plants, lawn grasses prefer some types of soils over others. They do best in moist, well-draining soil that is just slightly acid (pH 6.0 to 7.0). If the soil is too acid, as is often the case in the North, it is necessary to add limestone to "sweeten" it. Bluegrass, Bermuda grass, and ryegrasses—a bit less able to handle soil acidity—need more lime than fescues and bent grasses. Consequently, it is really helpful to be aware of the type of soil on your property.

The easiest way to get a reading on the acidity or alkalinity of soil is to find a neighbor who is an experienced gardener. Most serious gardeners know the pH of the soil in the area, and while it can vary even within the neighborhood, it is not likely to vary much. Simple pH meters designed for home use are available in some garden centers and from various mail-order catalog firms. Although they give only a rough indication of possible extremes in pH, they are useful in alerting homeowners to possible problems.

Soil test. A more precise indication of soil pH is available for five dollars from the local county extension service or, oftentimes, the local botanic garden. In addition to an accurate soil pH reading, a soil test usually includes recommendations for correcting any problems that are identified. For instance, if the soil tests fairly acid, the report will suggest, as we've mentioned, that lime be added to the turf.

Lawn soil is often too acid. This is partly a function of the action of plant roots which release hydrogen as they take up nutrients from the soil. The accumulation of hydrogen over time increases the acidity of the soil. Also, acid rain contributes to the problem, leaching out those elements in the soil, like magnesium and calcium, which help neutralize soil acidity. Whatever you do, though, do not add limestone to the lawn just because the neighbors do unless a soil test indicates excessive acidity. If the soil is already somewhat alkaline, the addition of limestone will cause rather than solve a problem.

It is easy to treat a lawn with limestone. When establishing a new lawn, spread ground limestone on the seedbed before seeding, mixing it in five to six inches deep. To "sweeten" the soil of existing turfgrass that is chronically too acid, spread lime in the late fall, winter, or very early spring. WARNING!! Do not use a limestone product with magnesium in it more than once or twice. Using a magnesium-

Guidelines for Limestone Application

POUNDS OF LIMESTONE FOR 1,000 SQ. FT.

SOIL pH	SANDY SOIL	CLAY SOIL
Over 6.2	*0*	*0*
5.2 to 6.2	*25 to 50*	*50 to 75*
Under 5.2	*50 to 75*	*100 to 150*

supplemented limestone year in and year out can create a magnesium excess and upset the desirable chemical balance in soil. Bear in mind, too, that limestone is sold in many forms, but only ground or granulated limestone is suitable for lawns. Since it takes at least five or six months for limestone to be absorbed into the soil and take effect, the very best time to spread it is the fall.

If the soil test indicates that the soil in the lawn is too alkaline (pH above 8.0), make it a bit more acid by adding ammonium sulfate, iron sulfate, or elemental sulfur. These amendments come in a powdered form that can be spread by hand or with a grass seed spreader. Spread elemental sulfur at 3 to 5 pounds per 1,000 square feet to increase acidity to acceptable levels. Information about the amounts of the other products to spread will be on the package labels.

NOW THE SOIL IS TERRIFIC!

Taking the steps recommended above will substantially improve the soil under an existing lawn and send it well on its way to self-sufficiency. Freed from dependence on costly fertilizer fixes and your constant labor, it will support the vigorous growth of grass plants over the whole season. Which kind of grass plants you have or choose is another important consideration. That is what this next section is all about.

RENOVATING THE LAWN

If your turf has become thin, damaged, or weedy, the decision to renovate by upgrading the quality of the grass is fairly easy to make. However, many homeowners are reluctant to undertake a lawn renovation project when the lawn looks to be in pretty good shape—albeit requiring lots of water, fertilizer, and time. It seems like an awful lot of work. There are varying degrees of renovation, though, and improvement in the turf may be possible with a minimum of effort. Renovation does not have to mean starting over. The key in all cases is to upgrade the turfgrass by introducing one or more of the newer, modern grass varieties.

Developed twenty-five years ago, the grass varieties growing in residential lawns in both the North and the South are outmoded. In the North, Kentucky bluegrass has been king, and in the South, Bermuda grass has ruled for decades. Unfortunately both these varieties of grass (especially their earlier generations) require considerable supplemental water and fertilizer to be at their best, even in optimum growing areas. Even though these old standbys may be basically satisfactory, enormous improvements in seed development in recent years make it advisable to change over to the newer ones. Modern low-maintenance/low-water lawn grass varieties are so much more desirable that it is definitely worth spending some time reseeding the lawn.

This is a very controversial recommendation, especially since the lawn-care industry and the county extension services of the state agriculture universities still routinely recommend Kentucky bluegrass and Bermuda grass in their respective regions of the country as they have been doing for decades. Of course, up until the last ten years there have been no satisfactory substitutes for these grasses, but with the advent of the 1990s, sturdy new ones have arrived on the scene. It is time to take advantage of new technology in this area.

Renovating an existing lawn, either by starting over or doing a less labor-intensive overseeding with modern grass varieties, will yield lower-maintenance lawns. Selecting the appropriate grasses for the region is the critical first step. Lawn grasses are classified according to climate: types that grow well in the cooler northern climates of the United States and types that grow well in the warmer southern climates. A description plus planting and care instructions for the varieties appropriate for the North follows. The insect, disease, and cultural problems are discussed at the end of the chapter.

Lawn Renovation in the North

In the North it is best to use a mixture of cool-climate grass varieties to achieve maximum insect and disease resistance and satisfactory appearance over an entire lawn. Each type of grass seed has its particular assets, and several in combination yield the best-of-all-possible-worlds lawnwise. This idea has been common for many years, a modern lawn just representing a change in the traditional mixture.

While there is no need to completely replace Kentucky bluegrass in a lawn, it is desirable to reduce its traditional starring role. By all

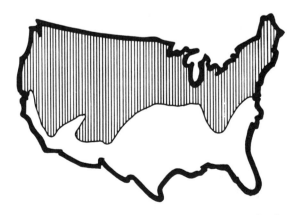

Certain grass seed varieties are only appropriate for the North and others are best for the South. The varieties discussed in this book will generally thrive in the northern section outlined on this map.

means, use the latest variety of Kentucky bluegrass, new and improved—but make it just one of the players. These grasses are heavy users of increasingly scarce water and large amounts of fertilizer, *irrespective of the soil they grow in*. The new tall turf-type fescues, on the other hand, require only 30 percent of the water needed by the Kentucky blues, and, in the North, most of this will typically be provided by rainfall.

Here are recommendations for lawns in northern climates. As suggested above, they include only a small amount of Kentucky bluegrass.

NORTHERN GRASSES

The most common cool-season types of lawn grass include:

TALL FESCUE (FESTUCA ARUNDINACEA). A turf-type tall fescue is a good alternative to Kentucky bluegrass as the primary grass in a lawn. This is a tough grass that is excellent for play areas. It withstands foot traffic and relatively heavy use, although, of course, no grass can handle repeated heavy traffic. Tall fescue is useful as a shade grass in both the South and the North. It is somewhat coarsely textured, but it has good color, good drought tolerance, and is quite resistant to diseases and insects. This grass does not spread by stolons—underground runners—which, as we pointed out earlier, are the true cause of thatch. Tall turf-type fescue does not cause thatch. At the same time, a lawn with only tall fescue can develop a "clumpy" look, so that is why some Kentucky blue (10 to 20 percent) is ideal to fill in the gaps and smooth out that clumpiness. Tall fescue is especially appropriate for the transitional area of the country where northern and southern climates meet. It is not good in mixtures unless it makes up more than 80 percent of the total (so use 10 percent Kentucky blue and 10 percent perennial rye to complete the mixture). Use 5 to 6 pounds of seed for 1,000 square feet of lawn. Popular varieties include 'Houndog', 'Arid', and 'Rebel II'.

TURF-TYPE PERENNIAL RYE (LOLIUM PERENNE). New varieties of this grass are attractive because they are quite resistant to diseases and insects. Perennial ryegrass germinates and establishes itself quickly, getting a new lawn off to a quick start. Planted as part of a seed mixture, it is eventually overtaken by the more desirable slow-growing fescues which should be the mainstay of the lawn. For this reason, ryegrass should not comprise more than 20 percent of a total seed mixture, 10 percent being sufficient in most cases. It has medium shade tolerance and is an excellent grass for overseeding a poor existing turf. This grass produces very little thatch. Use 3 to 4 pounds of seed to cover 1,000 square feet of lawn. Popular varieties include 'All Star', 'Pennant', 'Derby', 'Elka', 'Gator', and 'Regal'.

RED FESCUE OR TURF-TYPE FINE-BLADED FESCUE (FESTUCA RUBRA). Fine-bladed fescue is a fine-textured grass traditionally seeded in combination with Kentucky bluegrass. Try mixing it half and half with the tall fescue for a nice look. Its assets—lower nitrogen requirements and vigorous growth that effectively chokes out weeds—complement those of a tall fescue/bluegrass mixture. Its deep roots provide excellent drought resistance and it has almost no disease or insect problems. Fine fescue is excellent for overseeding poor lawns to improve turf quality. Seeded alone, it is good for shade areas. Fine fescue can be used in the South to overseed Bermuda grasses during winter months. Use about 3 to 4 pounds for every 1,000 square feet of lawn. Popular varieties include 'Falcon', 'Finelawn', 'Jamestown', and 'Jaguar'. 'Pennlawn' is less susceptible to leaf spot than others.

KENTUCKY BLUEGRASS (POA PRATENSIS). Kentucky bluegrass is a slow-creeping, sod-forming perennial grass. It propagates by means of stolons (runners under the soil), tillers (plantlets on a stem), and seeds. Its foliage color is medium to very dark green. It grows best in areas with mild summers and ample water, so it is not really suitable for areas with hot summers. Kentucky bluegrass prefers full sun, but will turn brown in drought periods. Its growth stops when soil temperatures exceed 85° to 90° F. Where it is feasible to continue to use bluegrass, use at least two Kentucky bluegrass varieties, along with 20 percent ryegrass variety in a new lawn. This will reduce the chances of a total wipeout by a disease or insect

that is specific to one of the grasses. Use 1½ to 2 pounds of seed to cover 1,000 square feet. Powdery mildew frequently infects Kentucky bluegrass growing in shady locations where air circulation is limited. Several of the improved varieties of Kentucky bluegrass are resistant to leaf spot ('Adelphi'), stripe smut ('Majestic'), and fusarium blight ('Merion'). Popular varieties include 'Estate', 'Fylking', 'Glade', 'Merit', 'Nassau', and 'Sydsport'.

CHOOSING A MIXTURE

It is impossible to recommend just one grass seed combination that will work everywhere in the country and on every property. Not only do grass varieties for the North perform poorly in the South, but even in the North grass mixtures have varying success, depending on the climate, the altitude, the presence of shade or sun, and other environmental factors. When in doubt about what to plant, contact your local county extension agent or a reputable lawn-mower repair and sales dealer for some advice. In the meantime, here are some general formulas for grass mixtures in various parts of the North.

NORTHEAST AND NORTHERN MIDWEST. North of North Carolina and Tennessee (Zone 6), a good lawn-seed mixture should contain two kinds of seed with no less than 80 percent turf-type tall fescue as the basic grass. It will provide the dominant texture and color to a lawn. The second grass in the mix could be turf-type perennial ryegrass. Limit it to no more than 10 to 20 percent of the seed mixture, because it is so aggressive early on that it may offer too much competition to the other grasses. Ryegrass provides quick green cover and erosion control while the slower-germinating and slower-growing fescues are coming in underneath.

We should observe here that most people in the Northeast and northern Midwest probably have Kentucky bluegrass as the primary type of plant in their lawn. If you wish to simply overseed and not do any major renovation, then you should continue using Kentucky bluegrass even though it may require more water and fertilizer than other grasses. Tall turf-type fescues do not grow well when overseeded in lawns composed predominantly of Kentucky bluegrass. The fescues do best when they are the predominant grass.

NORTHERN PLAINS AND MOUNTAIN AREAS. In nonirrigated areas in the northern plains states crested wheat grass mixed with a fine fescue makes a good combination. In irrigated lawns use the mixtures described for the Northeast.

COASTAL NORTHWEST. Substitute colonial bent grass ('Exeter') for the ryegrass in the mixture described for the Northeast. The bent grass can better hold off annual weeds in the moist environment of this part of the country.

NORTHERN GRASS VARIETIES ACCORDING TO LIGHT AVAILABILITY

Full sun. The basic tall fescue/perennial rye/ Kentucky bluegrass blend is best for lawns that get plenty of sun.

Part shade. Tall fescue likes part shade, and is often used as shade grass in the South. Perennial ryegrass prefers full sun, but tolerates part shade. Red, or fine-bladed, fescue does best in part shade; it does not like full sun. The most shade-tolerant of the cool-climate grasses though, is meadow bluegrass (*Poa trivialis*). It will accept more shade, especially in moist soil, than will red fescue. Substitute some meadow bluegrass for half of the fescue for shady areas. Unfortunately, meadow bluegrass is sometimes difficult to find in retail stores. See Resources at the back of the book for mail-order sources.

Full shade. No grass will grow well in full shade. Find a ground cover such as ivy or pachysandra for such areas.

NORTHERN GRASS VARIETIES
FOR POOR SOIL

In its capacity as a ground cover, lawn grass is often expected to cope with awful soil conditions. Sand or clay, excess acidity, infertility, and compaction all may exist in certain areas on the property. Fortunately, some grass varieties are tough enough to persist in these substandard conditions.

- tall fescue—tolerates poor soil and a pH range of 5.5 to 7.0.

- perennial ryegrass—tolerates almost any kind of soil and a pH level of 5.8 to 7.4.

- red fescue—tolerates almost any kind of soil with a pH range of 5.6 to 6.8.

Doing the Job

There are two ways to renovate a lawn. Overseeding existing grass with one or more modern varieties that will thicken the turf and eventually overtake the old grass is often effective for lawns that have no major weed problems. It is obviously considerably less work than a total overhaul. However, complete renewal may be necessary for severely weed-infested lawns. This requires killing all the existing grass and weeds with a safe herbicide and reseeding the lawn with newer grass seed varieties. While this involves a lot more work, it offers an opportunity to thoroughly recondition the soil as well.

Whichever method you choose, in the North lawn renovation is best done in late August or early September so there is time for the new grass to get established before the ground freezes. If it is not possible to do it in the fall, then do it very early in the spring, just after last frost. Be sure to do it before the leaves appear on the lilacs. By the time the lilacs bloom it is getting too late for any major lawn renovation.

Renovation by Overseeding

1. Mow the lawn very closely to remove as much foliage as possible. Set the mower at its lowest setting, down to about one-half to one-quarter inch.

2. Vigorously rake the mown grass to dislodge any thatch, the layer of accumulated organic material down among the blades of grass. Removing it permits the new seed to come in contact with the soil. For large lawns it may be worth it to rent machines called power rakes, turf thinners, dethatchers, or vertical mowers, to make this job easier. These tools tear out weeds and thatch but leave the grass intact. At the same time they cut shallow grooves into the soil that catch newly sown seed and facilitate its germination. They also aerate the soil. This equipment is available at most rental agencies and is easy to use. Mantis sells a suburban tiller that has dethatching and

This mulching mower chops grass clippings so fine that they can be left on the lawn to help fertilize it. Here the mower is set at its very lowest cut to prepare a lawn for overseeding.

soil slicing attachments to do this job (see Resources). This type of machine is not essential, but saves a lot of labor.

3. This is a good time to carry out the soil improvement steps that were described in the beginning of this chapter—aerating, adding humic acid products, adding organic materials, adding microorganisms.

4. Either at this time or the following weekend, spread slow-release fertilizer and grass seed combined, both at half the rate recommended for making new lawns. This will be about 2 pounds of seed per 1,000 square feet. Spread the seed and fertilizer together. While hand sowing is perfectly okay, the best sowing tool is a cyclone seeder. Either hand-held or on wheels, this spreader broadcasts the seed evenly over the turf. Hand-held spreaders of any kind, most of which are inexpensive, usually do a more even job than hand sowing. When hand sowing, take only an ounce or two of seed at a time and cast it in a semicircle ahead of you as you pace the length of the lawn. Try to cover as much area as possible with each handful. Go over the area several times in different directions for even coverage.

5. Lightly drag a leaf rake over the lawn surface to insure that the seed falls down into contact with the top eighth inch of moist soil. This will assure successful germination.

6. While it is not essential, it helps to firm the seedbed by going over the area once with a lawn roller filled with water to give it weight. This will press the seed into the soil. Grass seed does not germinate and grow well in loose soil which dries out quickly. Substitute frequent watering if a lawn roller is not available.

7. MOST IMPORTANT STEP!!! After sowing, a thorough gentle watering is essential. Follow up with frequent sprinklings—daily or more often—to keep the top layer of soil moist until the young grass plants are established. Letting the soil dry out just once can significantly reduce the germination rate of the seed. Proper watering is absolutely critical to the success of this project.

8. A very light covering of straw, hay, or peat moss will protect the seeds from wind, birds, or heavy rain. Mulches of this sort should be so thin that the grass and soil are visible through the mulch. This way the grass seedlings can see the sun. Mulch helps to retain moisture. There is no need to remove these organic mulches later, the first mowing will simply turn the mulch into finer mulch which will eventually break down into humus. One bale of straw or hay should be enough to cover 1,000 square feet.

An effective alternative mulch is a layer of woven netting or the new white, spunbound garden fabrics (fleece) developed to protect vegetable seedlings from frost and hard rains. Research has indicated that new seedbeds covered with this material have a 200 percent better germination rate than seedbeds left uncovered. It admits light, air, and water to the seedbed, simultaneously protecting the seeds from birds and heavy rain. Lay the fabric gently over the seeded area and fasten the

Patch bare spots in the lawn promptly lest weeds fill them in. After seeding, temporarily cover the spots with agricultural fleece or another protective material that permits air, light, and water to reach the germinating seeds.

corners to prevent the wind from blowing it away. Do not stretch it tightly over the area. As the new grass grows, it will push up under the light fabric. Leave these fleece mulches on until the new grass is three or four inches high and ready for its first mowing.

Renovation by Starting Over

Lawns composed of much more than 50 percent weeds and weak grass really need to be totally renewed. Consider wiping the slate clean and starting a new lawn from scratch. The easiest way to do this is to kill all the weeds and grass with a glyphosphate herbicide (sold under the brand names of Roundup or Kleenup). At least two weeks before lawn renovation is to begin, spray this herbicide over the lawn. Choose a day when it is not windy so the spray will not drift onto other plants.

Although absolutely safe for people, pets, and soil ecosystems, the glyphosphate causes any plant it touches to be unable to produce its own protein, essentially "starving" it to death. When all turf plants are brown and dead, follow steps 2 through 7 for renovation by overseeding.

Spot Patching Your Lawn

Sometimes some repair of worn or diseased spots is all that is needed to significantly upgrade a lawn. Patching is relatively simple and results in rapid improvement of localized areas. You can get away with overseeding small areas of existing sod or seeding in small bare patches in the lawn virtually any time of the year. Follow the program outlined above. Remember to water frequently during dry spells and to pull any weeds that intrude into the patches. A product called Super Lawn Repair Kit is now available that makes spot patching even simpler. It is a preseeded growing mat that can be cut to fit the bare area to be seeded. Newly germinating seed, blends of tall fescues

DAYS TO GERMINATE	
Kentucky bluegrass	6 to 12 days
Red fescue	10 to 14 days
Perennial ryegrass	3 to 5 days
Tall fescue	6 to 7 days

and Kentucky bluegrass embedded in a feltlike fabric, is protected from erosion and birds and germinates quickly to fill in the lawn.

HOW TO CARE FOR THAT GREAT LAWN

Once the quality of the lawn soil and the varieties of grasses growing in it are improved, annual maintenance will get easier and become less time-consuming. The discussion below proposes a radically different maintenance program from the one that most Americans currently follow. It reflects the results of intensive research on grass and turf maintenance over the last few years. It rejects most of the conventional practices and wisdom of the past and embraces the new knowledge and technological breakthroughs in lawn care. The "don't's" are:

1. Do not feed the lawn four times a year.
2. Do not routinely mow the grass down to only one inch tall and collect the grass clippings in a bag.
3. Do not water the lawn a little bit each day during hot weather.
4. Do not automatically apply herbicides or pesticides as preventive measures each year.

All of these practices have proven harmful to lawns in the long run, taking more time, costing more money, and yielding mediocre results.

The "do's" are:

1. Aerate once or twice a year.
2. Fertilize only once or twice a year.
3. Mow your grass higher and leave the clippings behind.
4. Water the lawn less frequently but more deeply.
5. Spread limestone only if it has been determined that the soil is excessively acidic.
6. Use pesticides only for a specific problem present in the grass.

Restoring a lawn to health and beauty is time-consuming, but once that goal is reached the maintenance job should get easier.

Aerating

The key to creating healthy soil is also the key to maintaining healthy soil, so aerating is recommended as an important routine measure for lawn care. It is a new step for most American homeowners and is discussed thoroughly earlier in this chapter.

Feeding

Americans feed their lawns much too much. Overfertilization results in excessive leaf growth (resulting in more mowing) and reduced root growth. It ultimately produces weaker, more vulnerable lawn grass plants. As indicated earlier in this chapter, conditioning the soil under the grass is a long-term form of fertilizing. At most fertilize only twice a year, in the spring and in the fall. Grass that is aerated at least once a year, receives a topdressing of organic material every year or two, and benefits from mowed clippings will likely need only one dose of fertilizer annually. Provide this in the fall.

Feeding the lawn can take three forms—a main meal, a snack, or a "vitamin" supplement. The fall or spring fertilization, a main meal, is all the lawn really requires. However, sometimes a snack during the growing season is justified when special situations such as a big outdoor party may be scheduled. Also, a dose of "vitamins" or tonic, while optional, will enhance the ability of the grass to utilize the nutrients available to it, the same way vitamins aid human metabolism. There can be too much of a good thing, however, so resist the temptation to fertilize heavily and often.

THE MAIN MEAL

Use a nitrogen fertilizer that is labeled "slow-release." Other fertilizer products deliver nitrogen in a form that is too rapidly absorbed by grass plants. Grass root systems pay a price for the immediate visible greening and growth of the grass blades after such a nitrogen "fix." A fertilizer containing a slow-acting form of nitrogen releases nitrogen slowly, providing steady nutrition to the grass plants over a longer period of time (ten to fourteen weeks) while they build sturdy root systems. Slow-

release fertilizer is considered to be ideal for lawn grasses, both northern and southern. It is now readily available in garden centers and other stores. Most products are clearly labeled as having a slow-release, or "slow-acting," form of nitrogen. As of 1990 liquid fertilizers have still not been formulated with this form of nitrogen, so expect to use a granular or powdered product. (See Resources for suggested mail-order sources.)

As mentioned, give the lawn its main meal in the spring and/or fall. Early spring fertilization promotes grass leaf growth before annual weeds germinate, giving the grass plants a head start and reducing the need for any herbicide. Fall fertilization encourages root growth that will help carry the plants through dry spells the following summer. In all cases a maximum of two main meals is all that is necessary for a healthy lawn.

Of course, additional fertilizer for the lawn comes from natural sources. A thin layer of composted municipal sludge or other form of humus, described earlier in this chapter, will contribute some nutrients to the soil as it is incorporated into the turf. Also, leaving grass clippings on the lawn to decompose after mowing can supply up to 50 percent of a turfgrass's nitrogen requirements. Researchers also find that weeds are worse when clippings are removed.

SNACKS

While liquid fertilizers are not appropriate for the main meal because of their fast-acting nitrogen, they are ideal for supplemental feeding in certain situations. Anytime after about eight weeks into the growing season, as summer heat sets in, the lawn might benefit from a snack. To give it a boost, spray a liquid fertilizer over the grass at half the strength advised on the bottle. This will invigorate the grass without straining it. Do this once or twice before late summer, maybe in late June and again in late July. Be sure, however, that the grass is not experiencing drought or other stress at the time. Also, liquid fertilizers at half strength are handy for greening up a lawn just before a big party or putting the house up for sale. Spray the diluted fertilizer on the lawn about one week before the grass must look its best. A snack for the lawn is an optional step and is not essential for a healthy lawn.

VITAMINS

Certain products on the market for lawns are not actually fertilizers, but facilitators. They are designed to improve the ability of grass plants to absorb nutrients from the soil. They also bolster disease, drought, and insect resistance. Although most of these "bioactivator" or "growth enhancer" products function slightly differently, they all have a tonic effect on the lawn. They contain vitamins, enzymes, hormones, and/or trace minerals.

Some of these products are sprayed on the blades of grass (Roots by Gardener's Supply, Spray and Gro by Spray and Gro, and FoliaGro by Necessary Trading, for example). Others (Thorvin by Necessary Trading Company,

Kelp Meal by Nitron) are in granular form to be spread over the turf for the rain to soak in. All are designed to be used only two or three times during the growing season. Dose the lawn first just before the grass greens up in the spring. Provide a second dose in July to improve drought resistance, and spray a third time in late August to help grass prepare for winter dormancy. Remember, this is an optional measure, only for those willing to spend a little extra time and money. Vitamins do make a difference in the health of your lawn.

A BALANCED FEEDING SCHEDULE

An ideal feeding routine is to spread a slow-release fertilizer supplemented with microorganisms (e.g., Ringer's Winterize or Lawn Restore) in the fall, then to spread a layer of composted municipal sludge over the lawn in the spring to condition the soil and add some nutrients. Throughout the season leave the grass clippings on the lawn, and provide some vitamin-type product over the summer. Coupled with regular aeration, this regimen will produce a beautiful, nearly problem-free lawn.

Mowing the Grass

A casual drive through a suburban residential neighborhood suggests that most homeowners mow their lawns too closely. They virtually shear the grass plants and then remove the clippings. This is a serious mistake if the objective is to have an attractive lawn. Cutting the grass close to the soil reduces the size of the leaf blade so dramatically that it impairs the grass plant's ability to metabolize food and to shade out threatening weeds. It also exposes its roots to the drying sun, increasing its risk from heat and drought.

MOWING HEIGHT. The height of the cut is a critical issue in keeping grass healthy. Small adjustments in mowing height make a big difference, because, like all plants, grass uses the leaf surface for intercepting the light necessary for photosynthesis. Increasing the height of the grass by only an eighth of an inch yields almost three hundred square feet more leaf surface for each one thousand square feet of lawn. This represents an enormous increase in a lawn's ability to produce food and increase vigor.

Never mow northern lawns closer than 1½ inches. Studies show that mowing northern turfgrasses two inches high results in a tenfold reduction in weeds over mowing one inch high. Allowing the grass to grow up as tall as two inches also encourages its roots to grow down. That gives grass plants more staying power during times of drought. Tall grass also helps shade the soil, cooling the crowns of the grass plants and reducing the evaporation of moisture from the soil.

For best results, vary the height of the mower according to the season. Set the mower lower in spring (about 1½ to 2 inches for bluegrass/rye/fescue lawns) while periodic rains and cooler temperatures prevail. Then gradually raise it to the top height (2 to 3 inches)

by mid-June when heat sets in. Always cut grass in shady areas at this higher height; it needs all the leaf surface it can muster to take advantage of the limited light in dim areas.

Keep the mower at this height until the last mowing of the season. Then, for the last mowing, lower the height to about 1 inch high. At that level the mower blades will cut off the growing points of the grass plants, encouraging each plant to send out basal shoots that will thicken up the turf the next spring. Also, shorter grass makes fall raking and overseeding easier.

Although, regrettably, it means extra work, it is best to mow the lawn lightly and frequently. Studies show that this causes less stress to grass plants. Try to remove no more than one-third of the grass blade at any one cutting. To maintain a lawn at two inches, mow before it reaches three inches. This may mean mowing every five days during the cool, moist spring months when the grass grows rapidly. Then gradually stretch it to every seven to ten days when hot weather arrives. During drought periods, several weeks may go by between mowings. Resume more frequent mowing in the fall.

CHOOSING LAWN MOWERS. Homeowners in the market for a new lawn mower face an array of choices these days. There are basically three categories of mowers: traditional rotary mowers with a bag, mulching rotary mowers with or without a bag, and reel-type mowers with a grass catcher. While each type has certain assets, for those who plan to leave clippings on the lawn as recommended, the mulching-type rotary mower with an optional bagging attachment is ideal.

For most of the season it is appropriate to leave grass clippings on the lawn and, as indicated earlier in this chapter, the mulching mower is the most effective way to do it. However, homeowners with shade trees on their property have to cope with leaves on the lawn every fall. During this season it is desirable to collect the grass/leaf combination in the mower bag rather than allow the leaves to remain on the lawn. Even chopped by the passing mower, leaves left on the lawn in volume harm the grass. The collected chopped leaves and grass clippings make an excellent winter mulch for shrubs and trees or a starter for a compost pile.

A word about reel-type mowers. Back on the scene in lighter, more maneuverable incarnations of their former selves, they definitely provide a cut on the grass blade that is superior to that of rotary mowers. Unlike the rotaries which tend to bruise the tips of the blades as they cut, reel mowers cut cleanly. Consequently, a lawn mowed with a reel-type mower is likely to be a bit healthier than one cut with a rotary. These days they are self-sharpening, so they maintain a clean, sharp cut all season.

For lawns with very few weeds and strong, thick grass, reel mowers may be the mower of choice. Mow frequently with them; they perform best on grass that is not overlong. This

---

Mowing Tips

Don't cut wet grass. It causes uneven mowing, the clippings are messy, and they mat rather than fall down among the grass plants.

Alternate mowing patterns for even wear on the lawn. Mowing in the same direction every time tends to compact the soil and causes wear patterns.

Keep rotary mower blades sharp to avoid bruising the grass and browning the lawn.

Since raising and lowering the mower at different times of the year is a value, choose a mower that is easy to adjust.

---

will also assure clippings that are short enough to fall into the lawn. Reel mowers cut a narrower swathe than most rotary types, so the job may take a bit more time. People with small yards (under two thousand square feet) with good grass find the reel mower ideal. Of course they are much quieter too, a major virtue.

Watering Grass

Proper lawn irrigation not only creates sturdier grass plants, it reduces insect problems and certain fungal problems as well. Deep, infre-

The easiest way to tell how long your sprinkler takes to deliver an inch of water to the lawn is to set a container or two under it when it is on. Watch to see how soon they fill with an inch of water.

quent watering is better than frequent light sprinkling because it encourages deep, healthy root growth. Grass with deep root structure tolerates droughts much better. Furthermore, because Japanese beetles prefer to lay their eggs in lawns that are constantly moist, allowing the soil to dry out a bit between waterings discourages the development of their grubs.

Most lawns like from one to two inches of water a week unless the weather is extraordinarily hot and dry, in which case an even more generous watering is required. Morning is the best time to water. This way grass plants start the day with moisture, yet can dry off quickly in the midday sun and avoid fungus problems.

The actual goal of watering is to get moisture down into the soil deep enough so the plants have access to water for more than a day or so. Aim to water to a depth of at least six to eight inches each watering. The amount of water required to get to that depth will vary somewhat depending on the type of soil. In most areas, one inch of water penetrates twelve inches into sandy soil, seven inches into loam soil, and about five inches or so into clay soil. Therefore, try to water long enough to assure one inch of water.

To determine how much water is landing on the grass, place an empty coffee can out on the lawn under the sprinkler. When it is one-inch full, that much water has been sprinkled on the lawn. A clever device called a Daisee will also do this (see Resources).

Once you have determined how long it takes your particular watering device to lay down an inch of water, you can save your own time and worry by attaching your lawn watering system to one of the many computerized timers that are available on the market. These timing devices allow you to set the watering of the lawn for a predetermined time and then will turn the water off when that time has expired. They are particularly helpful when you're renovating a lawn and have to water newly seeded areas every day.

CHOOSING A WATERING SYSTEM

There are a number of different types of lawn watering devices available and each has its advantages and disadvantages. Unfortunately, drip irrigation systems, ideal for gardens, shrubs, and hedges, are not yet effective for giving the lawn a uniform watering.

Rotating sprinklers. The rotary sprinkler gives both round and square-cornered coverage, and those with locking arms and adjustable nozzles provide excellent spot coverage. It is an inexpensive sprinkler, but it often distributes water too quickly to allow the ground to absorb it. To avoid wasteful runoff, periodically turn off the rotating sprinkler (ten minutes on and twenty minutes off) to give the water a chance to soak into the soil.

Oscillating sprinklers. Oscillating sprinklers sweep back and forth, giving broad coverage of the lawn and the surrounding gardens. They water in a rectangular or fan-shaped pattern which is adjustable on some models. While easy to move around the yard, their major drawback is that their high arc wastes water. Up to 30 percent is lost to evaporation before it gets into the soil. Oscillator types also tend to distribute water somewhat unevenly. Areas at the edge of the pattern usually receive the most water, while those closer to the sprinkler receive less.

Impulse sprinklers. Impulse types hurl streams in a low arc which waters large areas evenly. They are attractive because the better models are adjustable. It is possible to vary the size of the area covered and the shape or pattern of coverage. This is particularly handy in irregularly shaped yards or those with obstructions. Impulse sprinklers are the best devices for windy conditions because they throw water out low and flat, with great force.

Most lawns growing in good soil with lots of organic material need little additional watering by the homeowner. The grass may lose some of its green color during the dry season, but it will not die. You can tell if grass needs

water because it tends to get a bluish hue to its appearance. Also it will not bounce back up readily after being walked on. If you do decide to supplement the rain with watering, just remember to water deeply and only as much as is needed.

Maintaining Proper pH

It is important to monitor the condition of the soil under the lawn over time. The pH, described earlier in this chapter, can change and may need to be corrected after several seasons.

HOW TO SOLVE OCCASIONAL PROBLEMS

There is a direct relationship between the type of care a lawn receives and the number of problems it develops. Lawns with healthy soil and modern varieties of grass that are cared for with proper management techniques will have fewer difficulties over the years.

Because the overuse of pesticides often causes many chronic lawn problems, it is important to abandon the routine use of these powerful compounds. Never apply any pesticide—whether an insecticide, herbicide, or fungicide—unless there is a specific reason for doing so. Avoid fertilizers that include a pesticide or herbicide, such as a preemergent crabgrass killer. Use these products only in

Lawn Problems by Symptom

OVERALL LAWN HAS POOR COLOR

SYMPTOM	PROBABLE CAUSE
Grass turns brown	Excessive thatch buildup
Irregular brown streaks	Mole, crickets
Grass dull gray-green color	Needs water
Blades yellowed and pale	Needs food
Blades pale green, stunted	Leaf smuts
Grass yellow-orange color	Aphids or greenbugs
Lawn looks bleached	Leafhoppers
White coating on grass	Powdery mildew
Blackened, greasy coating	Pythium blight
Lawn has rust-colored tinge	Rust

SPOTS, CIRCLES, OR PATCHES OF SOME KIND

Green-ringed dead spots	Dog urine
Green circles, brown edges	Fairy ring
Yellow circular patches	Cinch bugs
Small irregular dead spots	Cutworms
Small dead circles	Sod webworms
Irregular dead patches	White grubs
Yellow, dead grass patches	Billbug grubs
Small pale circles	Dollar spot
Brown circles	Brownpatch
Brown rings, tattered blades	Necrotic ring spot

GRASS BLADES HAVE PROBLEMS

Holes in grass blades	Earwigs
Ragged holes along blades	Slugs or snails
Dark spots on leaves	Leaf spot

OTHER GENERAL PROBLEMS

Moss in bare spots	Soil deficiency
Grass lacks vigor, is thin	Soil compaction
Weeds taking over lawn	Improper lawn care
Bare areas in lawn	Armyworms
Grass plants look sickly	Nematodes
Dead matted grass in spring	Snow mold
Tunnels in lawn	Gophers or moles

response to a particular problem, not as a preventive, and use them only on the localized portion of the lawn that is in trouble. This approach requires that you become a fairly sophisticated observer, spotting and diagnosing problems, but it is worth the effort. Actually, most lawn problems are eventually solved not by pesticides and herbicides, but by changing lawn-care practices.

There are a number of approaches to looking at possible problems occurring in the lawn. The table opposite organizes some of the most common problems in groups of similar symptoms to help you get some clues to what is really going on so you can find the proper solution.

Diagnosing Lawn Problems by Inspection

Another way to learn about problems is to give your lawn a systematic evaluation in an effort to spot problems early so they are easier to solve. It is a rare lawn that does not have its problem spots: shady patches, boggy areas, heavy traffic, or weed-infested tracks. Often homeowners are dissatisfied with the overall appearance of the lawn, even though there are no obvious bare spots. Close inspection of grass plants visually above and below the surface of the soil provides information that helps solve problems before they become serious.

VISUAL INSPECTION ABOVE GROUND
Take a good look at your grass, even getting down on your hands and knees to check out the details. Here are some things to look for.

Color of grass. Grass blades should have a uniform, rich color. However, if they are exceptionally lush and green and are growing very rapidly, they may be receiving too much nitrogen fertilizer. Resist the temptation to fertilize lawns repeatedly over the season. If it is bluish in tint, the lawn probably needs watering. If the grass is turning yellow or brown, then there could be any number of causes, from dormancy to some kind of disease or insect problem.

Clippings. Notice if grass clippings disappear from the surface of the turf quickly, within at least a week of mowing. Clippings normally decompose naturally and provide nutritional benefit to the grass. Their accumulation in the grass is a sign that something is wrong. As they get packed among the grass blades, normal air circulation is blocked, and the plants become vulnerable to disease. This accumulation of matted, dead grass can lead to a thatch problem.

Water runoff. Poor or compacted soil may be the cause of an inferior lawn. Water should be absorbed immediately. Look for water runoff. It suggests that the soil needs aeration and additional organic material. Clay-based soils typically have this problem, but they can be improved by a topdressing of peat moss, compost, or other humus-type material that absorbs water. Treating a soil problem often solves the grass problem.

Discolored spots. Circles or rings of brown, or a gray to black powdery coating on grass blades anywhere in the lawn can indicate lawn disease. They are usually caused by fungi and require treatment with a fungicide.

Abundant weeds. A lawn with 50 percent or more weeds and bare spots has either infertile or poorly drained soil, sometimes both. Weeds can survive these conditions, but turfgrass plants can't. If this is the situation, the lawn may need complete renovation.

VISUAL INSPECTION BELOW GROUND
Take a few minutes to check out the conditions below the surface of the lawn. A chunk of turf reveals a lot about the health and well-being

Visual inspection of a core of your turf will reveal a lot about the health of the grass and the soil it grows in. Healthy grass roots should be at least four, preferably six, inches long and they should be thickly dispersed through the soil.

of turfgrass. After a substantial rain, cut out a triangular core of sod three to four inches deep with a heavy-duty knife. Examine it closely for signs of plant or soil difficulties.

Moisture retention and penetration. The core of the turf sample should be moist all the way through. If it is not, excessive thatch may be preventing water from entering the soil. Also, the soil may be too compacted to support grass plants. Moisture should penetrate at least four inches into the plug of turf.

Depth of roots. If the grass roots penetrate to less than four inches into the soil, it is too compacted. If grass roots in the turf sample are at least four but no more than six inches deep, the soil is probably okay but the grass needs to be fertilized and/or mowed higher. If the roots of grass exceed six inches then you should have a healthy lawn.

Thickness of thatch layer. A certain amount of thatch is desirable. Less than one-quarter inch in the turf sample is okay. If there is more than a quarter inch, then it must be removed

There is no systematic way to list all the possible problems you may experience in managing your lawn. We've organized some brief discussions about what we feel are the more common frustrations in trying to achieve the perfect lawn.

Most Common Cultural Problems

Since many of the most common lawn problems are not caused by insects or disease, a simple change in lawn care and maintenance practices may be the answer.

LAWN TURNS BROWN — EXCESSIVE THATCH BUILDUP. Most lawns that have been on intensive chemical fertilizing programs eventually develop a layer of organic material just above the soil level. This "thatch," if it is too thick, is a symptom of distress. Thatch consists mostly of living, and some dead, undecomposed roots and matted grass clippings that form a porous layer which dries out rapidly after a rain or sprinkling. The soil underneath the thatch layer becomes compacted, reducing moisture penetration. Rapid runoff will occur during rains or watering. Thatch acts as a barrier to healthy air circulation near the soil, and it provides a habitat for various diseases and pest insects. You must keep thatch from getting too thick to assure a healthy lawn.

A thatch layer one-quarter inch or less indicates that the soil is healthy and is routinely breaking thatch down naturally. A thatch layer of more than a quarter inch suggests that the soil under the lawn is in trouble. Soil lacking enough organic matter to support the microlife and earthworms necessary to convert organic matter like thatch into soil is essentially dead. An accumulation of thatch signals this and must be removed. To do this, rake the lawn or use a power rake or dethatching tool. Where thatch is severe, an alternative to hand or power raking is a biological product (Lawn Rx by Ringer and D-Thatch by Sudbury are two examples) which contains microorganisms and enzymes that decompose thatch. Aeration is occasionally advised where the soil has become unusually compacted. Experts say that to appreciably improve grass rooting, punch aeration holes at least eight inches deep. Use the cores of soil that the aerating machine surfaces as a topdressing for thatch control and reseeding.

An annual quarter-inch topdressing of good topsoil or a half inch of sludge or compost spread on an ailing lawn will help correct the soil problems that cause thatch buildup. A one-time application of lime spread lightly on the lawn will also encourage thatch decay, as will beer (1 pint per 500 square feet diluted with a thorough watering).

GRASS YELLOWED AND PALE — NEEDS FOOD. Lack of nitrogen makes grass turn yellowish or pale green. It grows slowly and becomes thin. To rectify this, follow the feeding guidelines on pages 19 to 21. Be sure to use a slow-acting nitrogen form of fertilizer to provide sufficient nitrogen over the entire season.

MOSS IN BARE SPOTS — SOIL PROBLEMS. Moss in lawns is the result of shading, soil compaction, low fertility, and acidic soil reaction. Power raking will correct all of these conditions and, combined with the use of a ferrous ammonium sulfate moss killer, will keep moss growth to a minimum. Moss killer is usually applied in combination with fertilizer to give uniform coverage. The fertilizer improves control by stimulating grass growth. In extremely wet, cool seasons moss will even grow in unshaded lawns.

GRASS GROWS POORLY AND IS THIN — SOIL COMPACTION. Determine soil compaction with the screwdriver test. Take a screwdriver and try to push it into the soil. If it penetrates easily (notwithstanding occasional stones), there is no problem. If there is much resistance, the soil is compacted. Loosen compacted soil by aerating the turf as described on pages 4 to 6. This will stimulate the microbiological activity that is necessary to keep the soil healthy. When aerating a compacted area, leave the holes open; grass roots will fill them in. Rake a thin layer of humus, topsoil, or compost over the affected area in the lawn to help lighten the soil. Try a topdressing containing between 50 and 100 percent fine sand (not ocean sand).

WEEDS TAKING OVER LAWN — IMPROPER LAWN CARE. Rampant weeds are a signal that something is amiss. Normally, healthy soil keeps the grass growing vigorously enough to crowd out most of the weeds automatically. When the soil is poor, though, weeds rapidly begin to take over, so part of the treatment of a weed problem should be improving the quality of the soil and the grass planted in it. If it seems as if an annual application of herbicide over the whole lawn is necessary, then renovation measures may be needed.

Of course, some percentage of weed growth in a lawn is inevitable, so it is important to establish a "weed tolerance level" and then monitor your lawn against that standard. Decide which weeds are acceptable in small numbers and which weeds must go when even one appears. Most people can tolerate a 5 to 10 percent weed incidence without even noticing it in the overall appearance of the lawn. With weeds that have a grasslike form, up to 25 percent might be tolerable. On the other hand, a weed like plantain (*Plantago*) is generally regarded as intolerable to homeowners.

Crabgrass also has few friends. It is unwelcome because it is capable of completely taking over a lawn in just a few years, negating all previous efforts to improve a lawn's appearance. Because crabgrass has difficulty establishing itself in a lawn that is healthy and thick with desirable grass plants, the first step, predictably, is to get both soil and lawn in good condition. Then, when a few crabgrass plants show up, remove them immediately, either with a mechanical tool or with a spot application of an herbicide spray sold specifically for crabgrass. Be sure to deal with interlopers before they set seed, otherwise they will leave behind a crop of crabgrass for next year. Crabgrass is one of the reasons you should always patch seed any bare spots in your lawn as they develop because crabgrass will pop up in those bare patches just as sure as the sun shines.

Very often an outbreak of a particular variety of weed is indicative of some other environmental problem in the lawn's ecosystem. For example, prostrate knotweed (*Polygonum aviculare*) indicates compacted, droughty soil, whereas yellow nutsedge (*Cyperus esculentus*) indicates waterlogged soil. A higher incidence of all weeds may indicate overfertilization. Too much fertilizer harms the soil, weakening the grass, which then gives way to weeds more readily.

Until recently the only environmentally safe way to eradicate weeds was to pull them by hand. Currently, there are a number of weeding tools on the market which are effective for small numbers of weeds. If weeds make up more than 25 percent of the lawn, a safe herbicide is a more efficient, practical approach to solving the problem.

There are now several environmentally safe herbicides that are very effective against dandelion, plantain, thistle, and other pesky perennial weeds. One product, called Sharp-Shooter, is a soap-based material that desiccates the plant on contact. Another product, called Roundup, uses a glyphosate salt to cause the plant to stop producing protein, starving it to death in a week to ten days. Both products are contact killers and nonselective —meaning they will kill *any* plant they touch, not just weeds. They will kill lawn grass if they touch it. When spraying these products, be sure to shield neighboring plants or healthy grass that is in proximity to the target weeds. Do not spray on a windy day. Better yet, try

painting the material onto the individual plants. These herbicides are most effective when the air temperature is over 70°F. Remember, if the dying weeds leave a bare spot on the lawn, it is important to reseed that area; otherwise opportunistic new weeds will move in and take over again.

Numerous broad-leaved weeds in the lawn make the use of the soap-based or glyphosphate-based herbicides impractical. Here's a situation where judicious use of a traditional herbicide such as 2,4-D might be most practical. Careful spot treatment of specific weeds will eliminate them promptly and, if healthy grass is encouraged to fill in their space, will solve the problem permanently. Such limited use in accordance with the instructions on the product label will not harm the environment.

Most Common Animal Pests

SMALL DEAD SPOTS RINGED GREEN—DOG URINE. The urine of female dogs will kill grass. The urine creates small dead spots often surrounded by a ring of very green grass. Soak the spots with water, and the grass should grow again. If it does not, reseed the spot.

TUNNELS IN THE LAWN—GOPHERS AND MOLES. In some regions of the country, gophers are a lawn problem. They push soil out of their holes, creating distinctive fan- or crescent-shaped mounds around their entrance holes that mar lawns. After digging they may close up the hole with a soil plug. One gopher can create several mounds a day. Gopher tunnels, about two inches in diameter, follow no pattern, running from a few inches to two feet below the soil. The critters themselves range in length from six to twelve inches. They have thick bodies with small eyes and ears and an excellent sense of smell. They are seldom found above the ground. You can drive these pests away by fumigating their holes. Place a small ammonia-soaked sponge into each gopher hole and then seal it. The gopher will dig out and abandon the tunnel system. The best time to do this is in early spring. Trapping is also an effective method for eliminating gophers. Place regular wooden-based rattraps in shallow pits near burrow entrances and lure the gophers by sprinkling small amounts of grain on the thin layer of dirt covering the trap trigger.

In their search for food, moles also make an extensive network of tunnels, many of which are used only once. Moles do not eat plants, so lawn grass is only an incidental victim of their search for grubs, beetles, and other soil dwellers. Their most favorite food is earthworms. Because they are solitary animals, it is likely that only one or two moles are responsible for the damage to a lawn. Active all year long, moles tunnel deep into the earth when cold weather drives the earthworms deep below frostline.

Control moles by denying them one of their favorite foods, white grubs. Introducing milky spore disease (*Bacillus popilliae*) into the lawn will gradually eliminate most grubs over the next three or four years. Traps can be effective, but they require vigilance and persistence. Early spring when the first mole ridges appear in the lawn is the best time for trapping. Identify the "travel lanes" by stepping lightly on a small section of several tunnels. Disturb but don't completely collapse them. Then mark these sections with stones or garden stakes. Within two days those that are raised again indicate active runs and good locations for setting a trap. Restore the turf over unused tunnels with a lawn roller or by treading on them. Both choker traps and harpoon traps are effective for trapping moles. Install them according to the instructions that come with the devices. Another alternative is to dig out moles. Since moles may be active at any time of the day, it is often possible to spot the soil ridging up as the mole moves along. Shove a shovel into the soil right behind the mole, and flip him out into a bucket. Dispatch the culprit in whichever manner seems acceptable to you.

Disease Problems

Most diseases attacking a lawn are fungal in nature. As you could see in the table of all the symptoms on page 26, fungal diseases are manifested in many different ways, from circles, to patches, to whole sections of turf. In most cases, the problem can be eased, if not solved, by using a fungicide that is designed for the specific fungal disease causing your problem. All garden centers carry fungicides to deal with diseased lawns.

What is more important to remember is that most fungal diseases are caused by some environmental condition that you can control. Therefore, after you address the immediate symptom with an appropriate fungicide, you need to learn why you had the disease in the first place. In most cases, by changing some cultural practice (e.g., watering during the day instead of at night) or adjusting some environmental condition (e.g., cooling grass on very hot days with a brief noontime sprinkle) you can prevent the disease from coming back.

Insect Problems

Lawns can suffer from various pest insects from time to time. We have dealt with lawn pests in our detailed discussion of pest control in chapter six. As you will see in that chapter and, as we've alluded in this chapter, pesticides can be effective in reducing the symptoms of pest insects, but the real solution to a pest insect problem is almost always tied to improving the quality of the soil, improving the quality of the lawn grass, and maintaining the lawn properly.

Lawn-care practices will continue to change as technology responds to the concerns of all caretakers of turf. Two new products to reduce lawn-mowing frequency are newly available to homeowners. A "turf growth regulator" sprayed on the lawn inhibits grass growth. Also, a new type of slow-growing grass has been developed.

Turf growth regulators cause existing turf-grass to grow so slowly that treated lawns need mowing only every six to eight weeks. These products are liquids that are mixed with water and sprayed on turf within three weeks prior to the spring greenup of the lawn. They have been used successfully for years on parks, golf course roughs, airports, and cemeteries.

Cutlass (Dow/ElanCo) is taken up through grass leaves and translocated to the part of the grass stem that is actively growing. It interferes with the formation of the cells at the growing point of the plant and reduces the size of the cells. Limit (Monsanto) is primarily active through root uptake, so it can be applied even in the rain.

However, it is likely that growth regulators for lawns may be unnecessary in just a few short years. Slow-growing varieties of grass are on the horizon. Modern fescues—'Spartan', 'Reliant', 'Waldina', and 'Scaldis'—are already available. These cool-season grasses do best in the mid-Atlantic region and farther north, or in the high-altitude regions of the South. They tolerate a wide range of soil pH and low soil fertility. A typical low-growing grass will need mowing only every other week in the spring when rains are plentiful, then only monthly through the summer. Another group of new grasses, the hard fescues, will require mowing only a few times a season. These innovative products are really worth looking forward to.

GENETICALLY ENGINEERED GRASS NEXT? What next? Well, genetic engineers are addressing a number of agricultural problems, and lawn grasses are likely to get some attention from these gene-splitters. Genetic engineering produces improved products faster. Changes take only a few years, rather than the decades that normal hybridizing techniques require. Currently the commercial market—caretakers of golf courses, parks, and roadways—are influencing the ongoing research in turf. But homeowners are bound to reap the benefits as well. So maybe by the year 2000, there will be grass that doesn't grow much, has built-in insecticidal qualities, and is highly resistant to disease and drought.

It is not necessary to wait until this utopia arrives to enjoy a healthy, attractive, low-maintenance lawn. By taking advantage of the progress already achieved in the development of sturdy new lawn grass seed, soil conditioning products, and efficient aerating and mowing equipment, a handsome lawn is within the realm of possibility now.

CHAPTER 2
Taking Care of Trees and Shrubs

While caring for residential lawns has been a virtual national pastime in America for decades, caring for their trees and shrubs has not been a high priority for homeowners. Those plantings that the contractor installed when the house was built are likely to have been taken for granted all these years, cared for incidentally, if at all. Victims of benign neglect, they gradually become overgrown, sometimes overwhelming the front of the house, even obscuring it from the view of the street. However, as popular concern about the "greenhouse effect" has grown in recent years, so has appreciation of the importance of the trees and shrubs on a property. They not only add value and beauty to home landscapes, they are critical to the health of the planet.

Handsome shade trees and decorative shrubs represent enormous ornamental assets to a residential property. As a result they also have a significant dollar value. Ask anyone who has put a house on the market lately or has suffered fire or hurricane damage to his property how much his trees were worth. While the value of shade trees varies with their location, age, and species, realtors estimate that a home with ten shade trees and twenty shrubs of various kinds may derive $10,000 to $15,000 of added value just from those plants. As we begin a decade where the spotlight will be on planting millions of trees to help compensate for the loss of large portions of the rain forests, knowing how to properly care for trees and shrubs suddenly becomes even more urgent. The place to begin is in our own backyards, with the ones we already have.

Trees and shrubs are what are called "woody plants." They have stems which do not die back each season, but rather develop thick tissues that survive year after year, getting harder as they age. Of course, they are much more self-reliant than lawn grass plants and require nowhere near the amount of care and attention that grass does. However, to flourish in top form they do need attention from time to time each year. Neglected trees and shrubs are disease and insect prone, and usually die prematurely.

This chapter begins by providing help in assessing the condition of the trees and shrubs that are already on your property. We'll offer some tips about how to get them into shape —the renovating phase of things—and then how to properly care for them afterward. There is information on how to choose additional trees and shrubs for the landscape too. Finally, we'll discuss dealing with potential tree and shrub problems.

ASSESSING TREES AND SHRUBS

There are several ways to evaluate the condition of existing trees and shrubs in the yard that have never received much care and attention. One way is to examine them yourself and undertake a renovation project along the lines suggested later in this chapter. Another way is to hire a professional consulting arborist to evaluate each of the trees and larger shrubs and recommend measures for any remediation and ongoing care. A consultation can cost from $100 to $150, depending on the number of trees on the property, but it is a good investment. Because consultants do not do the renovation work, their recommendations are totally objective and will provide a reference

point for evaluating estimates from tree services. Finally, a third way, probably the way most homeowners use, is to ask a tree-care service to come in and do an evaluation of the property. This evaluation is usually free, but it is made in the expectation that they will be doing the work and is hardly objective.

Both professional consulting arborists and tree-care specialists can easily spot dead wood, disease, and insect problems, things obvious to someone who knows what to look for. A service particular to a professional arborist, however, is an assessment about the relative quality of your trees. Are they "good" trees or "not so good" trees for their location and the local weather and growing conditions? Maples make great shade trees, for example, and are available in a variety of sizes. But their large, shallow root systems discourage the growth of other plants under them. Silver maples, which tend to be brittle, cannot withstand strong winds or ice storms. For shade and fall color, a recommendation may be to eventually replace some maples with ash or oak. This is the kind of valuable information available from a local consulting arborist who knows the area and knows the best trees for it.

Whether a consultant or a homeowner assesses existing trees and shrubs, the procedure is basically the same:

1. What kind of tree or shrub is this?
2. Does it serve well in its location?
3. What is the condition of its roots, trunk, and foliage?

Reducing the Lifespan of a Shade Tree

A Norway maple has a life expectancy of 75 years. A young five-foot sapling costs $150. It takes ten years to grow tall enough to provide sufficient shade to give it a value of $1,000. By failing to provide routine care and maintenance, a homeowner will shorten its life and reduce its total value to the home.

Damage by lawn mower, trimmer, or kid's bicycle	*subtract 10–20 years*
Neglect to apply fertilizer	*subtract 5–10 years*
Fail to aerate	*subtract 5–10 years*
Fail to water during droughts	*subtract 5–10 years*
TOTAL YEARS LOST FROM TREE'S LIFESPAN	*25–50 YEARS*

4. How old is it? What is its normal life expectancy?

5. Is it a "low-maintenance" or "high-maintenance" type?

6. What is its current monetary value?

Identifying Trees and Shrubs on Your Property

In order to take proper care of a tree or shrub, it is important to know what it is. It is worth the effort to identify those that are on the property. Neighbors may know, as may a gardener friend. Take a leaf to the local nursery for some help. Find a book at the library on the identification of trees and shrubs. It is not necessary to discover the precise variety of each plant. Knowing that it is a maple tree or an oak tree, an arborvitae or a juniper is sufficient. Whether a tree is a Norway maple or a sugar maple is helpful, but not necessary to knowing how to care for it.

Evaluating the Location

Even the healthiest, most attractive tree or shrub is a liability if it is in the wrong place. Some may have been properly sited originally, but have become crowded or too large. Perhaps they are now shaded by a faster-growing neighbor and are suffering from lack of light. For each tree and shrub on the property, ask: Is this plant in the right place? What is it doing for me here? Can it thrive here? Again, these are the questions a professional can help you answer.

The shrubs which the builder installed years ago have a way of taking over the house while we are not looking. These evergreens must be removed to restore light, air, and accessibility to this home.

Aesthetic value. Trees and shrubs in the right place will be aesthetically pleasing from the street, from inside the house looking out a window, and from the neighbor's side. They will be in proportion to the buildings on the property and to each other.

Functional value. Trees and shrubs in the right place block utility areas and bare foundations from view. They save energy by casting shade on the house or blocking wind. Shrubs reduce lawn size, attract wildlife, and screen private areas, such as porches and patios.

Trees and shrubs near buildings. Typically, older established plantings are too close to the house or garage. After ten years the charming young shrub or sapling fresh from the nursery may completely overwhelm an ordinary house or yard. After twenty years it detracts so from the appearance of the house that it becomes a liability. Rather than representing added value to the home, it represents an expense—the price to have it cut down.

The branches and foliage of trees and shrubs should not touch the house at all. Also, in most cases, these plantings should not obstruct the view from any window. If it requires radical pruning to control its size, a tree or shrub is the wrong plant for that spot. It should be removed and replaced by one whose natural habit is appropriate to the space. While all large trees have extensive root systems as a function of their size, certain types, such as willows or poplars, have roots that are notorious for encroaching on underground pipes and fouling drains. If these are on the property, be sure they are not near the house.

Trees and shrubs in the lawn. Nothing is more attractive than a stately shade tree or lovely flowering shrub that is planted as a specimen in a lawn. However, these plants are at risk if the grass grows right up to the trunk or stem. Lawn grass is greedy for soil nutrients and will deprive tree and shrub roots of their share. Although most of a tree's feeder roots are found throughout the top forty inches of soil, the vast majority of those roots are located just below the soil surface, down to twelve to eighteen inches. Good lawn turf has six- to eight-inch roots. Therefore, half of the area that normally provides most of the nutrition for trees is coopted by grass roots.

Often the grass under many large shade trees is in terrible condition itself. In many cases tree roots have surfaced, causing unattractive bare areas in the yard. Solve this problem and assure better nutrition for trees and shrubs planted in the lawn by establishing a grass-free ring around their trunks. Make it about three feet in diameter for young trees and shrubs, and six feet for larger mature plants. Cover this area with three or four inches of some attractive organic mulch, such as chopped leaves, woodchips, or shredded bark, or plant it with a less competitive ground cover, such as pachysandra, vinca, or ivy.

Improper light conditions. All plants have light preferences. This has a direct bearing on their health. Some trees and shrubs thrive on day-long full sun, while others require indirect light and some shade. For instance, hot, dry sites in full sun put a great deal of stress on understory plants, such as dogwoods and rhododendrons. Any understory plant—one that is normally protected by taller plants in its natural habitat—will be reduced in vigor unless it has some shade from the afternoon sun, protection from hot, drying winds, and a cool, moist root environment. Dogwood trees growing in full sun are more than three times as likely to be attacked by borers as those in somewhat shaded sites. Check the trees and shrubs on your property to determine if some are improperly located.

Although poorly sited trees and shrubs can cause problems and take up extra maintenance time, do not give up on them. Consider moving them to a more appropriate setting, or selling them to nurseries which often have a market for mature, healthy shrubs and small trees, or give them to neighbors. Perhaps their current location can be modified to reduce some of the location problems.

The Condition of Trees and Shrubs

It is not difficult to tell if a tree or shrub is healthy. Do all the branches have a full set of leaves? Are there any bare or broken branches in the tree? Is the foliage a healthy green? If leaves are discolored, full of holes, or undersize or if they drop prematurely, there may be a problem. Examine the surface of the trunk or stem. Is its color and texture uniform? Are there any visible scars, stains, holes and sawdust, or egg masses? These, too, may indicate a problem. Since humans are the single most common cause of tree and shrub damage, check for injuries on the trunks from lawn mowers, string trimmers, and other yard-care equipment.

The condition of tree and shrub roots is a bit more difficult to evaluate, since they are out of sight. Eventually root problems show up as growth or foliage problems. Both the superficial feeder roots and the deeper supporting roots range through the soil to great distances. Roots of a healthy shade tree typically spread two to three times the distance from the trunk to the drip line. The drip line is the imaginary line around the tree demarcating the outside diameter of the foliage of

This dogwood trunk has been repeatedly damaged by yard-care equipment and has become vulnerable to disease. A circle of organic mulch such as woodchips or chopped leaves, or a patch of ground cover around the trunk would have protected it.

driveways are renewed, house additions are built or repaired, earth is graded, or similar construction takes place, the roots of nearby shade trees and shrubs may be damaged severely. These plants suffer from shock sometimes, even though they are not actually physically damaged by these activities. Such stressed trees and shrubs are extremely vulnerable to pest and disease problems.

Often the stress first shows as premature loss of leaves at the tips of branches, around the perimeter of the canopy of foliage. Later —sometimes a year or two later—the tree will begin to show more obvious symptoms of distress. If a tree or shrub shows severe symptoms, such as limp, distorted, or prematurely falling leaves, or oozing or dieback of trunk or stems, it is advisable to call in a tree-care professional. In many cases, however, a major renovation of the plant (see pages 41–48) is all that is needed to get it back on the road to good health.

Low- versus High-Maintenance Trees and Shrubs

Most homeowners have limited time to spend caring for the yard. Because lawns take a disproportionate amount of time and effort to maintain, it is worthwhile to select trees and shrubs with an eye to low maintenance as well as beauty. Trees vary in the degree of care they require. Of course young ones of all kinds need more attention than older ones. Fruit trees,

the tree. If water flowed down the outside surface of a tree's foliage, it would drip down to the ground around the "drip line." The roots of shrubs spread as much as twice the distance from the stem to the drip line. It is not unlikely therefore, that over half the root system is under the street or driveway, and that it may be experiencing problems.

Again, humans are a major cause of root damage. Whenever new sewer lines are dug,

especially, need regular pruning, feeding, and spraying every year. Then among shade trees there are those that are "messy," forever dripping twigs, bark, nuts, or seeds all over the landscape. Some are particularly brittle, prone to breakage in wind and rainstorms. Others are "weedy," enthusiastic growers that seem to constantly erupt in rangy branches and un-authorized shoots along the branches. It takes time to maintain and clean up after them. It is not difficult to determine whether this type of tree is on your property. They make themselves known immediately.

Shrubs as a group tend to be less problematic than trees. Needled evergreen shrubs such as junipers and dwarf Alberta spruce, for instance, have attractive natural habits and need no pruning for shape. While some drop a few cones, the squirrels often deal with them. Broad-leaf evergreens like rhododendrons benefit from occasional pruning for shape and the removal of dead flowers, but neither chore is absolutely essential. Small flowering or "garden" shrubs need annual pruning and mulching, but little else.

Valuing Trees and Shrubs in Dollars

While we look to trees and shrubs to provide beauty to a landscape, it makes no sense to ignore their monetary value, especially if the inventory of the yard suggests that it is time to replace some of them. A young sapling three inches in diameter costs roughly $50 to $100.

For every inch more in trunk diameter the price goes up by $100 or more. Next, add 50 percent of the price on top for installing the tree in the yard. A good white oak, with a trunk twenty inches in diameter, is worth $2,000 in 1990 dollars. A less desirable species of comparable age and size, such as silver maple, is worth only $500.

Having an idea of the monetary value of a specific tree or shrub will help you decide whether to spend money to renovate it or to remove it.

RENOVATING TREES AND SHRUBS

From the foregoing discussion, it becomes obvious that wherever possible, it is desirable to retain those plantings that are appropriately sited, not yet overaged, and in reasonably good health. It is highly likely that they can be rejuvenated and will continue to enhance the beauty and value of your property for many years to come.

In the case of large shade trees with physical problems, it is worth calling in qualified tree-care people to prune or spray as the work is dangerous and requires specialized equipment. Unfortunately, tree-care companies vary widely in terms of their professional expertise. There are an alarming number of incompetent tree surgeons around the country, as any drive down a tree-lined suburban street will verify. Just because a company is big does not mean

If you take extra care when selecting a company to prune valuable shade trees, you can avoid this situation. Rather than simply heading back the main limbs, which encourages multiple weak shoots to sprout around the outside of the tree from ugly knobbed branches, competent professionals will prune by judicious thinning of side branches. This results in a strong, open branching pattern and a natural tree profile.

it is reliable and competent. Talk to at least two companies for estimates and compare their advice. Neighbors, friends, and government foresters are good sources of referrals for a tree service. Ask prospective firms for references and take a look at their pruning work.

Sometimes a tree-care expert will determine that a tree is not worth retaining. The removal of a large shade tree will cost between $300 and $1,000, depending on how close it is to a house, wires, or other structures. By all means have a tree removed if it poses any danger to the house or to people on and around the property. If the tree is definitely in the wrong place and is too big to move, then it should be cut down. A tree that has been diagnosed with disease or insect problems that cannot be corrected should be considered expendable. It is better to get rid of a questionable tree and replace it with a carefully selected high-quality tree than risk the even greater expense of serious damage or injury in the future.

If a large tree can be saved, then develop a rehabilitation plan with the help of a tree-care professional. Consider what steps are necessary to restore it to health. Renovation can include aerating the soil under the tree, pruning trouble spots in the tree, providing some specialized fertilizer, and sometimes intensive watering. These are therapeutic measures, one-time activities, designed to get a tree back on the line. Once the tree is healthy and the problems have been solved, an annual maintenance program is sufficient to care for the tree. That regimen is described later in this chapter.

Renovation by Aeration

Tree roots need nearby small empty spaces in the soil into which they can release carbon dioxide and from which they can obtain the oxygen they need in order to grow. If the roots are in compacted soil with little oxygen, they tend to grow upward toward the surface, or they die. The surface roots that ruin so many lawns are signaling that they lack oxygen. A lawn over ten years old that has never been aerated and that surrounds an established tree or shrub almost certainly has compacted soil. Think of the number of times it has been walked on over the past ten years! The nearby trees will definitely need some help getting oxygen to their root systems.

Where human traffic passes beneath the drip line of the tree, the roots should be protected from compaction with a mulch of organic material. Renew already compacted soils by punching holes in the soil with an aerating tool and the application of any product containing humic acid such as Nitron or Roots. This is the most effective approach. Commercial tree surgeons will charge between $200 and $300 for aerating under a large tree, roughly a thousand square feet.

Two different tools will aerate the soil under and around a large tree or shrub.

Soil drill. Fastened to a handyman-type power drill, a soil drill will bore holes in the earth, removing the soil as it penetrates. Drill half- to two-inch holes that are eighteen to twenty-four inches deep in the soil around the circumference of the tree or shrub out at its drip line. Then do the same thing out twice the distance to the drip line. Make the holes about eighteen to thirty-six inches apart.

Hydraulic device. A tree root watering and feeding device, this hydraulic type of aerator is a hollow pipe that is fastened to a garden hose and held over the soil around tree roots. The pressure of the water forced out of the end of the pipe will bore holes, simultaneously watering and aerating the tree. Face away from the tree trunk. Position the hydraulic probe at a 30-degree angle to the soil and aim the stream of water into the soil. Hold the probe in position for a few seconds until muddy water begins to spurt out, indicating that the soil is being driven out of the hole. These holes should be angled because tree and shrub roots tend to grow at an incline rather than straight down. Angled holes also increase oxygenation of the soil over a longer horizontal distance. Make as many holes and locate them as recommended above for the soil drill.

BACKFILLING THE HOLES. There is no need to fill aeration holes with anything, but if the soil is very clayey or seriously compacted, introducing some perlite, sphagnum peat moss, compost, or composted sludge into the soil at these spots is beneficial. To fertilize at the same time, fill the hole halfway with perlite or compost, then one-quarter full with slow-release fertilizer, then the rest with perlite or other material. The fertilizer does not need to be very deep, since most feeder roots are very shallow. Aeration holes created by hydraulic means are usually too small to fill with anything.

Renovation by Pruning

Pruning involves cutting off part of a tree or shrub for the benefit of the entire plant. There is a big difference between pruning a tree or shrub to renovate it and pruning it every year

To shape growth

To improve health

To stimulate growth and flower/fruit production

Rule of Thumb: Prune weak plants severely, healthy plants lightly.

or two as part of general maintenance and care. Pruning to renovate is radical pruning. It requires removal of a large percentage of the branches from the tree or shrub. It often means cutting an overgrown shrub practically back to the ground, thereby removing all the overaged woody stems to stimulate new growth.

PRUNING TOOLS

Although professionals will likely be handling major tree work, you can handle the pruning of small trees and all shrubs on your property. For these jobs there are all kinds of pruning tools on the market. Only two are really essential for normal landscape maintenance: a pair of hand pruners and a pair of lopping shears. The latter are simply pruning blades on the end of long handles to give extra leverage for cutting branches up to 1½ inches

in diameter. A handsaw is also useful for pruning the occasional large branch.

It goes without saying that the sharpness of pruning tools is very, very important. A dull pair of pruners will pinch a stem or tear a branch rather than cut it, leaving a damaged end that is more vulnerable to rot and other diseases than a clean cut would be. The cleanliness of pruning tools is also very important. After all, they are sometimes used to cut away diseased branches from otherwise healthy plants. It is therefore prudent to always clean pruning tools after cutting a diseased plant. Better yet, routinely clean them after every pruning session.

Professional landscape gardeners use a number of disinfectants that are simple and available to homeowners as well. Isopropyl (rubbing) alcohol is an excellent disinfectant for grafting and pruning tools, diluted one part to four of water. A household disinfectant spray such as Lysol is also effective and easy to use. Give pruner blades a quick spritz between cuts. A bleach solution made up of one part common household bleach and four parts water is also effective. After use, disinfect all pruning tools and then coat them with oil to prevent rust.

WHEN TO RENOVATE

When to carry out renovation pruning is a critical issue. It is confusing because it varies somewhat, depending on the plant. Renovate most deciduous shrubs in the spring just before their new leaves emerge. Then they will have plenty of time to regenerate new growth before facing the winter. Deciduous trees can be renovated during the growing season, but the best time for most is during the late winter while they are dormant. The absence of foliage makes it easier to see the tree profile. Many trees, such as birch, maple, and yellowwood, leak sap from wounds made during the late winter and early spring, so it is best to prune them in the summer. Evergreens, such as yew and holly, respond to severe cutting back of overaged stems done in late spring or early summer.

RENOVATION PRUNING TECHNIQUES FOR SHRUBS

Shrubs that have been neglected—are full of suckers and are misshapen with tangles of weak growth—usually need the most drastic type of renovation—pruning the entire plant back down to the ground, leaving just a few inches of stem growth to produce all new growth. Do this type of pruning in the early spring. As the young shoots grow over the season, clip them to produce a shapely shrub. This procedure is effective for deciduous plants such as forsythia, snowberry, weigela, and others that are vigorous growers.

After the season is underway it is not too late to renovate less drastically. Shrubbery that has become too thick and too high is a common problem in foundation groupings where unfortunate plantings of large-growing shrub

Maintaining shrubs and young trees around the yard does not require fancy pruning equipment. A pair of good quality hand pruners will clip twigs and small stems. Sturdy long-handled lopping shears provide the leverage needed to cut through branches up to two inches in diameter. This bow saw is lightweight but strong enough to cut through substantial limbs. Leave the chain sawing to tree-care professionals.

varieties have been made. Individual shrubs in this situation may be salvaged by removing some and then renovating the remaining ones. Removing some of the old shrubs will provide better air circulation for the remaining ones, and provide space for new, more appropriate, lower-growing species. If the shrub to be re-

This mountain laurel shrub had grown thin and leggy over many years. A thorough renovation required cutting back its old woody stems almost to the ground. New growth is already evident. Notice that the shrub is mulched with a ground cover, pachysandra.

to improve their health and reinvigorate them. Sometimes they benefit from the removal of old woody stems from their centers by cutting them out at ground level. Sometimes just clipping back overlong branches and removing suckers that erupt along the branches is sufficient. Study the individual growth habit of each shrub and determine how to encourage it rather than restrain it.

RENOVATION PRUNING TECHNIQUES FOR TREES

Renovation pruning of mature trees is best done by tree-care professionals who have the training and equipment for the job. While this job often involves severe pruning, it does not require maiming trees. Young trees (five to ten years) can be topped to control their size and shape, but mature trees must not be topped. Experts can effectively cut back branches and judiciously prune away overgrowth without leaving a butchered specimen, naked of foliage. When it seems as if a mature tree needs topping to bring it under control, especially if it is situated under a power line, it is most certainly the wrong tree for that location. The pruning of a large shade tree can cost from $200 to $600, depending on the extent of the pruning required. However, because it often can rejuvenate a significant specimen, providing years of added life and beauty, it is well worth the price.

moved is healthy and attractive, contact a local nursery before cutting it down. Sometimes nurseries are searching for mature-size shrubs for certain customers and will pay you to remove it. They have the equipment to remove it safely. A good quality mature shrub of a desirable species may bring several hundred dollars.

Short of cutting them back to the ground, there are alternative ways to prune old shrubs

Most small trees can be renovated by homeowners. Big or small, tree-pruning principles are basically the same. Cleanly cut away all broken or diseased branches. Remove all limbs that cross one another or rub against another limb to prevent abrasions from forming on tree bark that can foster disease problems. Neglected trees often are overloaded with a tangle of interior branches and limbs. Renovation requires cutting off most of the smallest interior branches to improve air circulation and light penetration.

The key to the correct pruning of tree limbs is to locate the cut properly. While it is not desirable to leave an obvious stub where the branch was, it is also not desirable to make a cut that is flush against the trunk. The ideal cut is one that leaves the "branch collar," the swollen area of living callus tissue that forms around the base of the branch as it grows older. This callus tissue is actually trunk wood, not branch wood, and it should not be cut away.

Before pruning off a branch, study the tree and learn to identify the branch collar. Whether the limb to be removed is living, dying, or dead, do not prune off the branch collar. Removing the collar exposes the trunk wood to disease organisms. On slow-growing trees, or on trees that are less able to "compartmentalize" the trauma, that can spell death. Cut close to, but not through, the collar.

Also look for the branch bark ridge at the base of the branch to be cut off. This marking is usually a darkened line of rough bark running at an angle into the trunk bark from the branch-trunk crotch. All pruning cuts should be made at an angle (usually 45 to 60 degrees) to the ridge, on the branch side of the ridge.

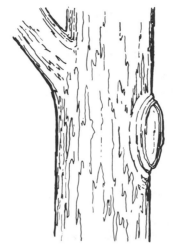
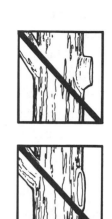

When pruning large limbs from trees, the placement of the cut is critical. Avoid cutting so closely to the trunk that trunk wood is cut. Conversely, do not leave too much of the limb.

The branch collar and the branch bark ridge serve as quick and easy guides for proper pruning cuts. When using a chain saw, stub back the branch first with a downcut, then finish with an upcut.

Needled evergreens (pine, juniper, fir, spruce, etc.) are best pruned only in the first years of growth. They rarely need extensive renovation because their natural growth habits automatically maintain their pleasing shapes. Sometimes a large old juniper or blue spruce gets a new lease on life, though, if raggedy bottom limbs that are lying on the lawn are cut off. Raising the canopy and exposing attractive trunk bark improves the appearance of these trees tremendously.

Improper pruning is a major cause of tree decay and can trigger insect attack. The branch collar mentioned above is a tree's first defense against disease organisms that may enter the trunk through dead, dying, or improperly pruned branches. When a tree is wounded, tissues in this collar form chemical barriers which compartmentalize decay organisms, limiting penetration and keeping new growth rings free from infection. The collar also appears to speed up the external closure of the wound by stimulating cambium tissue to form new bark and sapwood.

Consequently, contrary to longtime practice, there is no need to coat pruning wounds with tree paint or wound dressing. These materials do nothing to prevent decay, and little or nothing to promote wound closure. Some may reduce wood discoloration, but wood discoloration does not necessarily indicate wood decay and may, instead, be caused by naturally occurring chemicals stored in the tree cells.

RENOVATION PRUNING TECHNIQUES
FOR HEDGES

The best-looking hedge is one that is regularly pruned from the time it's planted. The unsightly holes in the base of many hedges result from years of improper pruning or no pruning at all. It is better to clip or shear a hedge every month, or even more frequently, than to do it only once or twice a year. More frequent clipping results in a denser growth habit and a better appearance.

Renovate a hedge that is leggy or skimpy with bare lower stems by hard pruning in the spring. Privet, barberry, Japanese holly, and other common hedge plants respond to this treatment by sending up many new shoots to fill in at the base of the plants. Cut woody stems back at least eight to twelve inches, more if the hedge has gotten completely out of control and is up to six or eight feet. Clip the sides of the hedge, but not as drastically. As the hedge fills in, shape it so it is narrower at its top than its sides. This way the foliage at the sides gets plenty of sun.

Of course, there is more to renovating trees and shrubs than pruning, but it is the fundamental first step. If neglected plants are to thrive once again, they must be cleaned up and stimulated to produce new, young growth. They need good light and air circulation to thrive. Pruning accomplishes this. It should be immediately followed up by fertilization with a good slow-release fertilizer and plenty of water.

ROUTINE MAINTENANCE OF TREES AND SHRUBS

Once renovated, the trees and shrubs on the property need regular attention. Annual maintenance of these plants is not anywhere near the job that lawn care or vegetable gardening is. In fact, you can divide the tasks up into two groups—the absolute minimum steps and those things that are helpful for the plant but not critical if not done each year.

Mulching Trees and Shrubs

A layer of organic mulch on the soil under trees and shrubs protects them from lawn mowers and string trimmers, discourages weeds, holds in moisture, cools the soil, conditions the soil, and looks attractive. Of all these, however, the most important role of the circle of mulch around plant stems or trunks is the protective one. Once injured by a lawn mower, string trimmer, or other yard-care equipment, the tree is at risk. There is no way to fix the wound and it is likely to provide access to insects and disease into the interior of the tree or shrub. It may be years before the effects of the injury are apparent, but this type of damage is the single most common cause of tree decline.

A ring of mulch around the bases of trees and shrubs creates a barrier against accidental injury. Effective mulch is about three to four inches deep—never deeper than four inches after it settles down. Spread it in a circle at least twenty-four inches in radius; it should not, however, come closer than two to four inches to the stem or trunk. Expand the mulched area as the plant grows larger, taking it out as far as six feet or to the drip line of the branches, if possible. If shrubs are grouped, mulch the entire group together. As noted in chapter one, another virtue of mulch is that it reduces the area of lawn that has to be cut. If the tree or shrub is surrounded by lawn grass when you decide to use a mulch, it is best to

> # ANNUAL TREE AND SHRUB MAINTENANCE
>
> ---
>
> MINIMUM STEPS:
> *Mulch soil around trunk or stem*
> *Fertilize once a year*
> *Water during drought*
>
> GOOD IF YOU HAVE THE TIME:
> *Aerate soil over root systems*
> *Prune to maintain shape; remove*
>   *damaged limbs*
> *Protect against harsh winter conditions*

kill the grass first. The best way is to use a glyphosate herbicide (like Roundup) which is very effective but safe for the environment.

There are several options for mulching around a tree or shrub. Use any number of organic materials, grow a living mulch, use a mulching fabric, or even a mulch of stones.

Organic mulches. Organic mulches, such as chopped leaves or woodchips, are easy to spread. You can produce these materials from yard waste with the help of a shredder, chipper, or mulching mower for a truly inexpensive mulch. As they slowly decompose, they add nutrients to the soil, reducing the fertilizer

The foliage canopies of these large shade trees have been pruned to allow more light to fall on the ground. This grouping, properly mulched with ground cover which thrives in the bright, indirect light, is a focal point in the yard.

Ground-cover mulches. Ground covers make a very attractive, low-maintenance mulch around trees and shrubs. Unlike turfgrass, they do not compete aggressively with tree and shrub roots for soil nutrients. Plants like pachysandra, vinca, ivy, and ajuga all require little care and little water or fertilizer, and they fill in thickly enough to prevent weeds from growing. Remove all established weeds before planting a ground cover bed, and expect to weed periodically until the new plants grow together. Spray the weeds in the planting area with Roundup, wait about two weeks, then plant the ground cover. It takes about two years for most ground covers to mature enough to prevent weeds on their own. Planting them more closely than the recommended spacing will shorten that time somewhat.

Geotextile mulches. "Geotextiles" or "mulching fabrics" have been available to homeowners for several years. Designed to be used around trees and shrubs as semipermanent mulching materials, they are usually used under organic mulches. These synthetic fabrics—permeable woven, nonwoven (feltlike), or knitted synthetics—resist decomposition and allow water and air to permeate them. They effectively suppress most weeds. Once covered with a nice organic mulch, they are not visible.

While these materials probably have appropriate applications in commercial and institutional settings, it is not clear how desirable they are for residential use. One concern is that they effectively block the slowly decom-

needs of the trees and shrubs. A layer of six or eight inches of freshly chopped dry leaves will settle to below the required maximum of four inches in a month or two. Bark chips or chopped bark mulches are available in most garden centers. These materials look nice and will need renewing each year. While organic mulch usually suppresses most weeds, stubborn perennial weeds may need a dose of Roundup herbicide once in a while.

posing organic mulch from entering the soil, denying the tree or shrub access to its valuable nutrients. Also, although manufacturers claim they allow water and air to penetrate into the soil, recent research suggests that the penetration rate is not uniform over the entire surface of the geotextile and that the plant suffers as a consequence. The only geotextile product that has passed all the tests of permeability and weed control to date is Dalen Corporation's Weed-X, found in most good garden centers.

Stone mulches. Japanese gardeners have shown how attractive various stone and gravel mulches can be. Young pines, apple trees, forsythia, and lots of other trees and shrubs thrive with stone mulches. Some are flat stones set close together, starting at least an inch out from the tree trunk; others are irregularly shaped stones or pebbles placed to direct rainwater down toward the roots. Coarse or fine gravel and rounded pebbles of various sizes and colors all make striking and effective mulches. They protect trees and shrubs from the inroads of power mowers and provide favorable conditions for soil bacteria and earthworms. Stone also holds midday heat and releases it gradually during the cooler night; on a cold night even one extra degree of warmth benefits plants, particularly if the temperature drops close to freezing.

Nutrition for Trees and Shrubs

Shrubs and trees in residential yards are routinely deprived of the nutrition found in their natural forest habitat, the decomposing organic debris on the forest floor. Homeowners do not usually mulch with organic material which adds some nutrients as it decomposes. They often rake up all leaves and keep the soil around the shrubs bare. Sometimes they unwittingly plant shrubs and trees in lawn turf which steals soil nutrients. After ten or fifteen years of this kind of nutrient deprivation, it is no wonder trees get sick, attract disease and insects, and begin to cost money for repairs and maintenance. Trees that are routinely fertilized, however, are not as likely to have those common problems.

Starting six months after they are planted, feed newly planted or transplanted trees and shrubs every fall for at least the first three or four years. This will cause them to grow vigorously, and probably increase the need for routine pruning somewhat, but their overall well-being will be greatly improved. After that, specifically feed established trees and shrubs every two or three years in the fall or feed them as part of a general feeding of the rest of the property every fall, as described below.

The best time to feed most trees and shrubs is the late fall just when the leaves are beginning to drop from the deciduous trees. This is about the time when the lawn and garden beds should be fertilized also, so the whole job can be done at the same time.

The root systems of large trees extend much further from the trunk than most people realize. Most of the roots that take up nutrients and moisture are near the soil surface.

Professional tree services usually use a special pressurized root-feeding tool that squirts slow-release liquid fertilizer down into the root zone. This is a very effective method for feeding trees but, unfortunately, the technology is too expensive for use by homeowners. A professional tree-care company will charge $75 to $150 for each large shade tree that is fed via this pressurized method. Professionals will also feed trees and shrubs using granular fertilizer, which costs much less than the liquid system.

A professional arborist will say that every large tree needs its very own fertilization program, because every tree is different; technically this is correct. However, for most of the trees and shrubs in the average home landscape, a standard feeding program such as the one described will work just fine in 95 percent of the cases. In the case of a particularly large and valuable tree, perhaps a historic tree, it may be worth hiring a professional to custom-

ize its diet. Otherwise, it's not that complicated to feed the trees and shrubs on your property. Spreading a granular, slow-release fertilizer is the next best thing to a professional application of liquid fertilizer.

To feed trees properly, it is necessary to understand a little about the root zone. Remember, it covers about twice the area as that covered by the area of the branches, configured underground much the same way as the branches are above. The large roots are near the trunk and the small fibrous hair roots that actually pull in the nutrients are farther away. These feeder roots radiate in a circle beginning about a foot or two from the trunk out to beyond the farthest spread of the branches. Therefore, any fertilizer spread close to the trunk is likely to be wasted. If that area is already mulched, there is no need to spread fertilizer over the mulch.

Because some homeowners may be interested in going beyond a minimum feeding program for their trees, but do not care to hire a professional tree-care service, the discussion below offers two regimens for feeding trees and shrubs. Trees and shrubs benefit from a feeding schedule modeled after the way humans get nutrition. Their primary source of nutrition comes from a "main meal" offered in the fall which is supplemented by occasional and optional "snacks" over the growing season to boost vigor if the tree or shrub is stressed. "Vitamins" in the form of seaweed or kelp products enable these plants to fully utilize the nutrients they receive. At the very least trees and shrubs need a "main meal" every two or three years, and annually is better. For those who choose to go a step further, snacks and vitamins foster optimum tree and shrub health.

PROVIDING THE MAIN MEAL

It is not difficult to provide adequate basic nutrition for trees and shrubs. The most common fertilizer sold in nurseries and garden centers specifically for trees and shrubs is available in the form of "spikes." They look like tent pegs and are designed to be pounded into the soil around the tree where they release nutrients slowly over time. They are not really satisfactory in most situations. They tend to concentrate the nutrition in a few small areas, out of reach of the many widespread feeder roots. Also, many, many more spikes than the number indicated on the label are needed to properly feed a single large tree. Although four or five spikes might be okay for a five-foot tall sapling, a full-size oak will require eighty to one hundred spikes to supply adequate nutrition, even though the box says ten are enough. At this rate the cost of spikes becomes prohibitive.

Granulated fertilizer can be spread more evenly and is less expensive than spikes. Granular fertilizer that is formulated just for trees and shrubs is a relatively new product and has recently become available only in some areas. However, the next best choice is any slow-release granular form of lawn fertilizer, which is available everywhere. That it contains the slow-release form of nitrogen should be prom-inently written on the bag label. All lawn fertilizer bags will indicate the ratio of nitrogen, phosphorous, and potatssium with series of numbers such as 10-6-10. The numbers indicate the percentage of each major nutrient in the mixture. The higher the numbers, the higher the percentage of that particular nutrient. The actual weight of each nutrient is calculated by multiplying the percentage of each one against the total weight of the bag of fertilizer.

A good ratio for fertilizing a tree or shrub is something around 3-1-2 or any multiple such as 9-3-6 or 15-5-10. Some tree companies even use a fertilizer with a 3-1-1 ratio. In other words, tree fertilizers tend to be higher in nitrogen than they are in phosphorous and potassium. Thus the ratio is not a precise standard but provides a guideline for shopping in the garden center.

HOW MUCH FERTILIZER?

As a general rule, spread granular fertilizer within an area at least one and a half times the size of the area under the plant's drip line. If the tree or shrub is in a garden or is surrounded by ground cover or other mulch, then use the amount per square foot recommended for lawns. If the tree or shrub is planted in turfgrass, then fertilize the lawn with just a bit more per square foot than is recommended on the package for lawns. Although the grass will get more than its share of the nutrition, the tree or shrub roots under the turf will get enough to stay healthy.

To Be More Precise

With trees, the problem is that the amount of fertilizer needed by the tree varies with each tree, being directly related to its size. To adjust fertilizing to the size of the individual trees, use ½ pound of granulated slow-release fertilizer for each ½ inch of trunk diameter measured/ estimated four feet up from the base of the tree. Spread the total amount of fertilizer needed in an area 1½ times the size of the area covered by the drip line.

PROVIDING SNACKS

Snacks for trees and shrubs during the growing season are offered in the form of a liquid fertilizer designed to be sprayed on plant foliage. While these products are inappropriate for main meals, they are ideal for giving plants a boost from time to time. Snacks are optional. They are not essential to plant survival or basic health. Delivered as foliar sprays they give trees and shrubs—actually, all plants—an extra kick that will help them better withstand drought periods, resist insect attack, and maybe even produce larger and brighter flowers or larger fruits. The nutrients are rapidly absorbed directly through leaf cells, invigorating the plants.

Not truly practical for large shade trees, snacks are most appropriate for flowering shrubs and small shade trees during their first five years. Use a pump sprayer (one gallon or more) and any fertilizer sold in the garden center that is easily diluted. Fish emulsion is the best, but there are many others that are satisfactory. Mix the spray and apply it in the morning before the sun gets hot. Spray to cover all the leaves lightly, both top and bottom. If time permits, a good routine is monthly snacks in May, June, and July. However, even just one snack a season is better than no snacks.

PROVIDING VITAMINS

Very often, although plants have sufficient sources of the major nutrients in their diets—nitrogen, phosphorous, and potassium—they sometimes lack certain materials called "micronutrients." These are trace elements such as zinc, boron, and magnesium that all plants need in minuscule amounts to grow and stay healthy. To avoid this deficit, which is very difficult to detect, give trees and shrubs a "vitamin" tonic spray once or twice a year. As with snacks, this step is optional but does make a difference in the overall health of trees and shrubs. All shrubs and small trees benefit from a spray of liquid seaweed or kelp extract in very dilute form, about one tablespoon of extract to a gallon of water. There are other "bioactivators" on the market that contain the enzymes, hormones, and trace minerals found in seaweed extracts. Any of these products will provide plants a boost and insure their having a balanced diet.

In summary then, fertilizing is not terribly complicated. The minimum for healthy trees and shrubs is a main meal of a slow-release form of granular fertilizer every two or three years applied over the entire area of the plant's root zone. This, and perhaps occasional snacks and some vitamins each season will assure sturdy, vigorous small trees and shrubs.

Watering Trees and Shrubs

The single most important thing you can do for the overall health of the trees and shrubs on your property is to be sure they have adequate water. Undoubtedly it offers them the best defense against insect attack in the heat of summer. Often their water needs are ignored because they do not immediately show distress like flowers, lawn grass, and vegetable plants do. Also, the average homeowner has no real sense of how these large plants use water. Arborists say that next to mechanical injury, drought is a primary factor in making trees vulnerable to attack by borers and other insect pests.

All trees, including evergreens, constantly lose water through their leaves during the process of transpiration. Water evaporates from the leaves at differing rates, depending on the air temperature, the humidity, the time of day, and the time of year. For example, a maple with a crown (drip line) diameter of twenty feet will lose about twenty gallons of water during an eight-hour period. On a hot day that amount can more than double. On the other end, if a good rain leaves an inch of water over the area of its root system, about 1,200 square feet, the area will be getting more than 700 gallons of water. That is one- to two-weeks' supply for the tree. However, the turfgrass will capture much of that water, leaving probably less than half the amount for the tree. In a hot summer, the tree will probably start feeling the lack of moisture after seven to ten days of no rain or other irrigation.

The soil's ability to hold and store water also makes a great difference in the water needs of trees and shrubs. If, over the year, the soil has been aerated and peat moss or compost has been put in the holes, the soil's ability to hold rainwater will be significantly enhanced. Routine supplemental watering may not be necessary very often.

SUMMER SOAKING

Common sense says that there are likely to be occasional extended dry periods when trees and shrubs will need to be watered. When does a big tree really need water? The answer is, when it has been hot, rainfall is sparse over several weeks, and flowers and lawns have required regular watering. Furthermore, when it is 85°F, city trees may experience temperatures of 130°F or more! Reflected heat from the pavement, roads, walls of buildings, and the metal bodies of cars hike up the surface temperature throughout a city. Even the surface temperature in suburbs can be 20°F higher than the day's reported temperature.

There are two situations in which it is important to water trees—low water conditions and drought conditions. A possible third is just before hard frost.

Low-Water-Demand Trees and Shrubs

Barberry, Japanese (*Berberis thunbergii*)

Bayberry (*Myrica pensylvanica*)

Bearberry (*Arctostaphylos uva-ursi*)

Birch, gray (*Betula populifolia*)

Box elder (*Acer negundo*)

Butterfly bush (*Buddleia*)

Chaste tree (*Vitex*)

Cherry, western sand (*Prunus besseyi*)

Cinquefoil (*Potentilla*)

Cotoneaster (*Cotoneaster*)

Dogwood, gray (*Cornus racemosa*)

Elm, Siberian (*Ulmus pumila*)

Goldenrain tree (*Koelreuteria paniculata*)

Hackberry, European (*Celtis australis*)

Honey locust, thornless (*Gleditsia triacanthos*)

Japanese angelica (*Aralia elata*)

Japanese pagoda tree (*Sophora japonica*)

Juniper (*Juniperus*)

Locust, black (*Robinia pseudoacacia*)

Maple, amur (*Acer ginnala*)

Mulberry, white (*Morus alba*)

Nannyberry (*Viburnum lentago*)

Oak (*Quercus*)

Olive, common (*Olea europaea*)

Osage orange (*Maclura pomifera*)

Pine, Japanese black (*Pinus thunbergiana*)

Poplar, white (*Populus alba*)

Privet (*Ligustrum vulgare*)

Quince, flowering (*Chaenomeles speciosa*)

Russian olive (*Elaeagnus angustifolia*)

Sassafras (*Sassafras albidum*)

Scotch broom (*Cytisus scoparius*)

Smoke tree (*Cotinus coggygria*)

Saint-John's-wort (*Hypericum*)

Sumac, fragrant (*Rhus aromatica*)

Tamarisk (*Tamarix*)

Tree of heaven (*Ailanthus altissima*)

Washington hawthorn (*Crataegus phaenopyrum*)

Witch hazel, common (*Hamamelis virginiana*)

LOW-WATER CONDITIONS. Less than one inch of rainfall during any ten-day period during the growing season, especially in the summer months, constitutes a low-water condition that will affect all plants. The easiest way to take care of trees and shrubs in this situation is to use a porous drip irrigation hose laid around the drip line of the tree or shrub. Run this irrigation long enough to assure that at least an inch of water soaks into the root zone and repeat every ten days until it rains again. If the drip hose unavoidably lies over turf, then two inches of water will be necessary to accommodate both the grass and the tree or shrub.

DROUGHT CONDITIONS. If the Department of Agriculture declares a "drought" in the area, then trees and shrubs are surely experiencing great stress and the soaker hose may not be able to deliver enough water to relieve it. In this instance, supplement soaker hose watering with root zone watering, using a root watering/feeder tool available from nurseries, garden centers, and mail-order catalogs.

A root zone watering device gets water down into the root system directly and quickly, easing the stress on a tree or shrub. To water most effectively, inject water in spots two or three feet apart throughout the entire root zone, that is, twice the distance of the trunk to the drip line. Insert the device into the ground about twelve to fifteen inches deep, and keep it there until water starts spurting up beside the probe. Then move to the next spot. A thorough watering such as this in soil that has any reasonable water-holding capacity should hold the tree in a drought for at least two weeks. In areas with sandy soil or little organic material in the soil, this technique may be necessary every week during a drought, especially for young trees and shrubs.

PREWINTER WATERING. In the northern parts of the country, where winter weather can be cold and harsh, all trees and shrubs—especially evergreens—suffer from desiccation, or loss of water through evaporation. Once the ground has frozen solid, the roots are no longer able to absorb water from the soil. At the same time, while things slow down, the plant is still transpiring or losing water through its leaves or needles. "Winterkill" is a catch-all term that is used to explain why a tree or shrub doesn't live through the winter, and very often the reason for the plant's death is dehydration.

While it is only one of several measures that should be taken for the winter protection of shrubs and trees, a final watering is a most important step. Some time during the period beginning a month after the first frost and before the ground freezes hard, water all trees and shrubs in the yard very, very well. In this instance a slow drip system is far superior to trying to do the job with an overhead sprinkling system. Run the drip system for several hours around every tree and shrub so that when they go into the winter they have the maximum amount of moisture in their systems.

Maintenance Pruning of Trees and Shrubs

In an earlier section we described aerating around trees as part of the renovation process (see pages 42–43). This practice is so beneficial it should be done as a maintenance measure at least every three to five years, ideally every year. Trees and shrubs growing in turfgrass need aerating at least every two years. Whether it is a shrub, or a small or very large tree, a plant growing in soil with a good source of oxygen will be far healthier than one living under compacted conditions. No doubt, aeration is something of an act of faith. It is impossible to see the impact directly. The same is true for qualities of drought resistance, insect pest resistance, or disease resistance inherent in plants. Trees growing in well-aerated soils will take less maintenance, will require less fertilizer, and will live longer than trees denied that care.

Maintenance Pruning of Trees and Shrubs

Pruning to renovate a tree or shrub has already been discussed. Once a tree or shrub is in good shape, pruning is necessary only as the need arises for maintenance. On large trees, routine pruning is rarely necessary more than every three to five years. On smaller trees and shrubs, some routine pruning is useful almost every year. The secret to keeping the pruning job

Proper pruning of shrubs assures them a healthier, longer life. Shearing has destroyed the natural, informal habit of these azaleas and caused them to develop dense growth inside the shrub. Clip branches individually to soften their profile and permit good air circulation around the foliage.

modest is to prune a little bit frequently, rather than waiting until the problems get serious. Maintenance pruning, as opposed to renovation pruning, is done for two reasons: to control the size of a tree or shrub, and to remove diseased or injured limbs.

PRUNING FOR SIZE

Most plants have a natural habit or shape. Each has a pattern of limbs and leaves that forms a shape distinctive to its particular species. This is especially true of trees and shrubs, which are often categorized as mound-shaped, columnar, urn-shaped, pyramidal, or weeping. The key to successful maintenance pruning of ornamental trees and shrubs (fruit– and nut-bearing trees require a different type of pruning) is to understand the basic natural habit of the tree or shrub at hand. Efforts to control

Spring Flowering Shrubs Pruned Just After Bloom

(avoid pruning off buds formed last season for this one)

———

Almond, dwarf flowering (*Prunus glandulosa*)

Azalea, evergreen (*Rhododendron*)

Broom (*Cytisus, Genista,* or *Spartium*)

Deutzia (*Deutzia scabra*)

Forsythia (*Forsythia* × *intermedia*)

Hydrangea, bigleaf (*Hydrangea macrophylla*)

Magnolia, saucer (*Magnolia* × *soulangiana*)

Rhododendron (*Rhododendron*)

Rose, climbing (*Rosa*)

Sand cherry (*Prunus* × *cistena*)

Spirea, Vanhoutte (*Spiraea* × *vanhouttei*)

Weigela (*Weigela*)

Spring Flowering Shrubs Pruned in Late Winter

(must have time to form flower buds on this season's new growth)

———

Abelia (*Abelia*)

Azalea, deciduous (*Rhododendron*), 'Mollis', 'Knapp Hill', Exbury hybrids, and natives

Butterfly bush (*Buddleia*)

Cotoneaster (*Cotoneaster*)

Dogwood, red twig (*Cornus sericea, C. stolonifera*)

Euonymus, winged (*Euonymus alata*)

Hydrangea (PeeGee) (*Hydrangea paniculata* 'Grandiflora')

Magnolia, star (*Magnolia stellata*)

Maple, cut-leaf (*Acer palmatum*)

Rose, bush (*Rosa*), hybrid tea, grandiflora, floribunda types

Spirea, Anthony Waterer, Japanese, Margarita (*Spiraea* × *bumalda, S. japonica, S.* × *margaritae*)

Viburnum (*Viburnum*)

Winterberry (*Ilex verticillata*)

the growth of a plant through the judicious clipping of twigs and branches should honor its natural habit. That is why, with the exception of hedges and specialty pruning such as

Spring Flowering Shrubs Pruned Either Time

Barberry, Japanese (*Berberis thunbergii*)

Lilac, common (*Syringa vulgaris*)

Mock orange (*Philadelphus coronarius*)

Quince, flowering (*Chaenomeles*)

Witch hazel (*Hamamelis*)

some forms of topiary, pruning is done with pruner/clippers or loppers which cut one branch at a time. Hedge shearers are for just that, shearing hedges, and should never be used to prune shrubs.

Annual maintenance pruning accomplishes several things. It neatens up the looks of shrubs and trees, especially those which habitually send out suckers or spindly weak secondary branches that sap the energy of the plants while contributing nothing to their appearance. It also benefits some shrubs, like rose of Sharon, pyracantha, or yew, by inducing them to form more branches, reducing legginess, making them more compact, and encouraging bloom. Sometimes overly dense shrubs benefit from being thinned out in the middle; this improves air circulation around the foliage, reducing the potential for disease problems. Other shrubs, such as butterfly bush and some roses, actually need to be cut back drastically at the end of every year as a maintenance measure. This stimulates new shoots from the crown and stems which form buds quickly.

While some annual pruning may be necessary to clean up some shrubs, it should not

be a big job. If a tree or shrub is planted in the correct place, its growth should not cause it to overgrow its location every year. If it is necessary to constantly prune back new growth hard lest the shrub overtake the space provided, or cover a window or doorway, then it is the wrong shrub for that spot and should be replaced.

Most trees and shrubs experience their most rapid growth in the spring, before summer heat slows them down. It is at this time that maintenance pruning is often undertaken, as part of the general sprucing up of the yard. In fact, certain spring-flowering shrubs must be pruned at this time, shortly after they bloom, so that newly forming buds are not clipped off, ruining next year's bloom. In the North it is safe to maintenance prune most shrubs from the spring through to mid-August or so. After that it is advisable to wait until late fall so that there is no chance that new growth will develop before frost.

Prune young conifers just after the new growth is completed, usually in late spring or early summer. Cut back the "candles," the new growth at the ends of branches, about one half.

Evergreens Pruned Just After Spring Growth/Bloom

Andromeda (*Pieris japonica*)

Daphne (*Daphne*)

Fir (*Abies*)

Heath (*Erica*)

Heather (*Calluna*)

Mountain laurel (*Kalmia latifolia*)

Pine (*Pinus*)

Evergreens Pruned Late Dormant (Winter) Season

Arborvitae (*Thuja occidentalis*)

Atlas cedar (*Cedrus atlantica*)

Bay laurel (*Laurus nobilis*)

Boxwood (*Buxus*)

Cherry laurel (*Prunus caroliniana*)

Chinese holly (*Ilex cornuta*)

Douglas fir (*Pseudotsuga menziesii*)

False cypress (*Chamaecyparis*)

Gold-dust plant (*Aucuba japonica*)

Heavenly bamboo (*Nandina domestica*)

Hemlock (*Tsuga*)

Holly (*Ilex opaca, I. aquifolium*)

Inkberry (*Ilex glabra*)

Japanese holly (*Ilex crenata*)

Juniper (*Juniperus*)

Oregon grape (*Mahonia aquifolium*)

Spruce (*Picea*)

Wintercreeper (*Euonymus fortunei*)

Evergreens Pruned Anytime

Cherry laurel (*Prunus laurocerasus*)

Euonymus, evergreen (*Euonymus japonica*)

Privet (*Ligustrum vulgare*)

Yew (*Taxus*)

Do not cut back past this point or the whole limb may die. This pruning regimen will keep the trees growing slowly and maintain them within the bounds of the space allotted to them in the landscape. When pruning these trees and shrubs, do not interfere with their natural habit. They are not likely to regenerate a limb or fill in a hole with foliage. Do not top them, either. This encourages them to form two leaders, or main stems, weakening the tree. If this occurs naturally, prune out the smaller of the two leaders.

PRUNING FOR HEALTH

At any time during the year it may become necessary to prune a tree or shrub for health reasons. Any branch or limb split or broken due to storm, wind, or damage from a flying object must be promptly removed. It is important that it is cut cleanly so that it can heal smoothly and quickly. Jagged, splintered breaks are prime locations for insect and disease access. Anytime it becomes obvious that a limb or branch is diseased, or the foliage in one area is covered with fungus, prune it out before the problem spreads. Wrap these cuttings and discard them in the trash so the disease does not spread. This is a time when it is essential to disinfect the pruners after use.

Winter Protection of Trees and Shrubs

The best protection for trees and shrubs in the winter is proper care during the rest of the year. The healthier they are before the cold weather hits, the better their chances of coming through the winter safely. Mulching around the trees and shrubs and deep watering just before hard freeze are two very important protection measures.

Stress from severe winters reduces the vigor of trees and shrubs. Extreme cold, harsh winds, and glaring sun can cause a variety of injuries to exposed trees and shrubs. Some kind of barrier is in order. Look in the garden center for windbreak material expressly designed for this purpose. Rigged around a shrub or along a hedge line, it allows some air through, but will buffer the greatest force of the wind, protecting the plant. Burlap supported by some kind of wooden frame will also protect smaller shrubs that are exposed to the elements. Snow fencing is also an excellent wind barrier. Do not use plastic of any kind. It does not permit the air circulation that is necessary to trees and shrubs even in the winter, and will cause intense heat buildup from the sun.

There are products on the market designed to protect evergreen foliage from winter wind and sun. Sprayed on leaves or needles, they coat them with a thin layer of plasticlike material. While the tree or shrub can still transpire, it does so more slowly so that it loses less water. These sprays, sometimes called antidesiccant sprays because they prevent drying out of the foliage, are not effective unless they are carefully applied so that all leaf surfaces are completely covered—tops and bottoms. Several of these products wear off after time and must be resprayed once or twice over the winter months. However, they do offer a measure of protection to evergreen shrubs and small evergreen trees if they sit in a vulnerable location, exposed to the winter wind and sun.

For optimium results, spray in the late fall when the air temperature is still above 40°F and will remain so for at least three or four hours after spraying. Then catch a mild day in January and sneak out to repeat the spray. Remember, the temperature must be above 40°F for three or four hours after applying the spray. Two coats, properly and thoroughly applied, will give a substantial measure of protection to most evergreen plants.

WINTER DAMAGE

Certain trees or shrubs will inevitably suffer some winter damage despite all precautions. When this happens, do not prune until the extent of the damage is known, usually by late spring. Plants with only foliage burn will appear normal again in May or June after new growth appears. Before cutting back limbs, scratch the bark with your thumbnail to distinguish healthy green tissue from brown, dead tissue. Or wait until spring buds begin to swell on the stems and then cut the limbs back to where the live buds indicate healthy tissue. Cut back shrubs that show extensive bark splitting and loose bark all the way around the stem promptly in early spring. If the soil is on the dry side, water affected plants.

It is important to remove any snow that accumulates on evergreen trees and shrubs after a storm. There is a right way and a wrong way to do this. Do not push the snow off the

---

Seasonal Care of Trees and Shrubs

SPRING

> *Plant certain trees and shrubs*
> *Prune certain shrubs*
> *Aerate soil over roots*
> *Remove any winter mulch cover slowly*

SUMMER

> *Water as needed*

FALL

> *Main feeding*
> *Water heavily just before hard freeze*
> *Prune certain shrubs*
> *Best planting time for most trees/shrubs*

WINTER

> *Renew mulch*
> *Prune most trees*

---

branches in a downward motion. If the branch is near the breaking point, this will simply finish the job. Instead, push the snow off the branches in an upward motion, taking the weight off the branches without forcing them to move any lower.

Shrubs or small trees located under roof overhangs are especially vulnerable to breakage from snow sliding off the roof in large chunks. Either move the shrubs out from under the overhang, or build some kind of a wooden frame around and over the plants to protect them from the falling snow. Such a frame must be sturdy enough to withstand the weight of wet snow, yet permit light to reach the shrub. A type of wooden Λ-shaped frame that resembles an opened step ladder over the shrub is available by mail order or can be made fairly easily.

In the North, severe late frosts occasionally catch early-flowering fruit and ornamental bushes, effectively wiping out the blossom display and expected fruit crops of these plants. Sometimes you can delay blossoming by spreading a couple of inches of sawdust over snow-covered plants in late winter for insulation. Slowing the snow melt this way can also reduce runoff and thus increase soil moisture reserves.

ADDING NEW TREES AND SHRUBS TO THE LANDSCAPE

This requires some forethought. Selecting appropriate plants for specific sites are important decisions, not to be left to impulse. In fact, for major changes in the plantings and organization of your property, it is wise to seek the advice of a professional landscape designer. Mistakes made with major landscape plantings can be expensive to correct and very disappointing.

On the other hand, most homeowners can select an occasional additional tree or shrub for the yard themselves, as long as they have thought about all the variables ahead of time. There are lots of reasons for selecting a particular tree for a particular site. The right kind of tree, planted in the right place, can provide cooling shade in the summer and deflect the wind in the winter, thereby affecting heating and air-conditioning bills. A line of a certain kind of tree or shrub can screen out noise and unsightly views. It is worth spending some time in advance thinking about choices.

It is important to choose species appropriate for the local climate and the soil, and the water-table level, as well as the wind and sun exposure of the intended site. Many homeowners want to have a specimen that is low-maintenance, a pleasing color and shape, and the correct size for the site. A plant in the wrong location attracts more insects, has more disease, is more vulnerable to physical damage, and will likely die prematurely. While it is possible to move trees and shrubs after they have already become established in a location, it is hard work. It is best to try and avoid this ordeal for the tree's sake, too.

Here is one way to go about selecting trees and shrubs:

Start with the site. Usually the process begins with some available space. Most people start with: "I'd like to have a tree (or shrub) in that spot." The next consideration must be whether the space is large enough for a mature tree or

Some Trees That Tolerate Wet Soil

Red maple (*Acer rubrum*)

Alder (*Alnus*)

Holly (*Ilex*)

Eastern larch (*Larix laricina*)

Sweet gum (*Liquidambar styraciflua*)

Sweet bay (*Magnolia viginiana*)

Willow (*Salix*)

Bald cypress (*Taxodium distichum*)

Arborvitae (*Thuja occidentalis*)

Some Small-Size Trees That Tolerate Shade

Vine maple (*Acer circinatum*)

Striped maple (*Acer pensylvanicum*)

Mountain maple (*Acer spicatum*)

Serviceberry (*Amelanchier*)

Redbud (*Cercis canadensis*)

Flowering dogwood (*Cornus florida*)

Holly (*Ilex*)

Wild red cherry (*Prunus pensylvanica*)

Rosebay rhododendron (*Rhododendron maximum*)

American arborvitae (*Thuja occidentalis*)

Hemlock (*Tsuga canadensis*)

shrub. It is easy to forget how large these plants grow, and how large the existing neighboring ones will also grow over the next few years. It is essential to plan ahead to avoid overcrowding. Do not depend on pruning to keep the new tree or shrub from outgrowing its site.

The other important consideration is light availability. Does the site offer full sun, part sun, or mostly shade? This information is critical to determining which tree or shrub will thrive there. Space and light are the primary site considerations because they are basically unalterable. Less than ideal soil at that spot can always be improved and sparse rainfall can be supplemented by watering.

Consider the purpose. Why would a tree or shrub be good in that spot? Of course, the primary purpose of such a planting would be to enhance the appearance of the landscape, so the answer might be, "Because it would look nice." But, of course, trees and shrubs have

Familiar Northern Broad-Leaved Evergreens

Abelia (*Abelia*)

Azalea (*Rhododendron*)

Barberry (*Berberis*)

Blueberry (some) (*Vaccinium*)

Boxwood (*Buxus*)

Cherry laurel (*Prunus laurocerasus*)

Cotoneaster (*Cotoneaster*)

Euonymous (*Euonymus*)

Firethorn (*Pyracantha*)

Holly (*Ilex*)

Japanese andromeda (*Pieris japonica*)

Mountain laurel (*Kalmia latifolia*)

Oregon grape (*Mahonia*)

Privet (*Ligustrum vulgare*)

Rhododendron (*Rhododendron*)

Viburnum (*Viburnum*)

functional as well as ornamental value, so it is a good idea to consider whether the new plant could also serve another purpose. Will it eventually provide shade, hold up a swing or hammock, block the view of the neighbors, accent the entrance to the driveway, reduce lawn size, produce cones or nuts, attract birds, provide evergreen boughs for indoor holiday decorations, shield the house from winter winds, produce flowers, etc.? Seeking answers to these questions will help define more clearly exactly what kind of tree or shrub is going to best fill the bill.

Consider the types of trees and shrubs. Trees and shrubs are usually divided into two main types: deciduous and evergreen. Deciduous trees and shrubs drop their leaves in the fall and winter over with bare trunks and branches. Although they require more maintenance—raking leaves comes to mind immediately—they are desirable for many reasons. Great shade trees, like oak, maple, ash, beech, and sycamore, and the smaller street trees, such as linden, hawthorn, and honey locust, are deciduous. The former produce stately, spreading canopies of foliage to cool the yard in the summer. Many deciduous trees offer attractive berries, nuts, or flowers, as well as stunning autumn color. Evergreens, both broad-leaved ones such as holly and rhododendron and needled ones such as spruce and pine, tend to be more compact and pyramidal in shape, and they generally require less maintenance. It is safe to say that evergreens of all kinds are the most important and versatile of the trees and shrubs in the landscape, not in the least because they are green year-round.

Some Small Shade Trees Suited to Residential Properties

Various maples (*Acer*) trident, hedge, coliseum, David, amur, fullmoon, lobel, Japanese, and others

American holly (*Ilex opaca*)

Ash (*Fraxinus*)

Crab apple (*Malus*)

Eastern redbud (*Cercis canadensis*)

English holly (*Ilex aquifolium*)

Flowering dogwood (*Cornus florida*)

Hawthorn (*Crataegus*)

Hemlock (*Tsuga canadensis*)

Hornbeam (*Carpinus*)

Japanese dogwood (*Cornus kousa*)

Japanese tree lilac (*Syringa reticulata*)

Magnolia (*Magnolia*)

Ornamental cherry (*Prunus serrulata, P. subhirtella*)

Sourwood (*Oxydendrum arboreum*)

Viburnum (*Viburnum*)

A trip to a local nursery will reveal the wide variety of tree and shrub forms. Many shrubs, both deciduous and evergreen, come in a wide range of sizes from full-size to dwarf, and some may have been hybridized to have a weeping form. There are types with blue, silver, or variegated foliage too. Others, like birches and sycamores, have particularly handsome peeling bark. While trees and shrubs of all kinds are also available by mail order, the local nursery is a good source of information about which varieties are suitable for the local area. Once they have been identified, it only remains to choose the one that is the appropriate size that appeals.

Other considerations. Tree safety is an issue few people think about. People who live in areas where severe thunderstorms are frequent should be aware that certain trees are likely to attract lightning and should be avoided. According to the American Society of Consulting Arborists, these are: oaks; tulip trees; silver, sugar, and Norway maples; pines; and hickories. Beech, sweet gum, and many others are less likely to be lightning victims.

Other tree species tend to be very brittle and cannot stand up to strong wind and ice storms. For this reason they are poor choices for street trees and should not be planted close to buildings. Examples of some that break and

Trees Suited to City Conditions

Norway maple (*Acer platanoides* 'Crimson King')

Fringe tree (*Chionanthus virginicus*)

Cornelian cherry (*Cornus mas*)

Lavelle hawthorn (*Crataegus × lavallei*)

Washington hawthorn (*Crataegus phaenopyrum*)

Ginkgo (*Ginkgo biloba*)

Honey locust (*Gleditsia triacanthos*)

Goldenrain tree (*Koelreuteria paniculata*)

Sweet gum (*Liquidambar styraciflua*)

Saucer magnolia (*Magnolia × soulangiana*)

Star magnolia (*Magnolia stellata*)

Crab apple/apple (*Prunus*)

Bradford pear (*Pyrus calleryana* 'Bradford')

Oak (*Quercus*)

Japanese pagoda tree (*Sophora japonica*)

Linden (*Tilia*)

Zelkova (*Zelkova*)

---

split easily are willows, silver maples, mulberries, and tulip trees.

Still other trees are terribly messy, dropping fruit, seeds, resin, or bark all over the yard. Anyone who has ever had a sycamore on the property knows this aggravation. Peeling bark litters the yard all season, followed by falling leaves in the fall and seed balls thereafter. Trees that bear fruits or nuts may be beautiful in the spring when in flower, but eventually they become a nuisance as the ripe fruits fall all over the lawn. Mulberries tracked into the house stain carpets badly. It is wise to inquire about these characteristics before purchasing a tree or shrub.

In addition, some trees are more susceptible to pest and disease problems than others. For instance, paper (or white) birches are plagued with borer problems outside of northern New England. Evergreen euonymus has chronic scale problems. Fruit trees are subject to a host of difficulties unless they are protected by regular spraying. Other trees that have persistent pest problems are buckeye, serviceberry, chestnut, hawthorn, English or American holly, larch, crab apple, lilac, linden, mountain ash, elm, and willow. Unless a homeowner is fully prepared to provide optimum, regular care to these trees, it is wise not to purchase them for the yard.

People in urban areas might think about planting trees that are considered tough and better able to withstand the harsher environmental conditions found in most urban environments. Species recommended for urban areas are quite attractive, and can more readily tolerate the hostile growing environments typical of many American cities than can many popular shade trees grown in more horticulturally benign suburban settings. They are better able to manage compacted soil, air pollution, highway salt, reduced air circulation, limited space, and reduced water.

Seeding advice. Upscale local nurseries have horticulturists on their staff who are familiar with trees and shrubs and are happy to give advice. Some homeowners have the good fortune to live near a public arboretum, an excellent place to see various tree and shrub varieties and learn about those suitable for the area. Also, a consulting arborist will know exactly what choices to consider. Finally, a very good way to identify some options is to drive around town and look for trees and shrubs that look terrific. If a particular one seems to be perfect for the spot at home in the yard, stop and ask the owner what that tree or shrub is. Most people are delighted to give that information.

When to Buy Trees and Shrubs

Once a decision is made about which tree or shrub is right for the yard, all that remains is to buy it and plant it. The best time to plant deciduous trees and shrubs is mid to late fall. During this time plants do not grow very much above ground, but their roots continue to de-velop until the ground freezes hard (about two months after planting). Planted at this time a deciduous tree or shrub has time to develop a root system that is capable of supporting the major spurt of top growth and the development of foliage in the spring. The best time to plant evergreen trees and shrubs is early spring because they make little root growth in fall.

The next best time to safely plant most trees and shrubs is in late winter or very early spring, as soon as the soil can be worked. At this time trees and shrubs are still dormant, so their roots do not have to work too hard just as the tree is adjusting to its new location and recovering from transplant shock. It is critically important that by late spring, when the plant is experiencing its main spring growth spurt, the roots have developed sufficiently so they are capable of providing enough moisture to support new top growth.

For this reason it is absolutely essential to water spring-planted trees or shrubs every three to five days during their heavy growth period in late spring. Be sure to spread a layer of mulch on the soil over the newly planted roots to help retain soil moisture. If watering is neglected, the shrub will not do very well for a whole year. Quite possibly it may die.

A possible, but least-desirable, planting time is late spring or during the summer. It is not the best time to plant a tree or shrub, but sometimes there is no choice. Minimize any moisture loss from the plant by spraying its foliage thoroughly with an antidesiccant before beginning the planting process. Follow that up with regular, generous watering for at least a month to get it through the planting shock. If the plant is relatively small (one to four feet tall), build a temporary protective canopy from burlap, an old bed sheet, agricultural fleece, or fine netting to protect it from the hot sun at a time when it is most vulnerable. Spray its foliage with seaweed or kelp extract; it acts like a tonic to help the plant overcome the trauma of transplating during warmer weather.

The best weather for transplanting shrubs or small trees is cool and overcast. Otherwise, wait until the late afternoon or early evening to plant, so that transplants do not have to cope with bright, hot sun on their first day in the ground.

Planting Trees and Shrubs

Planting a tree or shrub sometimes seems like an intimidating undertaking. However, planting small shade trees and most shrubs is a job well within the skills of the nongardening homeowner. Each year professionals in the horticultural field learn more about how roots grow and the techniques for planting trees and shrubs are modified in light of the new knowledge. About 25 percent of woody plant failures are due to poor planting techniques—letting the roots dry out, planting too high or too low

in the soil, not removing wrappings from the rootball, or failing to water. The other 75 percent are due to improper siting. Often a small move or a minor change in the above- or below-ground environment can make the difference between a thriving plant and one that declines. A careful analysis of the site can save much disappointment and replanting.

DIGGING THE HOLE

Regardless of whether the new tree or shrub comes from the nursery bare root, balled and burlapped, or container grown, the hole that it will be set in is the key to its future. Recent research has changed the rules for digging the hole considerably. There are now two steps to take—first, loosen the soil to a radius of five times the size of the plant's rootball and then dig a saucer-shaped hole for the plant.

Because modern housing developments are established with the use of very heavy earth-moving machinery, the soils around homes built in the past fifteen to twenty years are very badly compacted. Researchers have found that trees and shrubs planted in these compacted soils are unable to penetrate the soil with their roots. The result is that the roots grow around and around within the space of the hole, just as if the plant were planted in a container. Within a few years, the tree or shrub gets sick and usually dies. Homes more than twenty years old also have compacted soils, the result of the thousands of times people have walked over the lawn mowing the grass. It is important to deal with the compacted soil prior to planting a new tree or shrub.

Loosen the soil around the intended planting spot with a shovel or spading fork. A small tiller can also do the job. It is best to loosen the soil down at least twelve inches. In the middle of the area of loosened soil dig a saucer-shaped hole just as deep as the height of the rootball, no deeper. Once set in the hole, the rootball should sit on solid soil that has not been loosened. Score the sides of the hole with a garden fork, trowel, or some other implement so the soil is cracked and roughened. The saucer shape and the roughened sides encourage the roots to penetrate into the surrounding area. The saucer-shaped hole also makes it easier to firm the soil around the rootball by hand as you fill the hole.

The planting hole should be only as deep as is necessary to position the tree or shrub at the same level or slightly above (no more than one inch) the level that it was planted before. Whether the tree or shrub comes planted in a container, with its roots in soil and wrapped in burlap, or bare rooted in a plastic bag, it is usually fairly easy to discern the soil line on its trunk that indicates how deeply it was planted previously. Use that as a guide.

It is essential that the plant be at this correct depth. To check the depth of the hole, place a shovel handle or a yardstick across the open hole after setting the plant in it. Make sure the base of the shrub trunk or stem is, in fact, level

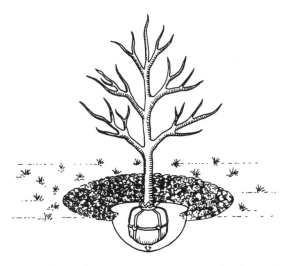

Dig a planting hole for a tree or shrub in the shape of a saucer to provide plenty of room for roots to spread and grow outward. If possible, rough up the soil around the hole another few feet. Position the plant on firm soil at the bottom of the hole so that it does not sink lower than the level of the soil surface. Once the tree is positioned in the hole, cut away as much burlap from around the rootball as possible. Fill the hole with soil and water it well. Then add a two- or three-inch layer of mulch over the root system.

with or only slightly above the surface of the surrounding soil.

Setting a shrub even just two or three inches below grade can slowly kill it. If the crown, the place where the stem meets the roots, is permitted to sink below grade, water will collect around it and promote rotting. The collected water also inhibits air from percolating into the soil to oxygenate the roots. The effect is to basically smother the roots. That is why there should be no loose soil or humus at the bottom of the planting hole, lest the tree or shrub gradually settle as the fill gets damp and compresses. It is better to have firm soil supporting the shrub's rootball. An exception to this is in the case of bare-root plants, which are discussed below.

THE SOIL MIX

If the soil at the planting site is either mostly clay or sand, it is beneficial to add some organic material to the soil mixture used to fill in the hole around the new plant. Work about one inch of this organic material into the surrounding area as you loosen the soil. Use peat moss, compost, leaf mold, municipal sludge, or chopped leaves. For the mixture in the hole use a ratio of about one part organic material to two parts soil. Add a handful of limestone to the peat moss if the new tree or shrub prefers a near neutral soil environment to offset the acidity of the peat moss. Use lots of peat moss without limestone for acid-loving plants such as azaleas or holly.

Recent research suggests that the introduction of any kind of fertilizer should be delayed until after the newly planted tree or shrub has been established for a year. Fertilizer at planting time stimulates early, rapid growth, which puts unnecessary pressure on the shocked root system to process nutrients and water.

TO PRUNE OR NOT TO PRUNE?

Some experts recommend pruning the roots or the branches of a newly purchased tree or shrub prior to planting it. This is not necessary in most cases. In fact, many plants come from the nursery already pruned. Do remove any broken or injured branches, stems, roots, or canes encountered during the transplant process. Also, remove one of any two branches that cross or touch each other. When transplanting a shrub or tree that has been elsewhere on the property, normal pruning of water sprouts, bad branches, and any diseased branches is fine, but no radical pruning is necessary. Excessive branch pruning can stimulate new top growth at a time when the burdened root system is struggling to establish itself.

THREE PLANTING SITUATIONS

Plants will come from the nursery in one of three conditions, each of which require a slightly different approach to planting. Plants will be in a bare-root condition, in a container, or wrapped in burlap.

BARE-ROOT PLANTS. Shrubs, roses, and some small trees often come from a mail-order nursery in a bare-root condition. The plant's roots have no soil around them and are packed in damp organic material of some kind and wrapped in a plastic bag. Store them in this packaging until planting time, then unwrap them and soak their roots in water for one to two hours (no longer) before planting them. Water to which some seaweed extract or root stimulator (available at garden centers) has been added does an even better job of fortifying the plant for the transplanting process. At this time prune any broken, twisted, or discolored roots.

When planting bare-root shrubs or trees,

build a mound of soil at the bottom of the hole to support the spread bare roots and establish the shrub at the correct height. This is the exception to the rule noted above, the only time when loose soil is put in the bottom of a planting hole. Set the plant in the hole over this mound and arrange the roots around it. Check that the shrub is high enough to position the graft union or root crown at the proper height relative to the surrounding soil surface. The height will vary by type of plant and by climatic zone for various plants, such as roses. Read the planting instructions on the label carefully.

CONTAINERIZED PLANTS. It is tempting with a shrub like an azalea or a small dogwood tree that comes in a container to simply remove the container, dig a hole, and plunk the plant into the hole as is. Avoid this tempatation.

Keep the soil in the container moist prior to planting time. Before removing the plant from the container, set it into the hole briefly to determine the right depth, then remove the container. Try to tip it sideways and slide the rootball out of the container, supporting the top of the soilball with your free hand. It may be necessary to give the container a stiff rap on the bottom to dislodge the plant. Many containerized shrubs and trees become pot-bound, the result of having their roots compressed in a restricted space over a period of time. Often many of the roots are grotesquely wrapped around the circumference of the root-ball and may even protrude from the container.

Once the plant is free from its pot, pull as many roots free as possible from the tight coil so they can be spread before the plant is set in the hole. If they are terribly matted and tangled, it is easier to score ¼-inch-deep vertical slices the length of the rootball at four or five places around its circumference to loosen the roots. It may even be necessary to clip off some of them to loosen the others. This may seem drastic but it encourages the roots to spread outward once they are planted. An alternative is to scrape the surface of the rootball with a screwdriver to loosen the roots. Cut away any dead or broken roots before setting the tree or shrub in its hole as described above.

BALLED AND BURLAPPED PLANTS. Plants whose roots and soilball are wrapped in burlap have already experienced the shock of having their roots severely pruned and bound. It is important to keep the soilball moist and to keep it covered to ease the shock to the roots. While conventional practice once dictated that the plant be planted with the burlap still covering the rootball, it is now recommended that the burlap and all other ties and wrapping be removed. Because it is important to keep the soilball intact around the plant roots, remove the burlap only after the plant has been lowered into its hole.

Place the burlapped plant into its hole. Then carefully untie or cut the strings holding the wrapping around the stem and pull them free. With a knife or scissors cut as much of the burlap away from around the soilball as pos-

When transplanting a tree or shrub, position it slightly higher than its depth in the soil at its previous site to encourage water to drain away from the stem. Before adding mulch, fashion a water-retaining ridge of soil several inches out from the stem to hold runoff water available to the rootball below.

biodegrade in the ground. If the wrapping around a rootball does not rot, it will strangle the root system over time. Next, adjust any exposed roots to aim them toward the sides of the hole. Roots that are not spread and are permitted to continue to grow in a circle will eventually strangle the tree or shrub.

THE PLANTING PROCESS

Once the tree or shrub is set in its hole properly, all that remains is to fill it with soil and water well. The process is the same, regardless of how the plant was packaged originally.

Fill the hole. Work the soil in between the roots, firming it periodically by hand. Then add more fill, always in such a way to eliminate any air pockets near the root ends. Do not tamp the soil with your feet or with water. This may bruise the tender roots and force oxygen from the soil which slows the growth of the roots. After the hole is full, tamp the soil down firmly by hand once more to eliminate air pockets.

Make a water-saver ring. Mound the extra fill soil mix around the trunk or stem of the plant, and then ten to twelve inches out from the trunk make a ridge of dirt around the whole plant. This creates a saucerlike space to catch water and hold it available for the tree or shrub. The mound of soil near the trunk prevents it from puddling there and possibly resulting in disease.

sible without disturbing it too much. All that should remain is a circular piece of burlap directly underneath the rootball which can be left in the hole. It is wise to remove as much of the wrapping as possible because common burlap-type material is being manufactured synthetically these days and therefore does not

Water very well. Only after the planting hole is filled with soil firmed over the root system is it time to water. Water the newly planted shrub or tree very slowly and very well. Set a hose into the water-saver ring and allow it to drip slowly for an hour or more. The goal is to have the soil thoroughly moistened, not utterly soggy.

Spread mulch. All newly planted trees and shrubs (and established ones too) benefit from a layer of organic mulch spread on the soil over their roots. It helps keep the soil moist by limiting runoff and evaporation and by absorbing water. At the same time it cools the roots so they can get a good start. Use woodchips, chopped leaves, shredded bark, pine needles, or compost. Spread a three- to four-inch layer around the plant out to its drip line, right over the top of the water-saving circle. Never pile more than four inches of mulch around any tree or shrub, as excessively thick mulch will prevent access to the soil by oxygen, critical to good root growth. A too-thick layer of mulch can kill a tree or shrub.

Keep moist, keep moist, and keep moist. Take pains to keep all newly transplanted trees and shrubs moist throughout the entire first season in their new locations. This step is the one most overlooked by homeowners and the cause of most lost trees and shrubs. If there is no rain, this may mean watering the new shrub

Too much mulch harms shrubs and trees. Limit the layer of woodchips, chopped leaves, shredded bark, or pine needles to a depth of 3 inches. Keep it away from plant stems to avoid problems with rot and rodents.

or tree as often as every three days in some parts of the country. Be sure to water especially well just before winter in northern climates.

Fertilizing the new planting. While offering granular fertilizer to a newly planted tree or shrub during its first six months in its new home is not recommended, it is a good idea to give it a boost with a dilute liquid fertilizer. Provide it either as a drench which is poured into the ground, or as a foliar spray which is sprayed on the leaves. Use any common liquid fertilizer, such as fish emulsion. Mix it at about half the normal strength—usually two teaspoons rather than a tablespoon in each gallon of water. Give the new plant this snack right after it is planted and about every three to four weeks until late summer. It is not essential, but it helps to assure a good start.

Staking the tree. There are two reasons for staking trees. One is to train them to grow straight, another is to assure that high winds do not uproot newly planted trees. Staking a tree to support it in its location is not always necessary. In fact, young trees need to bend a bit in the breeze to grow strong healthy trunks. However, a transplanted small tree taller than four or five feet that seems top-heavy with branches and foliage might appreciate some vertical support during its first season in its new location.

Anchoring the roots. Drive three 24-inch wooden stakes into the ground equidistant around the perimeter of the base of the new tree so that they are about twelve inches below the soil and twelve inches above the soil. Then loop lengths of thick, soft rope (or material designed especially for this purpose found at garden centers) around the plant stem and fasten them to the stakes. Be sure that each rope has about the same tension on it. Do not use

wire or nylon string because these materials will cut into the bark of the trunk. This arrangement holds the rootball firm, but still allows the top of the tree to flex in the wind and grow strong.

Supporting the trunk. Find two wooden stakes roughly two thirds the height of the tree and about 1 × 2 inches thick, and two lengths of strapping material a couple of feet long. Buy the strapping material from a garden center or use some woven belt fabric available in fabric stores. Drive the two stakes into the ground on opposite sides of the tree far enough beyond the perimeter of the hole to avoid accidentally putting the stakes into the rootball. Attach the straps low on the trunk, about a foot above

This is the correct method of staking a young tree to support its trunk. Check supports frequently to be sure they are not harming the tree.

the ground for evergreens and just below the first branches for a deciduous tree. Then fasten them to the stakes, again, with equal tension. Keep a very close eye on the condition of the bark under the straps, making sure no abrasion is occurring. Remove this rig as soon as it seems the roots have taken good hold, and do not leave it on longer than a year.

Protection from lawn mowers. A young tree's bark is very tender and vulnerable to injury, especially from lawn mowers and string trimmers. A small bump from a passing mower can develop into a major injury that can eventually kill the tree. A circle of mulch around the tree will keep mechanical yard-care equipment at bay. If, regrettably, there is grass growing right up to the trunk, place marker stakes around the tree to guard against mowing too closely. Clip any grass between the stakes and the trunk carefully with hand clippers.

Transplanting Trees and Shrubs

There are occasions when established plants begin to compete with some other plant or building and need to be moved. More commonly, an otherwise healthy, attractive shrub or tree simply does not look right in its current location. Sometimes moving a shrub that is a bit too close to the wall of a building just one foot forward in the bed will improve the health of the plant as well as the appearance of the landscape. While there are some exceptions, most common shrubs and trees found in residential landscapes are quite tolerant of being moved if the proper steps are taken.

If a shrub or tree has reached more than eight feet in height, professional help may be required to move it safely. However, because this is likely to be expensive (moving a fifteen-foot blue spruce could cost $500 or more), sometimes it is better to cut down the offending tree or shrub and plant a new tree in the location you prefer.

It is very easy to move a small shrub or tree. The same rules as to the timing and procedures for planting shrubs listed above apply to transplanting them. Early fall is the best time for moving most shrubs and trees, giving them an opportunity to generate some more roots and get settled before winter sets in. Move fast-growing and spring-flowering trees, such as magnolias and fruit trees, in the fall. Most shrubs and trees, however, can be moved in either early spring or during the fall, when the plants are dormant.

If transplanting is done in the spring, it's best done before any bud growth resumes, and especially before a plant leafs out. It is usually safe to assume that evergreens are in their dormant period two weeks after nearby deciduous trees have shed their leaves. They break dormancy roughly two weeks prior to the emergence of new growth on deciduous trees in the spring. The dormant period in southern areas may be the four to six weeks of late "winter." Avoid transplanting during wet weather. The digging may be easier but soil doesn't hold to

Some Trees That Are More Difficult to Transplant

Crape myrtle (*Lagerstroemia indica*)

Hawthorn (*Crataegus*)

Hickory (*Carya*)

Hornbeam (*Carpinus*)

Magnolia (*Magnolia*)

Oak, scarlet and white (*Quercus rubra, Q. alba*)

Pear (*Pyrus*)

Sweet gum (*Liquidambar styraciflua*)

Walnut (*Juglans*)

Yaupon (*Ilex vomitoria*)

Rule of Thumb: the younger the tree, the easier and safer it is to transplant. When in doubt, have a professional arborist plant a tree.

Shrubs Extremely Difficult to Move

Abelia (*Abelia*)

Bayberry, common (*Myrica pensylvanica*)

Buckthorn (*Rhamnus cathartica*)

Cotoneaster (*Cotoneaster*)

Inkberry (*Ilex glabra*)

Magnolia (*Magnolia*)

Rose of Sharon (*Hibiscus syriacus*)

Snowball (*Viburnum*)

Yew (*Taxus*)

Rule of Thumb: Always purchase balled and burlapped shrubs.

the roots as well and there could be soil compaction later.

The key to success is giving transplants a large enough rootball when digging them up. The bigger the plant the bigger the rootball needed to safely move the tree or shrub. For trees, the rootball should be a minimum of twelve inches in diameter for each inch of the trunk's diameter, measured at ground level. Thus a three-inch diameter tree would require a three-foot diameter ball. A multistemmed shrub or small tree up to eight feet in height should have a ball twenty-four inches across and eighteen to twenty inches deep. Make every effort to assure that the soil does not fall away and expose the roots of the transplant. Use burlap, geotextile mulch, or even an old beach towel or blanket as a temporary wrap. Follow the same planting techniques outlined for the burlap-covered shrubs described earlier. It's a good idea to dig the new planting hole a day or so ahead and fill it with water, planting in it only after all the water has drained away.

Again, generous watering is vitally important. Remember, shrubs and trees moved in warm weather will have a much better chance of survival if their foliage is sprayed with an antidesiccant just before transplanting.

TROUBLESHOOTING OF TREES AND SHRUBS

The rest of this chapter addresses some of the most common cultural problems that plague trees and shrubs in residential landscapes. Insect and disease problems for all the plants in the yard and garden, including trees and shrubs, are addressed in chapter six.

Homeowners can handle problems with small trees, but, of course, problems with large mature trees are better left to professional tree-care specialists. Most problems of large trees need specialized equipment available only from tree-care companies.

Cultural problems are those difficulties caused by the environment. Unusual or extreme weather, for instance, will sap tree and shrub vigor. Of significant danger are spells of unusual cold, periods of great dryness and/or heat, and wind storms. Extreme fluctuations in temperatures also take their toll. The winter protection measures discussed earlier in this chapter are helpful in minimizing this damage. Loosely wrap or shelter young trees to protect them from cold, and deeply water trees and shrubs during unusually dry periods. Whitewash the bark of young trees to forestall possible damage from sunburn which invites insect and disease.

Surface roots. Surface rooting is brought on by heavy, poorly drained, and/or shallow soils that have a low oxygen content. Because tree roots need oxygen to grow, they move to the surface of the soil, bulging above the soil surface as they become larger. Surface roots may be exposed by soil erosion. Then they get skinned by the lawn mower, they buckle sidewalks, they trip people walking in the yard, and they look unsightly. Although aerating the soil under trees prevents surface roots in the lawn, once they appear, what can be done?

One way to solve the problem is to cover the surface roots with "light" soil (topsoil mixed with peat moss or sand, for instance). Spread the soil to a depth of about two inches, no deeper. Burying the roots deeper harms the tree. If this fails to cover them completely, or if the yard still looks unsightly, why not plant a ground cover under the tree? While they may not be suited to high traffic areas, patches of evergreen pachysandra, vinca, or ivy will def-

Tree roots that snake over the surface of the soil signal a serious soil problem. Severe compaction denies oxygen to these roots. Aerate around trees and then mulch with organic material or ground cover to protect against lawn mower and pedestrian traffic that hardens the soil. Do not cover the roots with soil; such action can slowly kill the tree.

initely improve the appearance of the yard and obviate the need for mowing, and thus risking harm to the exposed roots. A coarse mulch, such as woodchips or bark nuggets, is an alternative to living ground covers. Limit them to a depth of four inches and avoid placing the mulch right up against the trunk as it then makes an inviting nest for mice and voles which feed on tree and shrub bark.

Soil pH. Soil pH is an environmental variable that can lead to tree and shrub problems. Some common trees such as pin oak, red maple, white oak, American beech, and tulip trees prefer acidic soil. If they are located in an alkaline soil they will not thrive. Urban areas, with their high concentration of concrete buildings, tend to have soils that are alkaline due to the leaching of lime from walls and mortar by rain which carries it into the soil. It is very difficult to modify the pH of the soil around a large tree. About the only solution to a major soil pH imbalance is to change trees. There are many popular trees that prefer an alkaline environment around their root systems. They include hackberry, sycamore, black locust, American elm, honey locust, and many hawthorns.

Can vines kill trees? Some vines can and do kill trees by strangulation or girdling. Not all vines are killers, but the vigorous twining vines, such as bittersweet, honeysuckle, and wisteria, can twist around a tree trunk and cut off translocation of water and nutrients as the tree grows bigger. If a vine is vigorous enough to make a foliage canopy over a tree, it can kill it by "smothering," which really is simply excessive shading. Wild grapevines in natural stands can wipe out large areas of trees in this way.

On the other hand, Virginia creeper, with its brilliant red fall foliage, English ivy, and climbing forms of *Euonymus fortunei* seldom grow fast enough to cover a tree's leaves, though they may cover the trunk with harmless foliage. Clematis and climbing hydrangea are often encouraged to climb up trees, the better to show off their flowers.

Air pollution. Areas with air pollution problems (sulfur dioxides, fluorides, and other oxidants from industry, cars, and such) present problems to trees and shrubs on residential

Trees Sensitive to Air Pollution

Aspen, quaking (*Populus tremuloides*)

Catalpa (*Catalpa speciosa*)

Elm, American (*Ulmus americana*)

Larch (*Larix*)

Pine, jack (*Pinus banksiana*)

Pine, white (*Pinus strobus*)

Poplar, Lombardy (*Populus nigra* 'Italica')

Willow (*Salix*)

Trees Relatively Tolerant of Air Pollution

Arborvitae (*Thuja*)

Box elder (*Acer negundo*)

Dogwood, white (*Cornus*)

Fir, Douglas (*Pseudotsuga menziesii*)

Magnolia (*Magnolia*)

Maple, Norway (*Acer platanoides*)

Oak, English (*Quercus robur*)

Oak, red (*Quercus rubra*)

Spruce, white (*Picea glauca*)

properties as well as to those growing in public parks and along streets. Fortunately, certain trees are more resistant to these compounds than others, and it is advisable to replace ailing trees with these tougher ones.

Salt damage. De-icing compounds used on highways, driveways, and sidewalks in the winter contain sodium chloride (table salt) and/or calcium chloride, both toxic to many trees and shrub. Plants near the street are injured when salt, dissolved in melting snow and ice, is absorbed by the foliage and roots. The sodium chloride in rock salt absorbs water in the soil and dehydrates tree and shrub roots, causing damage (twig dieback, stunted growth, and brown and black scorching of leaves). Often this damage is not evident until spring.

While it may not be possible to control what the municipal government chooses to use on the streets, it is possible to control what is used on local sidewalks. Use sand, fertilizer, wood ashes, or fresh kitty litter, rather than salt. There is now a product on the market called Safe Step that works as well as salt but is not made of salt. It causes no harm to grass, trees, or shrubs.

Trees Tolerant of Salt Spray or Runoff

Ash, mountain (*Sorbus*)

Ash, white (*Fraxinus americana*)

Aspen, big-tooth (*Populus grandidentata*)

Aspen, quaking (*Populus tremuloides*)

Birch (*Betula*)

Cedar, Eastern red (*Juniperus virginiana*)

Cherry, black (*Prunus serotina*)

Honey locust (*Gleditsia triacanthos*)

Larch, European (*Larix decidua*)

Locust, black (*Robinia pseudoacacia*)

Maple, Norway (*Acer platanoides*)

Maple, silver (*Acer saccharinum*)

Oak, red (*Quercus rubra*)

Oak, white (*Quercus alba*)

Pine, Austrian (*Pinus nigra*)

Pine, jack (*Pinus banksiana*)

Russian olive (*Elaeagnus angustifolia*)

Spruce, Colorado (*Picea pungens*)

Walnut, black (*Juglans nigra*)

Shrubs Tolerant of Some Salt

Buckthorn (*Rhamnus cathartica*)

Euonymus, winged (*Euonymus alata*)

Juniper, Pfitzer (*Juniperus chinensis*)

Sumac, fragrant (*Rhus aromatica*)

Sumac, staghorn (*Rhus typhina*)

Consider erecting barriers to reduce the impact of salt problems. Isolate roadside plantings from salt on the ground by digging a drainage ditch to carry away salt runoff. A simple barrier of plywood or burlap will keep spray caused by passing vehicles from hitting vulnerable curbside plants. If rock salt is broadcast on the street or sidewalk, remove all the snow from around the tree trunks or pits.

Then, early in the spring, when soil and air temperatures warm above freezing, water the soil around the trees to leach out the salt.

Algae and lichens. Occasionally a tree or shrub will develop a crusty gray or greenish white coating on its bark. This is probably algae or lichens. These primitive plants do not harm the host plants. Because both algae and lichens

Trees Sensitive to Salt Spray and Runoff

Alder, speckled (*Alnus incana*)

Arborvitae, American (*Thuja occidentalis*)

Beech, American (*Fagus grandifolia*)

Cherry, black (*Prunus serotina*)

Crab apple (*Malus*)

Fir, balsam (*Abies balsamea*)

Fir, Douglas (*Pseudotsuga menziesii*)

Hackberry (*Celtis*)

Hawthorn (*Crataegus*)

Hemlock, Canada (*Tsuga canadensis*)

Hickory, shagbark (*Carya ovata*)

Hornbeam, American (*Carpinus caroliniana*)

Linden, American (*Tilia americana*)

Linden, little-leaf (*Tilia cordata*)

Maple, red (*Acer rubrum*)

Maple, sugar (*Acer saccharum*)

Oak, pin (*Quercus palustris*)

Pine, eastern white (*Pinus strobus*)

Pine, red (*Pinus resinosa*)

Pine, Scotch (*Pinus sylvestris*)

Redbud, Eastern (*Cercis canadensis*)

Spruce, white (*Picea glauca*)

Yew (*Taxus*)

Shrubs Sensitive to Salt

Barberry, Japanese (*Berberis thunbergii*)

Boxwood, common (*Buxus sempervirens*)

Dogwood (*Cornus*)

Elder, American (*Sambucus canadensis*)

Euonymus, European (*Euonymus europaea*)

Indian currant (*Symphoricarpos orbiculatus*)

Quince, flowering (*Chaenomeles speciosa*)

Spirea (*Spiraea*)

manufacture their own foods, they are not parasitic. They grow anywhere there is sufficient moisture. Only a heavy covering of algae or lichen could lead to tree or shrub injury, possibly by suffocation or interception of sunlight. This problem can be safely ignored, unless it is so severe that the appearance of the tree or shrub is marred. To remove unsightly algae or lichen growth, spray it with a copper-based fungicide, such as Bordeaux mixture, several times at two-week intervals. According to some experts, algae and lichens on the bark of a tree or shrub often indicate stress on that plant. Look for possible problems with soil compaction, poor drainage, or insufficient fertilizer.

Lightning damage. Since lightning likes isolated, tall targets like telephone poles, antennae, towers, tall buildings, and trees, valued specimen trees are often victims. Those whose branches overhang buildings are particularly vulnerable because the wiring and plumbing in the building act as good conductors. Because trees protrude into the air and are more conductive of electricity than air, they are often struck. However, because wood basically resists conducting electricity that hits it, trees suffer severely. Instantaneously, the bolt of electricity causes tree sap to boil and turn to steam. The steam expands and blows apart the bark and possibly the tree stems as well. As the moisture is dried up, the charge of electricity then affects the cells in the tree tissues, causing them to expand and rupture and scorch.

Effective lightning protection systems for trees are based on the same principles as lightning rods for buildings. They are not intended to attract or repel lightning per se, but if it

should hit, they offer a path of least resistance to the electrical charge, down to the ground. Typically, a lightning protection system is composed of copper cabling and clamps fastened to vulnerable trees, leading to a ground rod which is buried in the soil. This type of system requires inspection every two or three years to assure that the tree does not grow around the cables. Professional tree-care companies install these protective systems.

THE PAYOFF

Undoubtedly trees and shrubs are the backbone of an attractive residential yard. They provide the essential framework for the landscape, defining edges and boundaries while providing a background for all the other plants in it. They also attract and support the presence of wildlife on the property. Truly effective trees and shrubs provide an understated balance to the landscape design, and they soften angles, screen unsightly views, and moderate the climate on the property. Occasionally a truly wonderful specimen tree or shrub serves as a focal point for the entire landscape. But, because their role is so often to be in the background, trees and shrubs are often overlooked and underappreciated. If there is any doubt remaining that they are worth the time, energy, and money it takes to renovate, maintain, and replace them, just go outside on the front walk and study your yard. Imagine how it would look if there were no trees and shrubs on it.

CHAPTER 3
Flowers in the Landscape

O f all the landscape plants that they might have on their property, flowers are regarded by many homeowners as the most difficult to deal with. Often they have been intimidated by the jargon and elaborate practices that have grown up around flower gardening and shy away from using flowers because they do not feel expert enough. This is a shame because, by and large, of all landscape plants flowers are the easiest, least expensive, most flexible, and most fun. Also, as with lawns, trees and shrubs, and vegetables, modern technology has made growing flowers easier. New hybrids, as well as planting tools and products, now available at the local garden center make it even easier for you to grow flowers confidently.

Think in terms of "decorating" your yard with flowers, rather than "starting a garden." Consider using flowering plants as an extension of the other decorative features of your house—the colorful trim on shutters and doorway, the seasonal wreath on the door, the white picket fence bordering the lawn, the charming mailbox at the end of the walk, the wrought-iron railing around the balcony. With their wonderful shapes and colors flowers are eyecatching and expressive. Just as it is easy to decorate the inside of your home with flowers, it is easy to decorate the outside. Whether they are in containers or in the ground they enhance your surroundings and frame of mind.

Flowering plants are valuable ornamental assets to the outdoor landscape in many ways. While they do not play as great a utilitarian role in the yard as the trees, shrubs, and vines which serve a structural function, they contribute more than their share in their decorative role. They provide colorful accents, fill in spaces, and add an element of delight to the landscape. They also celebrate the seasons and holidays. All the while their presence enriches the overall ecosystem in the yard by adding to its diversity and attracting and supporting desirable wildlife. By taking advantage of the incredible variety of flowers you can also easily change the look of your landscape with a very small investment of time and money.

KINDS OF FLOWERS

Although there are certain trees, shrubs, and vines that bear showy flowers sometime during their growing season, the term "flower" commonly refers to those plants which bear showy blooms and then die back at the end of the season. Conventional usage divides these plants into types: annuals, perennials, and bulbs. An understanding of the differences in these types really helps when it is time to select flowers for your yard.

Those flowers that die totally at the end of the season are called *annuals* because they complete their life cycle in one year. Although they leave numerous seeds behind that sometimes germinate the following year, providing new plants, the original plants die. In cold

The general term "bulb" includes several types of nutrient-storing plant structures. A true bulb such as a daffodil is a modified bud, whereas corms, rhizomes, and tuberous roots are really swollen stems or roots.

regions their roots cannot withstand winter temperatures. Although annuals live only one season, they are valuable because most bloom steadily the whole time. They are eminently satisfactory as decorative flowers for the yard because they give almost constant color. Abundantly available in garden centers, grocery stores, street corners, and outdoor markets in the spring, they are generally inexpensive and their death in the fall does not represent a significant financial loss. Properly placed in the yard, annuals are extremely easy to grow.

Some flowers die back to the ground at the end of the season, but their roots are hardy and are able to withstand winter temperatures. Come spring, they generate new young shoots that emerge from the warming soil and the plant lives on through a new season. Flowers of this sort that return over three or more seasons are called *perennials*. (There are a few flowers such as foxgloves and hollyhocks that take two seasons to complete their life cycle. While they are called *biennials* they are usually treated as annuals and will be included in discussions of annuals.) While flowering perennial plants offer the advantage of repeat appearances in the yard over many seasons, they usually do not provide continuous bloom for extended periods like annuals do. Typically they bloom for two or three weeks and then show only foliage the rest of the season. Although their foliage may have some decorative appeal, the value of their attractive flowers is short-lived. Most perennials are not very difficult to grow, but they require more ongoing

Some Familiar Annual Plants

Ageratum (*Ageratum*)

Alyssum, sweet (*Lobularia maritima*)

Bachelor's button (*Centaurea*)

Begonia, wax (*Begonia* × *semperflorens* = *cultorum*)

Carnation (*Dianthus*)

China aster (*Callistephus*)

Cockscomb (*Celosia*)

Evening primrose (*Oenothera*)

Forget-me-not (*Myosotis*)*

Four-o'clock (*Mirabilis jalapa*)*

Impatiens (*Impatiens*)

Larkspur (*Delphinium*)

Love-in-a-mist (*Nigelia*)

Lupine (*Lupinus*)

Marigold (*Tagetes*)

Nasturtium (*Tropaeolum*)

Pansy (*Viola* × *wittrockiana*)*

Petunia (*Petunia*)

Phlox (*Phlox drummondii*)

Portulaca (*Portulaca*)

Salvia (*Salvia*)

Snapdragon (*Antirrhinum*)

Spider flower (*Cleome*)*

Statice (*Limonium*)

Sunflower (*Helianthus*)

Sweet pea (*Lathyrus odoratus*)

Tobacco, flowering (*Nicotiana*)

Verbena (*Verbena* × *hortensis*)

Wallflower (*Cheiranthus*)

Zinnia (*Zinnia*)

*prolific self-seeders

care, since they are semi-permanent features of the yard. Perennials are more expensive and somewhat more difficult to find at garden centers than annuals.

Some flowers are in a class of their own. These are the *bulbs*. Although there are exceptions, most flowers that grow roots from bulb-like structures called variously bulbs, corms, or rhizomes, depending on their structure, die back after each season and return in succeeding seasons to bloom again and thus are technically perennials. However, because of their unique "bulb" structure, their storage sites for nutrients to be used the following season, this group of plants is distinguished from the other flowers. Known collectively as "bulbs," the

Familiar Perennial Flowers Having Color for Six Weeks or More

---

Aster, hybrid (*Aster × frikartii*) 'Monch', 'Wonder of Stafa'

Aster, New England (*Aster novae-angeliae*) 'Treasurer'

Baby's breath (*Gypsophila paniculata*)

Bee balm (*Monarda didyma*) 'Cambridge Scarlet'

Black-eyed Susan (*Rudbeckia*) 'Autumn Glory', 'Goldsturm'

Blanket flower (*Gaillardia*) 'Baby Cole'

Bleeding heart, fringed (*Dicentra eximia*) 'Alba', 'Luxuriant'

Catmint, hybrid (*Nepeta*) 'Dropmore'

Coneflower, purple (*Echinacea purpurea*) 'Bright Star'

Coreopsis, lance (*Coreopsis lanceolata*) 'Early Sunrise', 'Sunray'

Coreopsis, thread-leaf (*Coreopsis verticillata*) 'Moonbeam', 'Zagreb'

Daylily (*Hemerocallis*) 'Happy Returns', 'Stella d'Oro'

Evening primrose (*Oenothera*) 'Fireworks'

Loosestrife (*Lythrum salicaria*) 'Morden's Pink'

Phlox (*Phlox paniculata*) 'Eva Cullum', 'Sandra', Franz Schubert'

Sedum (*Sedum spectabile*) 'Autumn Joy'

Sundrops, Ozark (*Oenothera missourensis*)

Veronica (*Veronica longifolia*) 'Sunny Border Blue'

Yarrow (*Achillea*) 'Fire King'

---

spring ones and some summer ones are cold hardy, having the ability to survive winters in the ground. Like perennials they have a bloom period counted in weeks rather than season-long display.

Among the most familiar summer bulbs, only a few, such as lilies, are winter hardy and can be left in the ground year-round like spring bulbs. Other summer bulbs, such as dahlias, gladiolas, cannas, and tuberous begonias, are tender. They must be dug up in the fall, stored indoors over the cold winter, and replanted in the spring. Some yardeners choose to treat them as annuals and simply buy and plant new tender summer bulbs every year to avoid this extra work.

Familiar Spring (Hardy) Bulbs

Crocus (*Crocus*)

Daffodil and narcissus (*Narcissus*)

Glory-of-the-snow (*Chionodoxa luciliae*)

Grape hyacinth (*Muscari botryoides*)

Hyacinth (*Hyancinthus orientalis*)

Iris (*Iris*)

Lily-of-the-valley (*Convallaria majalis*)

Snowdrops (*Galanthus nivalis*)

Squill (*Scilla siberica*)

Star-of-Bethlehem (*Ornithogalum umbellatum*)

Tulip (*Tulipa*)

Winter aconite (*Eranthis hyemalis*)

The hardy spring bulbs are the easiest of all the types of flowers to grow, so they will be the ones discussed below. They are especially warmly welcomed by homeowners who have endured a drab winter landscape for months. While top-quality bulbs are sometimes more expensive than seedlings, they are a sound investment. Bulbs are widely available and come in a multitude of sizes and colors.

Flowers, whether annual, perennial, or bulb, are also categorized in other ways that help people choose which are the most appropriate for their yards. Like lawn grasses, trees, and shrubs, flowers have particular light requirements. Certain ones must have strong light and/or full sun almost all day to bloom at their best. Others can manage with somewhat less light, or sunshine only a small part of the day. As a general rule annuals and most perennials need sunshine during the time they are in bloom. Relatively few flowers bloom happily in partial shade. None will grow in total shade, although sun-loving bulbs do fine in the early spring in areas that eventually become shady when the leaves come out on the trees, as they are finished blooming by the time their site turns shady.

Another useful way that flowers are often grouped is by the size and shape of the mature plant. Certain ones are tall and narrow or bushy, others are short and narrow or bushy, while others virtually crawl on the ground. When thinking about which flowers would look best where, it is useful to take these factors into account. Whether a flowering plant is an annual, perennial, or bulb, to know if it needs sun or accepts some shade, and if it will properly fill the spot where it is planted is helpful. However, the nice thing about flowers is that most are quickly and easily moved if adjustments are necessary.

Common Flowers That Accept Some Shade

ANNUALS	PERENNIALS	BULBS
Ageratum	Aster	Daffodil and narcissus
Foxglove	Astilbe	Glory-of-the-snow
Impatiens	Bleeding heart	Lily-of-the-valley
Johnny-jump-ups	Columbine	Snowdrops
Pansies	Hosta	Squill
Sweet alyssum	Solomon's seal	
Torenia	Virginia bluebells	
Wax begonia		

INTRODUCING FLOWERS INTO THE LANDSCAPE

Many people feel that selecting flowers for the yard is half the fun. They enjoy browsing around the garden center and picking out young colorful plants for specific sites. Others are not willing or able to devote the time to the shopping, preferring instead to rely on a professional landscape designer, contractor, or gardener for recommendations. As is true with tree and lawn care, professionals will both give advice and provide planting and maintenance services for flowers for busy homeowners. However, choosing flowers to decorate the yard is not difficult and need not be very time-consuming, taken one step at a time.

Evaluating Flowers Already in Your Yard

A good place to start is to take a look at what is already on the property. People who move into homes with established yards are often delighted to discover that some flowers are already growing there. After a year these plants have all had a chance to do their thing and it is possible to evaluate how healthy they are. More importantly, it will be possible to determine whether you like them or where they're located.

Starting with the bulbs which make their presence known early in the season as their jaunty flowers soften the lingering chill of winter, through to the last mums in the fall, watch and enjoy whatever appears in the yard. Make a note of their location, especially the bulbs which will not be visible most of the season, for reference next year. Record which are your favorites and potential locations for planting more of them.

After a year it should be possible to determine which flowers on the property are keepers and which aren't. In evaluating which ones to keep, be sure to consider whether they promote the look, formal or informal, that you want in your yard. Using as many existing flowers as possible makes good sense, economically and laborwise. Some annuals will cooperate by self-sowing their seeds and will return on their own. Flowers such as spider flower, love-in-a-mist, and four-o'clocks do this frequently. The fact that they are thriving in the yard suggests that they are good choices for that particular area.

Identifying Areas to Decorate

Not everyone is lucky enough to have a house surrounded by plantings from a previous owner. Some of us move into newly built homes or homes that belonged to people who took no interest whatsoever in their yard. In these cases flowers will save the day. While they are always welcome and appropriate, in undeveloped landscapes they are even more useful. Until the few shrubs and trees the builder put in mature, or renovated ones recover, and until the lawn is established, dec-

Tuck flowers in among the shrubs along the foundation of the house to fill the space and add color to the landscape. Low-growing carpets of annuals soften the edges of the beds.

orative flowers, along with other plants, such as ground covers and ornamental grasses, will enhance the yard.

In any case, think about the areas to be decorated with flowers. On most properties there is a natural break between the front and backyards, so they can be treated as separate "rooms" with their own "decor." Side yards are often transition areas as well as popular locations for utilities such as air-conditioner compressors, trash receptacles, and firewood storage, and judicious use of flowers in these areas will definitely soften the view.

Don't forget the distinctive landscape features on the property. Natural ones, such as slopes or banks, wooded areas, and undeveloped areas, are perfect places to use flowers. So are man-made features, such as doorways, walkways, play areas, pools, porches and patios, fireplaces, garages, and toolsheds. It only remains to choose the flowers from the garden center and sit back and enjoy the pleasure they bring. Of course, while they are always decorative, flowers simultaneously serve other purposes in the yard as well. Before discussing specific planting techniques, it is worthwhile to think about the various uses of flowers in the landscape.

Using Flowers in the Landscape

Flowers offer flexibility in designing a landscape. Unlike mature trees and shrubs which are pretty much permanently in place, flowers are easily changed. Bulbs can be dug up at the end of the season and replanted in a different location. The same is true of perennials. Annuals are easiest of all. At little expense they can be replaced several times over the growing season to reflect the changes from spring to summer to fall. Because they die in the fall, they can be changed the following year to a different color or variety if last year's choice was not satisfactory. Because of the diversity of flower types and varieties, decorating with flowers outdoors offers endless possibilities.

It is easy to change annuals over the course of one season. A typical succession of annuals might begin with pansies in the very early spring. With the onset of summer heat, these pansies become weak and leggy, so they are best pulled up and replaced with petunias or geraniums or something similar. If the intense heat of late summer saps the freshness and vigor from these flowers, replace them with late summer and fall bloomers such as cocks-

comb or marigolds. Many people treat chrysanthemums as annuals, buying young plants in full bloom and planting them in the fall in place of other annuals, then discarding them when frost causes them to die back. For apartment dwellers who plant in containers, the flexibility and versatility of annuals are even more valuable. Window boxes, hanging baskets, and planters can be changed quickly and easily for a continual fresh display.

FLOWERS PROVIDE ACCENTS. Whether they are planted in containers or in the ground, flowers can be used in many ways. Because of their distinctive colors, they are ideal for accenting certain areas of the landscape. Just as a brightly colored throw pillow provides a color accent to the living room, strategically placed pots of bulbs or annuals, or masses of flowering plants punctuate the yard. They draw the eye to landscape features, such as the front door, steps, and paths. They also brighten shady spots and out-of-the-way corners. Planted in rows, they are commonly used to delineate the edges of walkways, patios, or lawn area. Nothing focuses attention on a special area of the yard like a mass of brightly colored impatiens or petunias. Plant low-growing flowers between shrubs to take advantage of the handsome backdrop their green foliage provides. Flowers in colors that coordinate with the paint trim on the house provide transition from front to side to backyards and pull the whole landscape together. Window boxes or hanging baskets of distinctively colored flowers just as effectively accent individual apartment, row-house, or condo facades.

As landscape accents flowers also help celebrate the seasons and holidays. Colorful crocuses, daffodils, tulips, and other spring bulbs mark the waning of winter and help us celebrate the arrival of spring. For many, they are the hallmark of Easter. Putting out cold-hardy field-grown pansies from the local garden center is an effective way of announcing that winter is over, at least in your yard! Similarly, the flood of blooming flowers, both annuals and perennials, that begins in many regions in May signals the onset of summer. As the heat turns up, the strong colors of sturdy marigolds, zinnias, petunias and salvias take over, followed by black-eyed Susans. When fall arrives, asters, chrysanthemums, and cockscomb are at their glorious best.

FLOWERS FILL IN SPACES. Another use for flowers is to fill in bare or empty spaces on the property. Flowers tucked between foundation shrubs will fill in around bare trunks and screen utilities and cellar windows. Around and in front of evergreen shrubs is an ideal place to plant small bulbs, such as crocuses, glory-in-the-snow, or grape hyacinths. They will peek out from under snow and mulch early in the spring when things are still pretty bare and colorless. Similarly some bulbs can be used to fill in open spaces in the yard. Some people plant crocuses in the lawn, although they have to hold back on mowing the grass until the crocus foliage dies back. Also,

Containerized plants make effective transitions from garden bed to lawn area. A focal point as well, they signal the presence of steps and draw the eye to an expanse of lawn. Plants in containers can be easily changed to fit the seasons.

nothing brightens an empty, wintry apartment balcony like a pot of brightly colored tulips.

Another way to use flowers to fill in spaces is to "naturalize" them. Perfect for marginal, undeveloped, or neglected areas, especially on large properties, naturalizing involves scattering large quantities of spring bulbs randomly over an extensive area and planting them where they fall. This creates a natural-looking planting pattern which fills in over the years as the bulbs multiply. Naturalized areas look lovely with virtually no care. This approach does not work with wildflower seed mixes. While they are ideal for these areas of the property, they require careful site preparation. This is discussed in the landscaping chapter.

Another way flowers can fill in spaces in the yard is as a small flower bed. Choose one of the packaged gardens widely available in garden centers or by mail order for an essentially carefree flower garden. These products offer assortments of bulbs, herbs, or perennials that are selected to provide a pleasing design and low maintenance. Ideal for nongardening homeowners who want to border an area along the fence or fill in a patch next to the pool or deck with an assortment of flowers, these packaged gardens provide compatible bulbs or young seedlings complete with planting instructions and a chart on how to lay them out.

FLOWERS ADD DELIGHT. Of course flowers in the yard do more than simply accent and fill in areas. They also offer occasions of pleasure and delight to the senses. It is a bonus when the pot of annuals near the doorway or the clump of herbs under the kitchen window is also aromatic. Although one of the prices paid for modern hybrid types of flowers is often loss of fragrance, there are still many old-fashioned favorites available to perfume the yard.

Homeowners who chose homes with a nice piece of property usually do so because they appreciate the opportunity natural surroundings afford for a taste of wildlife. Even though suburban and exurban yards require considerable work, there is a perceived value to being able to enjoy wildlife and nature up close. Many flowers attract visitors that add this extra element of delight. Brightly colored blooms on annuals and perennials as well as those on flowering shrubs and vines are favorites of butterflies and even hummingbirds. Hummingbirds look for vibrant color and tubular or trumpet shapes and will visit time and again as long as these flowers are producing blooms.

FLOWERS PROTECT THE ECOSYSTEM. Adding flowers to a landscape that has lawn grass, trees, and shrubs not only maximizes the potential for attracting hummingbirds and butterflies, but it makes the landscape healthier for all the plants. The greater the diversity of plants, the more likely it is that desirable insects will be attracted to the yard. Some insects are valued because they pollinate plants, making possible seed production and survival. Attracted by the color and fragrance of flowers, bees of all types, particularly honeybees, and many kinds of flies will regularly provide this service.

Although ladybugs, dragonflies, spiders, and praying mantises are easily recognized, most "beneficial" insects are so tiny that they are virtually invisible. Nevertheless, they shoulder the major responsibility for policing the landscape against harmful insect pests. Because some pest insects also carry disease, the desirable predators that attack them are also helping to ward off plant diseases in the yard. This natural process is at work even in the smallest ecosystems, such as an apartment balcony full of container plants, or in a window box over a city street filled with a variety of flowers.

While the activity of beneficial insects goes on wherever plants grow, certain flowers attract these allies and provide a built-in pesticide capability to a yard if they are planted there. Tiny beneficial wasps and flies are attracted to flowers with open blossoms, like daisies, and particularly those with flat clusters

Flowers Having Fragrance

ANNUALS

China pink (*Dianthus chinensis*)

Four-o'clock (*Mirabilis jalapa*)

Heliotrope (*Heliotropium arborescens*)

Mignonette (*Reseda odorata*)

Nasturtium (*Tropaeolum majus*)

Petunia, dwarf 'Resisto Blue' (*Petunia* × *hybrida*)

Snapdragon (*Antirrhinum*)

Spider flower (*Cleome spinosa*)

Stock (*Matthiola incana*)

Sweet alyssum (*Lobularia maritima*)

Sweet pea (*Lathyrus odoratus*)

Tobacco, flowering (*Nicotiana sylvestris*)

Verbena 'Royal Bouquet' (*Verbana* × *hybrida*)

HERBS

Basil, sweet (*Ocimum basilicum*)

Geranium, Scented (*Pelargonium* × *fragrans*)

Hyssop (*Hyssopus officinalis*)

Thyme (*Thymus vulgaris*)

BULBS

Freesia (*Freesia refracta*)

Grape hyacinth (*Muscari botryoides*)

Hyacinth (*Hyacinthus orientalis*)

Iris, hybrid bearded (*Iris*)

Iris, Spanish 'King of Blues' (*Iris xiphium*)

Jonquil (*Narcissus jonquilla*)

Madonna lily (*Lilium candidum*)

Siberian wallflower (*Erysimum asperum*)

Tulip 'Eros' (*Tulipa*)

Tulip, Florentine (*Tulipa sylvestris*)

PERENNIALS

Cottage/grass pink (*Dianthus plumarius*)

Honeysuckle, Hall's Japanese (vine) (*Lonicera japonica* 'Halliana')

Hosta (*Hosta*)

Lavender (herb) (*Lavandula angustifolia*)

Sweet William, wild (*Phlox maculata*)

Yucca (*Yucca*)

Flowers That Attract Butterflies

Ageratum (*Ageratum houstonianum*)

Aster, New England (*Aster novae-angliae*)

Butterfly weed (*Asclepias tuberosa*)

Coneflower, purple (*Echinacea purpurea*)

Hyssop (*Hyssopus officinalis*)

Marigold (*Tagetes patula*)

Phlox (*Phlox*)

Sage (*Salvia farinacea*)

Sedum 'Autumn joy' (*Sedum spectabile*)

Verbena 'Sissinghurst' (*Verbena*)

Zinnia (*Zinnia elegans*)

Flowers That Attract Hummingbirds

Bee balm (*Monarda*)

Blazing star (*Liatris*)

Cardinal flower (*Lobelia cardinalis*)

Century plant (*Agave americana*)

Columbine (*Aquilegia*)

Coralbells (*Heuchera*)

Delphinium/larkspur (*Delphinium*)

Four-o'clock (*Mirabilis jalapa*)

Fuchsia (*Fuchsia*)

Geranium, tender (*Pelargonium*)

Honeysuckle (*Lonicera*)

Impatiens (*Impatiens wallerana*)

Lantana (*Lantana camara*)

Nasturtium (*Tropaeolum majus*)

Nicotiana (*Nicotiana alata, N. sylvestris*)

Petunia (*Petunia*)

Phlox (*Phlox*)

Sage, scarlet (*Salvia splendens*)

Sweet William (*Dianthus barbatus*)

of tiny florets, such as Queen Anne's lace. Fortunately, many of the flowers that are attractive to beneficial insects are often the same ones that are attractive to homeowners as decorative plants and are available as seedlings or in wild-flower seed mixes at the garden center or at the nursery.

FLOWERS SOLVE LANDSCAPE PROBLEMS. Because there are flowers that will bloom in just

Flowers That Attract Beneficial Insects

Angelica (*Angelica*)

Baby blue eyes (*Nemophila menziesii*)

Bishop's weed (*Aegopodium podagraria*)

Black-eyed Susan (*Rudbeckia*)

Buckwheat (*Fagopyrum esculentum*)

Buttercup (*Ranunculus*)

Candytuft (*Iberis*)

Daisies (*Chrysanthemum*)

Evening primrose (*Oenothera*)

Goldenrod (*Solidago*)

Morning glory (vine) (*Ipomoea*)

Nasturtium (*Tropaeolum majus*)

Queen Anne's lace (*Daucus carota*)

White clover (*Melilotus alba*)

Yarrow (*Achillea*)

about any environment except deep shade, flowers sometimes offer perfect solutions for decorating problem yards. Flowering plants vary in their need for water. Some, such as daylilies, Japanese iris, primroses, and loosestrife, don't mind having their feet (roots) wet and are ideal for areas in the yard that are chronically soggy.

Flowers can solve landscape problems at the seashore. Decorating a yard that is windswept and possibly sprayed with salt seems like a difficult job, but many plants are able to thrive under these conditions.

Some flowers can actually manage on very little water. A landscape decorated with these will be lower maintenance because it will not need as much watering. They are perfect for areas of the yard beyond the reach of the hose, for yards in towns where residential water re-

strictions are in force, or for situations where maintenance of flowers is difficult, such as second homes in the mountains or at the shore that are visited infrequently. A landscape designed with an eye toward low water use is often called a "Xeriscape" landscape. On these properties not only the flowers, but the trees, shrubs, and lawn grass varieties are chosen because they are low-water-demand plants. Lots of plants are low-water demand, so there is no need for a Xeriscape landscape in New York State to resemble a yard in Arizona. Some of the most common are listed on page 99.

These flowers are, of course, very self-reliant. There are also many others that, aside from occasional watering, are virtually care-free. They are a perfect solution for the yard that is frequently unavoidably neglected by busy homeowners or people who travel often.

Some Flowers That Will Grow at the Seashore

Ageratum (*Ageratum houstonianum*)

Baby's breath (*Gypsophila paniculata*)

Bee balm (*Monarda didyma*)

Black-eyed Susan (*Rudbeckia fulgida, R. hirta*)

Bleeding heart (*Dicentra eximia, D. spectabilis*)

Butterfly weed (*Asclepias tuberosa*)

Candytuft (*Iberis*)

Chrysanthemum (*Chrysanthemum*)

Coralbells (*Heuchera sanguinea*)

Coreopsis (Tickseed) (*Coreopsis*)

Cosmos (*Cosmos*)

Daylily (*Hemerocallis fulva*)

Goldenrod (*Solidago*)

Heath (*Erica*)

Hollyhock (*Alcea rosea*)

Hosta (*Hosta*)

Iris, German bearded (*Iris* × *germanica*)

Lamb's ears (*Stachys byzantina*)

Oriental poppy (*Papaver orientale*)

Petunia (*Petunia*)

Phlox (*Phlox*)

Pinks (*Dianthus*)

Rose, wild (*Rosa rugosa*)

Sage (*Salvia*)

Sedum (*Sedum*)

Spider flower (*Cleome*)

Wormwood (*Artemesia*)

Yarrow (*Achillea*)

Yucca (*Yucca filamentosa*)

Numbered among them are some perennials that are so absolutely carefree that they deserve special mention. These are recommended for homeowners who may be interested in trying perennial flowers for the first time. Great values in terms of hardiness, ease of care, and wealth of blooms are listed on page 100.

Remember, you don't have to have a lot of space to have flowers. Containers of all kinds, especially hanging baskets or pots, make it possible to decorate a home that has limited or nonexistent yard space. Flowering plants in containers sitting on a porch or balcony offer all the decorative beauty of those planted in the soil, plus wonderful flexibility. Colorful bulbs, annuals, and perennials that spill out from hanging baskets, small pots, and patio planters, as well as less mobile window boxes

Flowers Needing 20 Inches of Water or Less a Year

Baby's breath (*Gypsophila elegans, G. repens*)

Bachelor's button (*Centaurea cyanus*)

Blanket flower (*Gaillardia aristata*)

Butterfly weed (*Asclepias tuberosa*)

Coreopsis (*Coreopsis tinctoria, C. verticillata*)

Cranesbill (*Geranium sanguineum*)

Desert four-o'clock (*Mirabilis multiflora*)

Dotted gayfeather (*Liatris punctata*)

English lavender (*Lavandula angustifolia*)

Garden cosmos (*Cosmos bipinnatus*)

Globe amaranth (*Gomphrena globosa*)

Gloriosa daisy (*Rudbeckia hirta*)

Grass pink (*Dianthus plumarius*)

Honeysuckle (*Lonicera japonica*)*

Ice plant (*Mesembryanthemum crystallinum*)

Iceland poppy (*Papaver nudicaule*)

Madagascar periwinkle (*Catharanthus roseus*)

Missouri evening primrose (*Oenothera missourensis*)

Morning glory (*Ipomoea tricolor*)*

Noble goldenrod (*Solidago speciosa*)

Penstemon (*Penstemon*)

Petunia (*Petunia* × *hybrida*)

Prairie coneflower (*Ratiba columnifera*)

Purple coneflower (*Echinacea purpurea*)

Red-hot poker plant (*Kniphofia uvaria*)

Silver lace vine (*Polygonum aubertii*)*

Spider flower (*Cleome hasslerana*)

Strawflower (*Helichrysum bracteatum*)

Sunflower (*Helianthus annuus*)

Western virgin's bower (*Clematis ligusticifolia*)*

Wild bergamot (*Monarda fistulosa*)

Yarrow (*Achillea millefolium*)

*vine

are truly a movable feast for the eyes. They can be positioned to accent many different areas of the landscape over the growing season. In yards where sun is limited, they can be moved on wheels to the sunnier areas as the day progresses. So easily planted, containers

Extremely Carefree Perennials

Bishop's hat (*Epimedium grandiflorum*)

Christmas fern (*Polystichum acrostichoides*)

Daylily (*Hemerocallis*)

Hosta (*Hosta*)

Lady's mantle (*Alchemilla vulgaris*)

Siberian iris (*Iris sibirica*)

Flowers That Are Hardiest, Easiest to Grow, Most Floriferous

PERENNIALS

Bee balm (*Monarda didyma*)

Black-eyed Susan (*Rudbeckia fulgida*)

Columbine (*Aquilegia* × *hybrida*)

Daylily (*Hemerocallis*)

Heliopsis (*Heliopsis*)

Hollyhock mallow (*Lavatera trimestris*)

Loosetrife (*Lythrum salicaria*)

Meadow rue (*Thalictrum aquilegifolium*)

New England aster (*Aster novae-angliae*)

Obedient plant (*Physostegia virginana*)

Sweet rocket (*Hesperis matronalis*)

Tickseed (*Coreopsis lanceolata*)

ANNUALS

Bachelor's button (*Centaurea cyanus*)

California poppy (*Eschscholzia californica*)

Cosmos (*Cosmos bipinnatus*)

Hollyhock (*Alcea*)*

*biennial

Oxeye daisy (*Buphthalum salicifolium*)*

Rose campion (*Lychnis coronaria*)*

Spider flower (*Cleome hasslerana*)

Some Flowers Suited to Hanging Containers

BULBS

Achimines (*Achimenes*)

Tuberous begonia (*Begonia* × *tuberhybrida*)

ANNUALS

Black-eyed Susan vine (*Thunbergia alata*)

Candytuft (*Iberis umbellata*)

Dwarf marigold (*Tagetes pumila*)

Geranium (*Pelargonium*)

Impatiens (*Impatiens wallerana*)

Ivy geranium (*Pelargonium peltatum*)

Lobelia (*Lobelia erinus*)

Nasturtium (*Tropaeolum majus*)

Pansy (*Viola* × *wittrockiana*)

Petunia (*Petunia* × *hybrida*)

Phlox (*Phlox drummondii*)

Portulaca (*Portulaca grandiflora*)

Trailing fuchsia (*Fuchsia procumbens*)

Verbena (*Verbena* × *hybrida*)

Vinca (*Vinca major*)

PERENNIALS

Basket-of-gold (*Alyssum*)

Italian bellflower (*Campanula isophylla*)

Moneywort (*Lysimachia nummularia*)

Serbian bellflower (*Campanula poscharskyana*)

---

can be repeatedly replanted, so that they represent a low-maintenance, fresh, and varied show of color and texture over the entire growing season.

Not the least of the show is the container itself. There are containers crafted in just about any style imaginable and in a wide variety of materials. The traditional and always tasteful terra-cotta or clay pots and urns have been joined by wooden boxes of all kinds. Now plastic, or resin, types of containers are available as hanging pots, stationary planters, and window boxes. Familiar artifacts from the home and farm make some of the most effective landscape planters. Wooden carts, wagons, wheelbarrows, animal watering troughs, pumps, half barrels, and kegs make striking containers for decorative plants around the yard, patio, or pool.

Almost any plant will grow in a container if it is the proper size. Certain flowers are ideal for hanging baskets and window boxes because they droop. Annuals are a first choice because of their season-long bloom and bright colors. Perennials are not so appropriate for containers unless they are treated like annuals and are removed from the container when they end their bloom period or are brought indoors over the winter. Those planted in generous-size containers can overwinter outdoors just as shrubs and trees do.

A final word on the general subject of choosing flowers. As a group, bulbs tend to be the easiest to care for, annuals tend to be the most prolific bloomers, and perennials tend to be the most unusual and enduring of the flowering plants. Why not try to use all three to advantage? Not only will they each bring distinctive beauty to different areas of the yard, but combined they will also do well in a decorative border or plot. In the fall, plant the bulbs first, perhaps near the front of the planting area, taking care to mark where they are located. Then plant perennial plants nearby, allowing space for their spread over two or three seasons. In the spring tuck annuals in among the perennials and bulbs to provide continuous color and to obscure the dying bulb foliage.

BUYING FLOWERS

While it is possible to turn the pleasant task of choosing plants into a highly complex and terribly significant activity, only "gardeners" need to do this. Typical homeowners or apartment dwellers who want to decorate the yard are free to simply indulge their whims and choose whatever looks good as long as they follow a few simple guidelines. The first one is to know why you are buying the plants. Be aware of the purpose, perhaps one or more of those mentioned above—as accents, to fill space, for fragrance, etc.—for the plant. Also have in mind where you're going to place the flowers, so you can choose the correct flowers favoring sun or shade.

When choosing flowers it is helpful, but not essential, to do some preliminary information gathering. Study the yards in your neighborhood that you like for ideas about plants you find attractive and which seem to do well in the area. Look through any plant catalogs that may come in the mail to get acquainted with flower names and types. If you don't care to get involved in choosing flowers, you can probably depend upon the horticulturist at the local garden center or nursery or a landscaper with good success. These professionals will recommend specific plants and buy and install them for you. Landscapers often provide follow-up maintenance too.

Choosing Bulbs

Choose hardy bulbs in late spring from mail-order catalogs or in the fall from catalogs or local retail stores and garden centers. Often mail-order houses will offer attractive discount prices on bulbs ordered in the spring for delivery in the fall. Most hardy bulbs are planted in the fall for bloom the following season and subsequent springs.

Bulbs are graded by size, the best quality ones being the largest or "topsized." Because the topsized ones are the best value, be sure to purchase bulbs from a reputable source and check the package for information on the grade of the bulb. What may appear to be a terrific bargain is probably inferior bulbs. An exception to the rule of buying the best quality bulbs is when the bulbs are intended for naturalizing. Here's a situation where it is most economical to purchase a slightly lower grade of bulb because they will be planted in large numbers over a large area. Many bulb producers offer special bulk rates and varietal or color assortments of narcissus or the various minor bulbs, such as crocus, snowdrops, squill, or glory-in-the-snow, commonly used for naturalizing. Often this is a very good deal.

Whether your purchases will ultimately be from a catalog or not, it is really helpful for planning purposes to become familiar with all the types of plants available. Catalogs often feature many types of the same plant lavishly illustrated, offering a good opportunity to learn about their differences.

For instance, there are two main kinds of tulips. The modern hybrids are the familiar ones—tall with single cup-shaped flowers held at the ends of slim stems. They are called variously Darwin tulips, Cottage tulips, and hybrid tulips and are available in wonderful colors. Unfortunately, they do not hold up year after year and are best treated as annuals and replaced every year or two. Those types of tulips called botanical or species tulips are better suited for nongardening homeowners because they bloom reliably year after year. Water-lily tulips (*Tulipa kaufmanniana*) are a good example of this type of "perennial" tulip. They are lower growing, some with handsome variegated leaves. Among the earliest bloomers every spring, their flowers open and close daily for two weeks or more. For carefree flowers, look for this type of tulip.

Catalogs also give information about the climate preferences of various flowers. Obviously perennials that are happy in Florida are not going to be able to survive Connecticut winters, so the United States Department of Agriculture (USDA) has developed a numbered zone system to indicate the northern limits of cold hardiness of perennials. Based on records of the United States Weather Bureau, regions on the map of the United States and Canada are numbered from one to eleven. One represents the very coldest region and eleven the warmest. Nurserymen and catalogs are careful to include this number on plant labels or in descriptions of perennial plants so that buyers do not make the mistake of purchasing a plant that is not suited to their climate. A copy of the hardiness map with the zone numbers is on page 261. When ordering plants by mail it is important to be aware of your zone number to assure that the perennials, as well as trees and shrubs, you order can handle the winters in your area.

Annuals and Perennials—Seedlings versus Seeds

Annuals and perennials are available in garden centers, nurseries, and mail-order catalogs, both as seeds and as seedlings. While seeds are less expensive, they require at least four to eight weeks of lead time before young plants are available for transplanting. As a result, if the seeds are not started indoors, the wait for warm planting weather outdoors delays plant growth and bloom until later in the season. Many feel that it is much easier to have the nursery start the seeds and provide seedlings ready for planting just as the weather gets nice.

Purchasing young plants as seedlings is much more practical for busy homeowners. It saves time and effort. On display at garden centers for purchase at the appropriate time for the season, the young plants have already developed strong root systems under the watchful eyes of professional growers. They are usually sold in "market packs" of four to six seedlings in a single container or in a set of small attached containers. At this stage they are quite inexpensive.

It is easy to select plants as seedlings since their foliage is already developed and, often, some flowers are beginning to bloom to give an idea of their color. Healthy, nursery-grown seedlings transplant well and begin producing blooms promptly. Choose compact seedlings with good, crisp, green foliage and mostly tight buds. Avoid those that are leggy, have yellowish or limp leaves, or that have fully blooming flowers and no buds. While they may seem awfully small when they are purchased, rest assured that they will increase in size many times over once they are planted in the ground.

Some annuals and many perennials are also available as full-size potted plants, especially later in the spring when the growing season is well under way. These plants are sold and priced according to the size of the container they are in. They are more expensive than seedlings, but planted as full-size, blooming, or nearly mature plants, they provide instant landscape decor. They are ideal for the impatient homeowner who wants areas accented or spaces filled in immediately. A situation where buying full-size flower plants is especially common is a seasonal changeover. Buy large potted blooming chrysanthemums to set in planters and around the yard wherever fall color is needed and tired summer bloomers need replacing.

When purchasing seedlings or potted annuals and perennials, be sure to check the label that accompanies them. Usually made of plastic or some other durable material, the label indicates whether the plant is an annual or perennial, whether it likes sun, partial sun, or shade, and how tall it grows. Ideally, it will also indicate how far apart to plant the annual or perennial. This information is extremely helpful at planting time, so be sure that all new plants have labels. Keep the labels after planting for future reference. They will be a reminder of the plant name for next year.

Good catalogs also provide key information about plant preferences and even offer planting instructions and design suggestions. Mail-order firms often offer a wider variety of flowers than may be found at the local nursery for those who want more choice. Also, many firms have helpful customer service operators who will answer questions about flowers over the phone.

PLANTING FLOWERS IN THE GROUND

It is not difficult to plant flowers if the correct tools are at hand. Usually a sturdy trowel and a watering can that holds at least a gallon of water are sufficient. When planting bulbs a trowel works fine, but a bulb-planting tool, available in garden centers or through mail order, is even better.

Selecting the Site

As we've said in the preceeding chapters, the most critical factor in the successful planting of flowers, or any plants for that matter, is the location. The two most important issues in location are the amount of light available at the site, and the quality of the soil there. As a general rule of thumb, plants that produce flowers, and annuals in particular, like sun. While there are some flowers that manage without much sun (see page 90), there are very few, and even these appreciate as much bright indirect light as they can get. It is important to have a general sense of how the sunlight moves across the yard as the day progresses, so that sun-loving plants can be located in the areas that receive the most sun over the day. Bulbs love sun, but the spring ones can be placed almost anywhere because they bloom before the leaves come out on the trees and cast shadows over the landscape. Near a wall or side of a building they benefit from the protection and warmth that heat-absorbing stone or brick provide.

TYPES OF SOIL

As for quality of soil, ideally it should be reasonably fertile, neutral to slightly acid, and loose enough to drain well after a hard rain or generous watering. Fortunately, many flowers are somewhat forgiving of less than ideal conditions, especially annuals which are in place for only a few months. If flowers have grown successfully on the property in the past, it is likely that the soil is just fine. On the property of newly built homes soil type and quality are often more problematic. The topsoil is likely to have been removed prior to construction and the existing soil will have been compacted by earth moving and construction equipment.

Some Flowers That Like Acid Soil

Auricula primrose (*Primula auricula*)

Butterfly weed (*Ascelpias tuberosa*)

Daffodil (*Narcissus cyclamineus*)

Dogtooth violet (*Erythronium dens-canis*)

English primrose (*Primula vulgaris*)

Heath (*Erica*)

Heather (*Calluna*)

Japanese iris (*Iris kaempferi*)

Leopard lily (*Lilium pardalinum*)

Lewesia (*Lewisia hybrids*)

Mahogany fawn lily (*Erythronium revolutum*)

Silverdust primrose (*Primula pulverulenta*)

Speciosum lily (*Lilium speciosum*)

Tiger lily (*Lilium tigrinum splendens*)

Toad lily (*Tricyrtis stolonifera*)

Virginia bluebells (*Mertensia virginica*)

Wake robin (*Trillium grandiflorum*)

Wax begonia (*Begonia* × *semperflorens-cultorum*)

Fortunately, though, while the soil may be unsatisfactory, or may vary in quality from site to site on the property, unlike availability of light, it can be altered without too much effort.

Enrich areas that are not very fertile—that lack nutrients—by adding compost, municipal sludge, or some peat moss mixed with some slow-release granular fertilizer at planting time. If the soil does not drain well—after a rain water tends to puddle on its surface for hours—these same soil amendments will improve that condition as well. Add sand to soil that seems to be mostly clay. If your soil is impossibly compacted, have a landscaper build a raised bed or two, especially for bulbs which cannot tolerate sticky clay or wet feet.

Planting Times

Plant spring-blooming bulbs in the fall. They need time to establish roots and many need a period of chill to trigger their bloom in the spring. Most can be planted as late as December or January, as long as the ground has not frozen solid to prevent digging. Annuals and perennial seedlings are planted in the spring, most when threat of frost is past.

Even though colorful annuals may be on display in the garden center, it may not quite be time to plant. When planting, pay attention to the weather. The key factor in timing spring planting is the temperature of the soil. The calendar may indicate that it is past the last frost date for the area, and the air temperature may confirm this. But it is the soil temperature that is critical to the survival and growth of seedlings. Gardeners sometimes measure the soil temperature with a thermometer designed for that purpose to determine if it is warm enough, but that is not necessary.

The best rule of thumb is to wait at least ten days after the date of the last expected spring frost in the area to even think about planting. Frost dates have been calculated by the USDA for all the regions in the country, and they are available from the United States Weather Bureau or from your local county extension service. There is nothing to be gained by rushing out to plant young plants prematurely, since they will simply not grow until the soil has warmed up to their liking.

Not only must the soil have time to warm up, but it must have time to dry out too. Soil that is still soggy from snow melt and spring rains is impossible to work with. When dug, it forms into clumps of mud that hinder planting and destroy the soil structure, as they will dry into hard chunks. Wait to plant until the soil is dry enough that a handful crumbles through your fingers.

When planting seedlings, make every effort to assure their survival. Their first ordeal will be the transplanting process itself. Close attention to the weather will help them through this. Choose a day to plant that is overcast. Although normally most flowering plants like plenty of sun, the day that they are transplanted they need protection from it. Bright sun forces them to speed their rate of transpiration which taxes the tender roots' ability to take up water at the very time when they are least able to because they are coping with the shock to their systems induced by the transplanting process. Newly transplanted seedlings go limp almost immediately in this situation and are in danger of simply drying up. If an overcast day is not available, then transplant seedlings in the late afternoon or early evening when the sun is not so harsh. They will then have at least twelve hours to recover from the transplant shock. In all cases it is essential to water seedlings well when they are planted and every day until they are established.

Planting Patterns

There are all kinds of ways to position flower seedlings and bulbs for decoration of your landscape. Group them, row them, drift them, or naturalize them. Set in informal groupings of three or five plants they will develop into colorful masses as they mature, ideal for accenting areas. Planted in rows either alone or alternating with low shrubs or other flowers, they dramatically mark off borders and edges. Planted as a drift of flowering plants they create a flowing band or wave of color over a large area. Naturalized plantings are informal and highlight undeveloped areas of the property. No matter how you plant your flowers, however, spacing is important.

As mentioned previously, every flowering

Cluster flowering plants in various patterns for best color impact: Plant them in rows in narrow areas along walks or walls (figure A); group them in clumps of three or five of the same kind in beds or wide borders (figure B); or, to fill even larger spaces, mass them in informal drifts that flow among other plantings and trace the contour of the ground (figure C).

plant has its own characteristic growth habit. Some are bushy, others grow vertically, while others clump or crawl on the ground. Each needs space to grow in its own way, and the space must be sufficiently large to permit air circulation around the plant when it is mature. If air cannot move freely around and between the flowers, moisture rising from the soil stagnates around the lower foliage and roots. This combination of stillness and moisture often encourages disease. In addition, plants growing too close together are forced to compete for air, space, light, and nutrients. Be sure to follow plant labels and seed packet recommendations for spacing to help prevent overcrowding.

For homeowners interested in trying a small bed or border of flowers, the size of the flower plants is especially important to the planting pattern. The general rule of thumb is that taller flowers belong in the back of the area, medium ones toward the middle, and small ones in the very front along its edge. Rather than lining flowers up in strict rows in this format, aim to group varieties of plants, three or five in a group for a natural look.

Planting Your Flowers

Once the plants are purchased, the soil is warm and dried, and the planting pattern determined, it is time to plant. Bulb planting differs somewhat from that of annuals and perennials, but none are at all difficult.

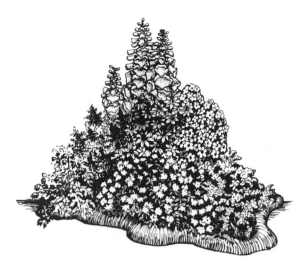

When planting flowers of varying heights together in a bed, locate the taller ones in groups toward the back so that they do not block the shorter ones. The medium-size plants should be in the middle of the bed, reserving the front edge for groups of low or creeping types.

PLANTING BULBS

Clear the ground of debris such as sticks, fallen leaves, and weeds. If only a few bulbs are to be planted in an area, use a trowel or bulb planter to dig individual holes somewhat deeper than the specified depth (see chart below) for the type of bulb and at the correct distance apart. In loose, sandy soil, plant bulbs three to four inches deeper than the depths recommended below. In fact, tulips do better when deeply planted. They like a minimum of six inches of soil over the top of the bulb, even ten inches or more in light, sandy soils.

Measure the planting depth from the bottom of the hole where the bulb roots will rest when the bulb is set in the hole. Set each bulb in its hole, taking care that the pointed part aims up and the flatter side rests on the soil.

Give the bulb a gentle twist to assure that the beginning roots at the base of the bulb make contact with the soil. Be sure to plant bulbs at the recommended distances apart because many of them need room to develop new off-shoots. Fill each hole with the soil that was removed when it was dug and gently firm and smooth the planting surface. Soak the soil after planting to start root growth.

In cases when a large number of bulbs are to be planted, it is easiest to simply dig a wide trench in the planting area to the correct depth for the type of bulb. Position all the bulbs on the bottom of the trench in the desired pattern and shovel the soil carefully over and around them until the bed is covered. Firm the soil over the bulbs and water.

ANNUAL AND PERENNIAL SEEDLINGS

Planting annuals and perennials involves similar procedures. It is most likely that these

When planting a cluster of bulbs, dig a trench to the proper depth for the bulb—in this case tulips—then position the bulbs in the desired pattern. Cover them with soil, tamp it lightly, and water thoroughly. Be sure to mulch bulb beds over the winter.

Planting Depths/Plant Heights for Some Bulbs

	BULB DEPTH	MATURE PLANT HEIGHT	SPACING
Crocus	4 inches	8 inches	4 inches
Daffodil	8–9 inches	24 inches	5 inches
Dutch iris	8 inches	22 inches	5 inches
Glory-of-the-snow	3 inches	4–6 inches	3 inches
Grape hyacinth	4 inches	8–9 inches	4 inches
Hyacinth	6 inches	1–12 inches	5 inches
Hybrid lily	8 inches	3–4 inches	12 inches
Hybrid tulip	8 inches	18–20 inches	5 inches
Lily-of-the-valley	4–6 inches	8 inches	4 inches
Narcissus	4 inches	16 inches	5 inches
Ornamental onion	8 inches	32 inches	5 inches
Snowdrop	4 inches	4–5 inches	4 inches
Species tulip	4 inches	10–12 inches	5 inches
Squill, Siberian	3 inches	4–6 inches	3 inches
Star-of-Bethlehem	4 inches	8–10 inches	6 inches
Winter aconite	2 inches	3–4 inches	3 inches

Rule of thumb: plant twice as deep as the height of the bulb itself.

flowers will be planted as seedlings early in the growing season, when air and soil conditions are right. They will come from the nursery in some sort of small container—either a plastic egg carton type of pack or a small peat box, each holding six to eight seedlings. Some-times larger seedlings come in individual peat cups. However you buy them, keep seedlings moist until planting time.

Prepare the soil much the same way as for bulbs. Remove all the sticks and twigs, stones, and rotted debris that have accumulated over

Sometimes plants begin to outgrow their containers before they come from the nursery or garden center. Before planting, loosen the roots of pot-bound flowers—scoring the tangle with a knife if necessary—so that their roots will grow down into the soil and not around in a strangling circle.

Some perennials come from the nursery bare root. Dig a hole that will accommodate their roots when they are spread out. Support the crown of the plant with a mound of soil that allows the roots to fan out naturally, while taking care that the crown is at the same depth in the soil, perhaps even a bit higher, than it was previously. Fill in with soil, firm it gently over the roots and around the stem, and water generously.

the winter. Dig into the soil with a trowel to loosen it down to about ten inches, breaking up any clumps of soil encountered in the process. If the soil is clayey, this is a good time to dig in some peat moss, compost, or sand to improve drainage. Once the soil is loosened and smoothed level, dig a hole for the seedling that is about the depth of the container it is in. Some flowers, such as peonies and daffodils, are extremely persnickety about their planting depth, so follow the directions on the package carefully.

Pop the seedling out of its market pack or peat pot, taking care not to harm the plant stem. Do not pull it up by its stem. Try pushing up on the bottom of the container to eject the seedling intact. Sometimes, however, seedlings have been in the small packs too long and their roots are wrapped and tangled around themselves. If this is the case, take a minute to loosen the fragile rootlets and spread them a bit so that, once in the ground, they are aimed outward toward the sides of the planting hole. Otherwise, they might continue to grow in a circle. If they have protruded from the drainage hole in the market pack, try to pull them back through when removing the seedling. If these longer root tendrils are broken, it is not a serious problem.

Although peat pots are designed to be planted directly into the soil as is, plant roots have an easier time penetrating the peat and reaching the soil if the pot if punctured or slit up along its sides prior to being set in the planting hole.

Place a seedling in each hole and check that

it is at the same approximate depth in the ground that it was in its nursery container. Fill in around it with soil, pressing it gently against and around the stem. Do this with each seedling, then water them all to encourage good root contact with the soil. Water is especially important to young plants during their first few days in their new location. Check them daily to see if they are drooping and need more moisture. Once they are established—when they look perky and begin to produce new foliage, buds, or stems—you can safely leave them on their own.

PLANTING FLOWERS IN CONTAINERS

Whatever the container, the key to successful container planting is drainage. Just as the ground soil must drain well to nurture flowers, so must containers. The most important thing a container must have is holes or spaces in its bottom to allow excess water to drain away from plant roots after a heavy rain or watering.

Similar to ground soil, the soil within the container must be capable of both holding water and draining well. In container planting this problem is easily solved by the choice of potting medium. Avoid using soil from the backyard in containers. It is likely to contain disease organisms, weed seeds, or insect eggs that will result in problems later in the season. More important, it is usually quite heavy, especially when wet, and makes moving planted containers difficult.

Choose a commercial soilless potting medium from the nursery or garden center. This will be sterile and light and easy to work with. Commercial soilless potting soils are specially formulated, with lots of material such as peat moss to help hold moisture mixed with lots of vermiculite and/or perlite which encourages good aeration and drainage. They have no dirt or soil in them. You can make your own potting mixture by combining equal parts of sphagnum peat moss, vermiculite, and either perlite or coarse sand.

Plant seedlings in outdoor containers in the same way and at the same time you are planting in the ground. You can get away with setting them a bit closer together in the container than in the garden bed in order to give a fuller look when the plants have matured. Make sure the planting medium is moistened thoroughly before planting the seeds or seedlings. In hanging baskets, arrange seedlings toward the edges so they will droop over them as they mature. Set one in the middle to fill in. Remember that containers tend to dry out much faster than the ground does, so attention to watering is extremely important to successful container growing.

CARING FOR FLOWERS

Properly planted, most flowering plants will grow quickly and produce abundant foliage and blooms with very little care. As long as they receive sufficient water and food, they can pretty much fend for themselves. To assure best success, however, a little bit of extra attention is in order. Flowers benefit from periodic grooming, protection against severe weather, and attention to their problems.

Fundamental to healthy plants of all kinds is sufficient water. Like grass, vegetables, trees, and shrubs, flowers need a regular supply of water. As described above, water is particularly important at planting time. Generous watering at that time helps the soil settle into contact with flower seedling roots, nourishing and supporting them. It also provides the extra moisture they need to overcome transplant shock.

The single most common cause of death of plants is insufficient water. Whether a homeowner or a landscape contractor plants them, the flower and bulb beds must be watered regularly over the growing season. A general rule of thumb for established plants is one inch of water a week. Of course some Xeriscape plants are able to do with considerably less if they have to (see page 99 for a list of them). During seasons when rainfall is regular, supplemental watering is rarely necessary, but in the summer when droughty periods are likely to occur, it is extremely important to water flowers every few days. Annuals, in particular, are shallow rooted and tend to dry out more quickly than perennials. And don't overlook the flowering plants in shady areas. Although they don't use as much water as flowers in sunshine do, they may need extra water because the leaves of the trees overhead often prevent light rains from reaching their soil.

Flowering plants in containers on patios,

decks, and windows are vulnerable to drying out because they are in the sun and have so little soil to hold moisture around them. Even with an ideal soil mix, an eight-inch pot of petunias can dry out within hours on a sunny day when the temperature is over 80°F.

Feeding

While flowering plants do not often die from malnutrition, they may fail to do their best because they are in soil that is not very fertile. This is particularly true of perennials and bulbs which are in place year after year in the same soil. To replenish soil, routinely fertilize flower and bulb beds once a year with whichever granular, slow-release fertilizer you have chosen for the lawn, trees, and shrubs. In the spring or fall sprinkle a handful of granular fertilizer around each perennial plant and sprinkle it at about the same rate over beds of bulbs. The box or bag of fertilizer will have more detailed instructions for that particular brand. This main meal should be sufficient for most situations. Because the vital nitrogen is released gradually into the soil over the entire growing season, this feeding will sustain most plants nicely. Take care to avoid getting fertilizer on the leaves or stems of plants, because it may burn the tissues and cause spots.

It is very tempting to fertilize flowers generously and often during the growing season, but to do so is a mistake. If their diet is too rich, most plants will respond by sprouting an overabundance of foliage at the expense of flowers. This excessive vegetative growth is lush and tender and is super vulnerable to pest insects and disease. One main meal is all that is necessary for most plants.

However, after saying that, note that most flowers benefit from an optional snack now and then, especially the annuals that are producing flowers steadily all summer. A snack is a very light feeding using a liquid fertilizer in foliar or spray form. Any liquid fertilizer will do. Use it at half strength no more than two or three times the entire season, about once a month or so. Since the nutrition enters the plant directly through the leaf tissues, the flowers enjoy an immediate boost. Snacks are best given in the morning.

Bulbs are a special case. If their foliage is left to age and turn brown naturally after their blooms have faded and been removed, they will manufacture and store nutrients themselves for use the following spring. The spring or fall main meal of granular fertilizer, or special bulb food available at the garden center instead, will supplement this system and assure vigorous blooming.

Flowers in containers that are planted in soilless mix require a different feeding regimen. Because the mix has no soil, it offers no nutrition to the plant. It is necessary to feed these containerized plants periodically over the season. Give your containerized plants diluted liquid fertilizer in their water or spray the foliage with the diluted mixture about every two weeks. An alternative is to use a time-release type of granular fertilizer sold for houseplants and containers. One application of this slow release material lasts for the whole season.

Primping and Protection

Some simple grooming tasks not only improve the appearance of flowering plants, but also contribute to their health. Those homeowners who take time to mulch, stake, and trim their flower plants, just as they do their shrubs and trees, help them to resist disease and insect problems and to withstand damage from the weather.

Mulching. Mulch annual and perennial flowers to save water. Covering the bare soil reduces water evaporation and runoff, helps maintain soil moisture after watering, and cools the soil during the hot summer. A two- or three-inch layer of chopped leaves, shredded bark, or some other attractive organic material spread on the soil around the plants keeps down weeds as well. Spring bulbs benefit most from mulch during the winter while they are dormant. It insulates the soil and moderates the extremes of freezing and thawing of the soil, typical of winter weather, which can disturb bulbs and even heave them up to the surface of the soil. However, in early spring it is a good idea to rake off this protective mulch from bulb beds and other areas where bulbs are planted

Some Plants That Need Support

Aster (*Aster*)

Bee balm (*Monarda didyma*)

Black-eyed Susan (*Rudbeckia fulgida*)

Chrysanthemum (*Chrysanthemum*)

Coneflower (*Echinacea purpurea*)

Coreopsis (*Coreopsis lanceolata*)

Cosmos (*Cosmos bipinnatus*)

Delphinium/larkspur (*Delphinium*)

Hollyhocks (*Alcea*)

Lilies (*Lilium*)

Lupine (*Lupinus*)

Monkshood (*Aconitum*)

Phlox (*Phlox*)

Spider flower (*Cleome hasslerana*)

Sunflower (*Helianthus*)

Zinnia (*Zinnia elegans*)

to allow the soil to warm in the sun. This will encourage the new shoots and they will not have to struggle to thrust up through a soggy layer of winter mulch.

Flower plants growing in containers can be mulched also. Use a fine material such as rounded pebbles, colorful aquarium gravel, or marble chips to hold water in the soil and discourage weeds.

Staking. Many flowering plants need support when they reach their mature size. Plants more than twenty-four inches tall sometimes flop over by the sheer weight of their blossoms, other times falling victim to heavy rain or wind from summer storms. Plants that have broken or split stems or whose flowers lie on the soil not only look unsightly, but are prime targets for pest insects and disease. Experience with various flowering plants soon reveals which ones need support. The time invested in staking tall plants is worth it.

Some flowers can be staked individually. Tie single-stemmed plants like delphiniums to stakes, one to a plant. Use green bamboo stakes that are sold at the garden center or improvise from materials at hand, perhaps sturdy narrow branches from tree prunings. It is important, though, to choose a stake that is substantial enough to support the mature plant and that will be within six inches of the expected height of the plant. If the stake is green or brown it is less obtrusive. Insert the stake into the soil near the plant stem at least ten or twelve inches deep so that it is secure. Use green string or another flexible material such as the paper-

Make a supporting matrix for large clumps of plants with stakes and string. Set this up before the plant grows very tall so its multiple stems can grow up through it for natural-looking support. This works well with peonies, black-eyed Susans, bee balm, and chrysanthemums.

coated wire available at garden centers for ties. Wrap the string around the stake once first, then loop it around the plant stem loosely, running it back to the stake to be knotted. Do this about two thirds to three quarters of the way up the stem from the ground.

Multistemmed or very bushy plants like chrysanthemums are best supported by several strategically placed stakes, connected by string. To avoid a crushed, bunched look, place stakes around the perimeter of the flower clump about eight inches apart. Then run string from one to the other in a circle, and also across to the opposite stakes. This will create a supporting grid of string through which the plant can grow, its individual stems being supported separately while the entire clump is held up. Garden centers and mail-order catalogs offer stiff wire supporting structures that offer this matrix pattern, un-

obtrusively holding the bushy flower plants in a very natural position.

Once the particular flower plants that will need staking are identified—probably from the previous season's experience—be prepared to set out stakes as soon as they are more than a foot tall, or are showing buds. While supports that are established before the plants are mature may be obtrusive for a short time, it is best to be prepared in the case of sudden stormy weather. It is possible to avoid this job by growing flowers which are able to support themselves or that remain more compact with pinching, and in some cases by fertilizing cautiously so as not to encourage excessive growth.

Pinching back. A third activity which not only helps flower plants to look their best, but also encourages their good health, is pinching. This is simply a form of pruning. Pinching or clipping off ends of stems helps shape a flowering plant. It is particularly beneficial to annuals, like petunias, which become leggy and lanky later in the season. Pinching, or "deadheading," the faded, spent flower heads improves bloom on perennials and maintains the vigor of bulbs.

Normally flower plants live to produce seed for the next generation, and having done so, they go into decline. By removing spent flowers before they have a chance to form seeds, it is possible to stimulate plants to extend their flowering season as they continually strive to produce seeds. This practice can prolong the life of pansies into early summer, for example. Many perennials that have a relatively limited bloom time can be spurred to repeat bloom by cutting back the mature blossoms and stems to the ground. It is extremely important to cut off bulb flowers before they can set seed, so that they can channel the energy produced in their foliage into storage in their bulbs and not into producing seeds.

Some flower plants, like many shrubs, respond to pinching or clipping by becoming bushier and more compact. Chrysanthemums, particularly, like to be pinched back two or three times during the early part of the growing season, well before they form flower buds. Removing the top two inches or so of tender new growth from each stem stimulates stems to branch so that the plant becomes denser and more rounded in form. It also forestalls bud formation, resulting in the traditional fall bloom. Those that are not routinely pinched grow very leggy and tall (requiring staking) and bloom before summer is over. Annuals in containers are often revitalized by pinching back their stems. While they may stop blooming for a short time, they soon resume, producing more colorful bloom on more compact plants.

Dividing flowers and bulbs. Perennials and large bulbs require some extra care every few years. Because they remain in the ground season after season, they develop into large clumps of plants. Eventually, they become so crowded that the plant suffers, or they run out of space.

Over three or four years, perennial plants tend to grow into oversized clumps, crowding themselves and their neighbors. This clump of Siberian iris is divided with a sharp spade into two plants. One is replanted at the original site, the bonus plant is located elsewhere on the property.

Flowers become smaller, foliage lacks good access to light and air, and roots become massed and tangled. Overall health declines as the plant is less able to take up nutrition from the soil and it becomes vulnerable to attack by insects and disease. Bulbs such as iris and species tulips produce numerous offshoots, or bulblets, which begin to grow and crowd one another with similar effect on the health and appearance of the flowers.

Therefore, every three or four years, depending on the plant, it is advisable to dig up clumps of perennials, such as chrysanthemums, astilbes, black-eyed Susans, or daylilies, that are oversize and split them into smaller chunks to be discarded, given away, or planted in new locations. This is done by gently digging down beside and around a plant clump to loosen the soil around its roots, and lifting it out of the ground. The roots of some plants can be pulled apart by hand, while others must be cut through with a sharp knife or a spade. Take care to insure that each new piece of plant has plenty of roots attached. Promptly replant the smaller chunks of plant.

This is true of bulbs as well. If they show signs of crowding—usually the flowers are undersize—they need to be thinned. Wait until the foliage has had a chance to age and die back, then dig them up, separate them, and replant some in the original bed and use the others around the property. Often the larger parent bulbs will have developed small offshoots, or bulblets. Gently detach these babies and plant them separately. It may be another year or two before they are mature enough to produce flowers. Sometimes iris rhizomes become so crowded that they protrude from the soil in tangled masses. Gently dig up clumps of rhizomes and cut through the tangle with a sharp knife. Discard the obviously older, woody ones, and cut the others into two- or three-inch chunks. Be sure each chunk has root fibers on it. Replant the iris in place or elsewhere on the property.

Splitting or dividing perennial plants is usually done in the fall, but can be done in the early spring if necessary in most cases. Divide bulbs anytime after their foliage has died back. The reward for this job is not only healthier perennials, but free extra plants.

Flowers are an easy, inexpensive way to decorate the landscape. Whether they are annuals, perennials, or bulbs, they are a source of color and delight, returning in generous measure the small amount of effort it takes to grow them. Take advantage of the flexibility and beauty of flowers to enhance your landscape.

CHAPTER 4
Growing Vegetables

This chapter is for folks who really enjoy eating fresh vegetables but have never tried growing any. Those who don't particularly like vegetables, or who are not inclined to take on this activity, may skip to the next chapter. It is worth exploring the subject, though, because growing a few veggies is easy. It is possible to produce a little food in the yard without getting heavily into vegetable gardening and all that that implies.

Because many food and herb plants have ornamental value as well, they can be integrated into a residential landscape very easily. They are treated basically the same way flowering plants, trees, shrubs, and grass are, but they offer a bonus of fresh, plant-ripened food—nothing tastes quite so good as a tomato straight from the yard. This chapter outlines a series of modest steps to introduce homeowners to growing vegetables. They represent varying degrees of involvement so that a beginner can choose an approach that does

not demand more time or effort than he or she is willing to commit.

Over the past ten years, an interesting thing has been happening to vegetable gardens in the United States—they are getting smaller and smaller. In 1980 the average garden in this country was about six hundred square feet. In 1990 the average garden was slightly under two hundred square feet, a major reduction. Does that mean we are growing fewer vegetables? No, it means we are learning to be more productive in less space. New techniques and vegetable garden designs enable homeowners to have lots of fresh vegetables and herbs during the summer months without monopolizing the backyard. In addition, new techniques help them to produce food with less time invested. These methods can be employed by nongardening homeowners as well. It may be time to consider trying to grow a few veggies yourself.

Growing a few vegetables, and maybe some fresh herbs, will not save any money; they are always cheap at the market in season. These

Nothing tastes better than homegrown vegetables. Sprinkled among other ornamental plants around the yard or in a small plot, a few vegetable plants will produce food and look attractive.

days, most people grow some of their own because they want the higher quality. The tomatoes have real flavor and more juice. The peppers are crisp and have a much deeper flavor than the store-bought versions shipped from California. Fresh basil or parsley, picked just before it is used, has more flavor than fresh herbs available in the store and their dried counterparts.

Not inconsequential is the fact that vegetables grown in the backyard and picked just before they are eaten have much more nutritional value than fresh vegetables from the supermarket. Store-bought produce typically spends days in transit after it has been harvested, and even fresh vegetables lose food value over time. Additionally, more and more people are concerned about the possible pesticide residues on fresh produce purchased in the store. If you grow your own you can control whether any pesticides even touch the veg-

gies you harvest. Vegetable plants in the yard means that fresh produce is just a few steps away. Salads, soups, and stews can be created by simply picking what is ripe at the moment. Better taste, better texture, greater nutrition, and ready access are why people like to grow some of their own vegetables.

Growing vegetables can be done on one of several levels of involvement:

1. *"Just for fun."* Tuck a few tomato, pepper, and herb plants in among other landscape plantings; you'll grow twenty to thirty pounds of fresh food during the summer season.

2. *The basic vegetable bed.* Set up a small bed dedicated to vegetable plants over the late spring and summer; in one hundred square feet grow fifty to seventy-five pounds of food.

3. *Adding a vertical growing area.* Add a trellis to the vegetable bed to increase productivity by 30 percent with no increase in the size of the garden itself; in 100 square feet with a 24-foot trellis grow 100 to 150 pounds of food.

4. *Extending the growing season.* Use devices such as cloches and plastic mulch in the garden bed to add a spring growing season and a fall growing season; double productivity in one hundred square feet, grow two hundred to three hundred pounds of food.

JUST FOR FUN

It is possible to grow almost any plant normally found in the typical vegetable garden in among shrubs or mixed with flowers in a flower bed. Perhaps the most common plants tucked in somewhere in the landscape are tomatoes, peppers, lettuce, parsley, and basil. These plants are annuals in most parts of the country and are no more difficult to grow than petunias. It is a simple matter to pick up a few vegetable seedlings at the market or garden center along with the flower seedlings. Vegetables and herbs also do well in containers—hanging in baskets, sitting around the patio, or lined up on the sunny side of the garage. They will thrive in a window box or on a balcony of the twenty-third floor of an apartment house. Just like most of the other plants discussed in this book, they require lots of sun (at least six hours a day), moisture, sufficient space, and appropriate soil. Vegetables will not grow in the shade.

The key to growing vegetables among other landscape plantings is to provide enough light and space for them to grow without harming the aesthetic appearance of the landscape in general. Like flowers, vegetable and herb plants have characteristic growing habits, such as tall and narrow, bushy, or vining and creeping. Take this into consideration when placing them in the yard.

Tomato plants will grow very tall and will probably need some support, so they are best located among tall shrubs where they will add to the green foliage background in that area of the landscape. Take care to provide access to them so it is easy to pick the ripe tomatoes when the time comes. When the tomatoes are

To enjoy fresh vegetables in yards where space is limited, plant vegetables among the ornamental plants where they can share the sun. Tuck tall tomatoes among lupines and dahlias or sneak in smaller pepper plants among the daisies or impatiens. Use lettuce, cabbages, and onions in the front at the edge of the border.

ripening, the red color adds a nice accent. Peppers, especially the various hot peppers with gorgeous yellow and red fruits, are also attractive set among other landscape plantings. They have nice deep green bushy foliage. There are also dwarf versions of pepper plants and other vegetables which are ideal for the front of a border of ornamental plants or for containers. Lettuces are low growing and offer various shades of green and red, and curly or flat foliage. These also make good edging plants. Peas are climbers and will twist up a fence or porch railing. Green beans are available as both climbers, called pole beans, or as bushy plants. The same is true for cucumbers. The possibilities for unobtrusive placement of vegetable plants among existing landscape plantings are endless.

Vegetables need to be in good soil. Like

flowers, they like soil that is capable of holding moisture, yet is well-draining when there is too much rain. This is true whether they grow in containers or in the ground. If they are planted among flowers and shrubs that are already flourishing, the soil is probably just fine. If soil drainage is doubtful, dig up the soil down to twelve to eighteen inches and mix in a few shovelfuls of peat moss or compost before planting in that area.

Containers for vegetables should be twelve to twenty-four inches deep, depending on the plant to be grown. Use a soilless medium rather than soil from the yard. It is lighter, if the container must be moved, and it both drains and holds water well. The best soil mix for growing plants in containers is a mixture of vermiculite, perlite, and peat moss (see page 112) that is sold in garden centers under the name of "Pro Mix." Because there is no dirt or actual soil in this mix, it is important to feed containerized plants regularly, using either a powdered, granulated, or liquid fertilizer. See Appendix D for lists of recommended container varieties and guidelines on the appropriate container sizes.

Seeds versus Seedlings

It is easiest for beginners to plant vegetable seedlings purchased from the local garden center rather than starting them at home from seed. Nursery-grown plants have had professional care and attention throughout the crucial stages of germination and are likely to be healthy and vigorous. They will also be varieties that are appropriate for the area. Many of the most common vegetables are widely available as seedlings, such as tomatoes, peppers, leaf lettuce, squash, and cabbage. They are sold in plastic market packs of six or eight to a pack or in small peat containers. It is a simple matter to set them into the bed. Some crops, such as spinach, peas, carrots, and beets, are not usually available as seedlings, but they are easy to grow from seed sown right in the bed. Follow the directions on the label of the seed packet, bearing in mind the advantages of intensive planting and closer spacing discussed below.

While seedlings are more expensive than seeds, they are cost effective because there is no need to buy more than is needed. Most seed packets have over one hundred seeds in them, enough to supply the whole neighborhood for a year. Since a small bed can accommodate only a few plants of each type of vegetable, seedlings are convenient. However, planting from seed offers the advantage of greater choice. There are many, many more varieties of each type of vegetable available as seed than as seedlings. The garden center might offer three varieties of tomatoes, while most seed catalogs will offer more than thirty varieties.

Plant vegetable seedlings the same as you do flower seedlings. Keep them moist until planting time. Choose a day that is overcast or plant late in the afternoon so that tender seedlings do not have to cope with the hot sun as they adjust to transplanting. Choose a site that will accommodate the particular plant's mature size and prepare the soil by digging it with a trowel to loosen it. Remove any stones and debris, then smooth the soil surface level.

With the trowel dig a hole as deep into the soil as the seedling's rootball is in its market pack or pot. Pop the seedling from its container by pushing from the bottom or rapping its side to loosen it so it will slide out when tipped. Loosen any matted roots to encourage them to grow outward in the soil, and then set the seedling in the hole at the same depth that it was in its container. Tomato and pepper seedlings are less finicky about this; in fact, they do better if they are set a bit lower in the ground than they were previously. Fill the hole with dirt, gently pressing it around the stem of the seedling. Water generously and daily until the plant shows signs that it has recovered from the transplant shock which may cause it to wilt.

Fertilizing and Watering

Whether in the ground or in containers, vegetables—unlike the grass, flowers, trees, and shrubs nearby in the landscape—need to be fed fairly often if they are to produce a good harvest. Use the same slow-release nitrogen granular fertilizer that is recommended for all the plants on the property, but give extra feedings to the vegetable plants. It is safest to follow a simple monthly feeding routine until the needs of the individual vegetable plants be-

Some Vegetables and Herbs for the Home Landscape

Basil	Mint	Radishes
Beans*	Parsley	Rhubarb
Eggplant	Peas*	Summer squash
Lettuce	Peppers	Tomatoes

*not available as seedlings

come familiar to you. Mix some granular fertilizer into the soil when planting vegetable seedlings, then use a liquid fertilizer every month to maintain plant vigor. Follow the instructions on the box or bottle and mix enough liquid fertilizer to spray the foliage thoroughly or to pour on the soil around the plant.

Vegetables wilt when they need water. Unfortunately, by the time they do this they have been stressed for a day or two already. Regular rainfall will normally provide sufficient water for vegetables and other annuals. When rain is scarce, watering once a week in the spring or fall and twice a week during the summer should be sufficient to guarantee enough water.

Tomatoes. These are the most popular vegetable grown at home. No surprise here. Just one or two tomato plants yield dozens of fresh

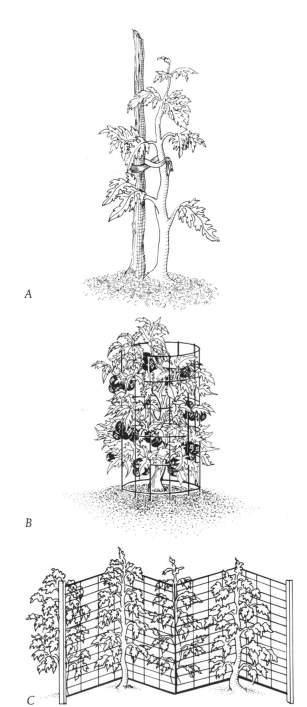

A

B

C

tomatoes from July through September in most parts of the country. There are two kinds of tomato plants. Indeterminate ones grow in long vines up to twenty feet. Once they begin to bear fruit, they continue until frost. Determinate tomato plants grow in bush form, rarely exceeding four feet in height. They stop growing when they set fruit on their topmost branch. They can be planted more closely together, need less support, and their fruit ripens faster. These latter, the bushlike determinate plants, are the easiest to grow for beginners. Labels on tomato plants sold in nurseries or garden centers indicate whether a tomato seedling is determinate or indeterminate and its variety, or name, within that category. Labels also list pest and disease-resistant qualities, indicated as V, F, N or T. These letters mean that the tomato variety has inherent resistance to Verticillium wilt, Fusarium wilt, nematodes, or tobacco mosaic virus. It is wise to select varieties that display some or all of these letters.

Tomatoes do best and look better when they

There are as many ways to support tomato plants are there are tomato growers. Here are three reliable methods: (A) Tie each individual tomato plant to its own sturdy stake. Use a soft fabric strip or special tie made for this purpose, available at garden centers. Loop it around the stake, then the tomato stem, then back to the stake to be fastened; (B) A tomato cage will support a single tomato plant, or two or three that have been planted in a group. Weave the branches around the wire, tying them where necessary. The wide openings in the wire make it easy to pick the tomatoes; (C) A sturdy trellis fence such as this will support a row of tomato plants. Tie them to the wire as described above.

are staked, and staking the bushlike determinate tomato is much easier than dealing with the long indeterminate vines, at least for a first attempt at agriculture. The determinate ones will blend best with nearby shrubs and other landscape plantings.

Peppers. These are an acquired taste, but for those who love them, nothing is better than home-grown peppers. Fortunately they are readily available as seedlings at garden centers. Growing them in the yard provides an opportunity to have several varieties, both hot and sweet. Their colors are decorative, blending nicely with marigolds, salvias, and other bright flowers. Sweet peppers form as bell-shaped green fruits and, if left to ripen thoroughly, turn yellowish or red over time. Both are tasty, but the reddened ones are sweeter and have more carotene and vitamin C than when they are green. Hot peppers tend to be narrower and more elongated in shape, although some varieties have small, round "cherry" shapes. Hot peppers may be yellow, red, or green and vary in degree of hotness. When the harvest is in, try them cautiously!

Pepper plants may need staking, as their fruits tend to weigh down their branches, which sometimes break off altogether if not supported.

Eggplants. These are delicious and ornamental. They have lovely gray-green foliage and small lavender flowers that turn into glossy oval purple fruits. Eggplants blend well with petunias

SOME RECOMMENDED TOMATO VARIETIES

INDETERMINATE	DETERMINATE
'Better Boy'	'Celebrity'
'Big Boy'	'Heinz'(ideal for canning)
'Roma' (sauce tomato)	'Pixie Hybrid II' (good for containers)
'Super Beefsteak'	'Tiny Tim' (dwarf cherry tomatoes)

SOME RECOMMENDED PEPPER VARIETIES

SWEET	HOT
'Bell Boy Hybrid'	'Hungarian Wax'
'CaliforniaWonder'	'Jalapeño M'
'Crispy Hybrid'	'Super Chili Hybrid'
'New Ace Hybrid' (good for stuffing),	'Long Red Cayenne'
'Sweet Banana'	'Zippy Hybrid'

in a flower border. They also do well in containers. If their fruits are picked promptly, they will continue to bear until frost. Japanese types of eggplant are elongated, measuring ten to twelve inches long and one to two inches in diameter. Some varieties such as 'Early Beauty' bear lots of small oval fruits over a long season.

Lettuce. This is so easy to grow that it is perfect for planting "just for fun." Available as seedlings in both the "leaf," or loosehead types, and the "head" types, they come in a variety of textures and colors. All have much more flavor and food value than the ubiquitous iceberg found in every grocery store in the country. Lettuce does not like the heat of the summer, so check the stores for seedlings in the early spring and plant as soon as frost danger is past. Once the weather heats up, lettuce "bolts"—it grows raggedy, bitter, and goes to seed. However, after summer heat is past, it is possible in many areas to sneak a few more lettuce plants in for fall eating.

Leaf lettuce plants will tolerate poor soil and are best for areas that experience hot summers. They mature rapidly. Harvest them by cutting the leaves off at soil level rather than pulling the plant out of the ground. Cut off at the crown, the plants will sprout new leaves. Grow both green leaf lettuce and red leaf lettuce for variety. You can plant a row of alternating green and red along the outside edge of the flower border in much the same manner petunias are used as a border. Used this way, when the lettuce is ready to pick, do not pick the entire plant, but just harvest a leaf or two from each plant down the line of the border. You can enjoy the ornamental value of the bright red-and-green border and great salads for weeks and weeks.

Summer Squash. Zucchini squash and its yellow cousins come by their reputation as prolific producers honestly. Summer squashes are mostly bush types and are very easy to grow. They mature rapidly. Because they take up a lot of space, it is important to limit the number of plants you plant. There will be plenty of squashes, even from only two plants. Plan on one plant per family member who likes squash. Plant three or four seeds or two seedlings in clusters on hills of soil that are four feet apart. Thin germinated seeds to the strongest two plants per hill once they show their true leaves. If you prefer rows, plant seedlings one plant per eighteen inches, allowing four feet of space on each side of the row. They also grow well in containers. Pick squashes when they are young, before they grow much bigger than six inches, to encourage a larger and longer harvest. Summer squash of all kinds is most flavorful and tender if harvested when it is immature. Squash flowers are edible too.

Culinary Herbs. They are easily grown in containers or tucked in among the flowers. The seedlings most commonly available are parsley, basil, dill, rosemary, and sage. Grow the

COMMON VARIETIES OF CULINARY HERBS

BASIL: cinnamon basil, 'Green Bouquet' (dwarf, mounded), lemon basil (silvery leaves), 'Purple Ruffles' (fringed, dark purple leaves), sweet basil (classic for tomato sauce)

PARSLEY: 'Extra Curled Dwarf' (classic curly leaves), 'Single Italian' (flat, deeply cut leaves, more flavorful than curled)

THYME: common thyme (for seasoning, as ground cover), creeping thyme (dwarf version of common, two inches tall), golden lemon thyme (lemon flavor great in tea, sauces; good in rock gardens)

cook's favorites. Put them in containers near the kitchen door or out among the annual flowers. When herb plants flower they add color to the yard and their foliage—in grays and all shades of greens—contributes color and texture to the landscape. Some, like rosemary, become woody over the season and take on the dimensions of a small shrub in the right conditions.

Prune off spent flowers on herb plants to encourage dense foliage growth. The repeated pinching of sprigs for use in the kitchen serves to keep plants compact and stimulates growth. Parsley grows in bunches of three stems. Pinch off only the middle stalk in the clump of three, which is usually the one having the fatter stem. Leave the other two stems intact. Clip off basil stems just above a pair of leaves. If basil show flowers, be sure to pinch them off promptly or the plants will grow spindly and weak. Systematically pinched, most herb plants will get bushier and have a better appearance.

Parsley sprigs store well in the refrigerator either with their stems in a glass of water or moistened and sealed in a Ziplock bag. Basil leaves will store nicely in the refrigerator too, but only for a week or so.

Generally annuals, most herbs are not hardy enough to winter over safely outdoors in the North, but they will grow indoors in a pot set in a sunny window until it is safe to put them out in the yard in the spring. If this is not possible, pinch herb plants before frost and dry the leaves (a microwave oven does a good job) for storage and use over the winter.

Of course, there are other common vegetables that are appropriate for planting around the landscape "just for fun." Some of these will be discussed later in this chapter.

STARTING A SMALL VEGETABLE BED

Not everyone will want to try growing vegetables throughout the landscape as suggested above. More adventurous homeowners may chose to dive right in and establish a small vegetable bed. Properly designed and cared for, a modest plot in a corner of the yard will produce a substantial amount of fresh produce with a relatively minor investment of time and effort. Growing vegetables on this scale is a good way to learn about food gardening. This section of the chapter will focus on vegetable growing during the standard growing season —roughly June to October, depending on the region of the country. In a small bed it is possible to grow lettuce, tomatoes, peppers, green peas, green beans, zucchini squash, eggplant, Swiss chard, cucumbers, carrots, spinach, green onions (scallions), and beets during this period of time.

The first step is finding the right location for the vegetable bed. Sunlight is critical; the more, the better. Six hours a day is considered minimum, eight to twelve hours a day is best. If there is a choice, site the garden bed on a north-south axis so that larger plants won't shade out the smaller plants for too much of the day. If the bed must unavoidably line up on an east-west axis, extra care is necessary when planting various crops to assure that all get a fair share of sun.

Size and Shape of the Bed

Traditional vegetable gardens are rectangular in shape, ranging in size from just thirty square feet to thousands of square feet. However there is no earthly reason they can't be circular or free-form in shape. The old patterns were established in response to cultivation practices and equipment, which are not terribly significant when plants are grown on a very small scale in the yard. There are some benefits to having the rectangular shape if the bed is to be boxed and trellises are to be added as described later on in this chapter.

Whatever its configuration, one hundred square feet is a good size for a beginning vegetable bed. This is enough space to grow plenty of fresh produce over the summer without becoming a burden to maintain. Once successful with a bed this size, it is easy for you to expand by simply adding new beds if the yard is large enough. A plot 4 feet wide and 24 feet long makes a nice 96-square-foot garden. An alternate design of three beds four feet wide and eight feet long represents the same total growing area, and may better accommodate the other activities that take place in the yard. While growing beds can be any width, four feet assures comfortable adult reach and lends itself to more advanced vegetable garden designs, described later in this chapter.

RAISED BEDS

Years ago, most vegetable gardens were flat plots of soil which were industriously tilled, or dug up each year at planting time. Plants were then planted in single rows separated from one another by paths. Inevitably the soil throughout the garden was compacted as the location of paths was altered from year to year.

The strenuous labor of digging or tilling the plot had to be repeated annually. Gardening was hard labor.

This old model has been replaced in recent years by a raised bed model. Raised beds are typically three or four inches higher than the surrounding soil. Three or four feet wide and of various lengths, raised beds are permanent. Garden paths that permit access to the raised beds are also permanent and are often attractively covered with woodchips, gravel, or bricks to minimize mud problems. They are designed to handle all garden traffic, so there is no need to ever step on the surface of the raised bed. Consequently, the raised garden bed does not ever suffer compacted soil and never needs to be dug up once it is established. These raised beds significantly reduce the amount of labor that is involved in growing vegetables.

Raised beds are better for plants too. Plants grow better in soil that is not compacted, whether they be lawn grass, flowers, trees and shrubs, or vegetables. The loose soil in raised beds drains better and has more air available to plant roots. The soil also heats up sooner in the spring, a consideration in growing food crops. Plants in raised beds are healthier and produce more food. When raised beds are boxed in with wood planks, they are not only easier to maintain, they are neat and attractive in the landscape. Whether a homeowner intends to have a small, trial vegetable bed, or to establish a more extensive garden, boxed beds are an ideal concept.

Raised beds do not have to be boxed to offer the benefits of good drainage, low maintenance, and increased production. They require some attention to keep the soil from slipping onto the paths after heavy rains.

EASY RAISED BEDS. The easiest way to make a raised bed is to lay out its dimensions with string or other markers, and then systematically move along the area, turning the soil with a shovel or spading fork. If the plot is to be established in an area that is lawn, it is probably easier to remove any pieces of sod and set them aside, rather than to try to incorporate them into the soil at this point. Working backward along the bed to avoid stepping on newly turned soil, dig up and turn shovelfuls of soil, removing any large rocks and breaking up large chunks of dirt along the way. Try to dig down at least a foot, mounding the soil in a loose pile within the measured dimensions of the bed.

Once the rough outline of the bed is established, set up pathways around the outside of the bed. Allow at least two feet—more, if possible—for the paths. Scrape or dig out the top few inches of topsoil from the paths and mound that on the bed to add to its height. Spread two to four inches of woodchips in the path areas, rake and level the surface of the mounded soil, and the raised bed garden is ready to plant.

BOXING THE BED. A raised bed, as described above, works just fine and does not need a box around it to produce happy plants. The box is for the homeowner, not the plants. A box made from planks that shore up the sides of the mounded soil saves some time over the years, and it also looks neater. The sides of simple raised beds tend to erode over the season. Heavy rains run off it, carrying some of the soil onto the paths. Plants tend to flop down onto the paths. Beds that are boxed do not require the annual sprucing needed to restore the mounded shape that plain ones do. Paths are kept clear of mud and more space is available for growing plants if beds are boxed.

Pressure-treated two-inch-by-eight-inch lumber planks nailed together with spikes make suitable boxes for raised beds. While the chemicals used for pressure treating lumber today do not create any toxic problems for vegetables growing nearby, one precaution you can take is to box all raised beds in the fall. By spring the soil microbes and weathering will have neutralized any traces of chemicals in the soil or the boards. As a matter of fact, it is a good idea to build the garden bed in the fall, anyway. This way the hard work of digging is accomplished when there is more time in the fall. The bed will be ready for planting first thing in the spring.

Choosing What to Grow

The most common mistake made by novice vegetable growers is overenthusiasm. They plant too many different kinds of vegetables. Because each type of vegetable has its own growing needs, management of lots of different kinds can get very complicated. For the first small bed, choose only six or eight types of vegetables to experiment with. Be sure to choose those which are favorites with the family. There is no point is growing radishes if no one likes them. Kohlrabi is great in salads, but if no one has ever had one, wait till next year to try growing it. Look over the list of family favorites and select a few; don't be tempted to plant a little bit of everything. The list below is offered to help you make some choices.

It is difficult to provide a list of those vegetables that are easiest to grow, because often what is easy in one part of the country may be difficult in another.

It is a good idea to make a rough sketch of the vegetable bed to plan where the various plants will go and how many will fit comfortably into the bed. Check the charts in the appendix of this book for help in estimating how much space individual vegetable plants will require when they are full-grown. Use the same general rule that was outlined in chapter three

---

Choosing Among Vegetables

HIGHEST NUTRITIONAL VALUE
(*highest listed first*)

Broccoli
Spinach
Brussels sprouts
Lima beans
Peas
Asparagus
Cauliflower
Sweet potatoes
Carrots

MOST PRODUCE PER SQUARE FOOT
(*most productive listed first*)

Tomatoes (staked)
Peppers
Squash
Green beans
Beets
Lettuce
Carrots
Cauliflower
Broccoli

---

for siting flowers in a bed; locate the taller plants toward the back, the medium ones in the middle, and the small ones along the edges of the bed. This way the tall ones do not shade or obscure the smaller ones from view. Plan to tuck a few herbs, such as parsley, basil, and dill, into corners of the vegetable bed where they are handy for the cook. The simple sketch below, based on a standard ninety-six-square-foot bed is an example of a planning sketch. Precision is not necessary here, just a general sense of where things are going to go.

The challenge of gardening for fresh produce for the table—and it takes a few years of experience to accomplish this goal—is to plant just enough of each vegetable so when it ripens there is just enough for the family to enjoy with little left over. Three tomato plants may do the job, while six tomato plants (which don't look very big in the spring when they are seedlings) may provide enough tomatoes for a small army. Be conservative. Unless someone is willing and able to cook up or freeze the excess harvest, it becomes a burden.

Like flowers, certain vegetable plants are more cold hardy and can be planted fairly early in the season while others must wait until it is much warmer. Although it is tempting to plant seedlings out in the yard the minute they are available in garden centers, avoid this temptation. There is no point in planting even hardy plants in soil that is too cold and wet and there is danger of frost. Weather temperature records from decades past enable agricultural experts to determine the likely dates of the first frost in the fall and last frost in the spring in all areas of the country. Check with gardening friends or the local county extension service for the date of last expected frost in your area. Obviously this is not a firm date, but it provides a guideline for early planting.

Vegetable Temperature Preferences

COLD WEATHER: beets, broccoli, cabbage, carrots, cauliflower, celery, Chinese cabbage, kale, kohlrabi, leeks, lettuce, onions, parsley, peas, radishes, spinach, Swiss chard

WARM WEATHER: beans, corn, cucumbers, eggplant, melon, peppers, squash (summer and winter), sweet potatoes, tomatoes

It is possible to plant spinach, peas, leaf lettuce, and onion sets several weeks before that expected last frost, but everything else should wait until two weeks or so after that last frost date. That is plenty of time for a successful summer garden.

Intensive Planting

One of the reasons American vegetable gardens have gotten smaller is that people have learned about intensive planting techniques. Traditionally vegetables were planted in rows and, because most vegetable gardens were in the country where space is not a problem, the distances recommended between plants were related more to making space for cultivating tools than to what each plant needed for healthy growth. It turns out that most plants can be planted much more closely than has traditionally been the case. Recommended guidelines for distance between plants on seed packets, in gardening books, and on plant labels refer to gardens planted in rows, rather than in beds. Again, the spacing is usually more generous than necessary. Grouping seedlings closer than these recommended distances is called "intensive" planting. This technique is particularly suited for raised beds.

While it is perfectly fine to plant raised beds in rows, it is not necessary. In fact, more plants will fit into the same bed area if they are grouped and spaced as close together as is possible for healthy growth. Notice in the garden plan drawing above, the plants are in groupings rather than in rows. The trick here is to space each plant equidistant from the same type plant, so each tomato plant is eighteen inches from each of the other tomato plants. Although the mature plants will seem to be a bit crowded, the superior soil afforded by the properly dug raised bed will accommodate the roots of so many plants. With several different kinds and shapes of plants in a relatively modest space this may seem chaotic, but the plants are happy. The charts at the back of this book list both the intensive planting distances as well as the traditional planting distances. Either approach will grow vegetables; the intensive approach will simply grow more food in less space.

Note that while vegetables planted more

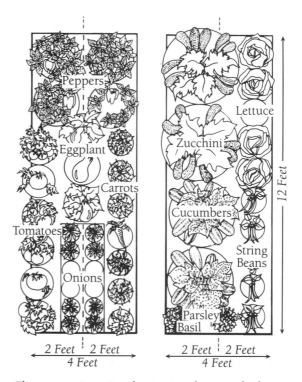

The secret to intensive planting is to locate each plant in the bed so that when it is mature its leaves just touch those of the adjacent plants.

Because raised beds have loose, rich soil it is possible to plant seedlings closer together than normal. This intensive system yields much more produce. Here regular cabbage and Chinese cabbage, cool-weather crops, thrive in tight quarters.

closely together produce more total crop, the individual vegetables are somewhat smaller than the maximum size that would be possible if the plant had lots of room and no competition. Here is a surprising statistic. Pea vines spaced one inch apart rather than the recommended 1½ or 2 inches will yield peas that are smaller than normal, but because there are more pea plants per square foot, the total weight of shelled peas per square foot from the intensively planted garden is greater than the total from the row garden. Tomatoes are a bit smaller, but there are more pounds of tomatoes. Cucumbers may be a bit smaller, but there are more pounds of cucumbers. Since the production of a volume of fresh produce, rather than large individual vegetables, is the objective here, intensive planting techniques makes sense for small backyard beds.

Managing the Small Vegetable Bed

While a single small vegetable bed of ninety-six square feet or so takes very little time to manage over the whole season, there are certain maintenance tasks that must be done. The pleasure of growing vegetables as well as all plants is reduced if the homeowner has to be out in the yard every day weeding, watering, and worrying about bugs. Fortunately there are a number of simple planting and maintenance techniques that contribute to the general health of the vegetable plants while minimizing the time invested by the gardener.

MULCHING

A simple technique which makes vegetable growing less work is mulching. There is no need for weeding to become a major burden, and the days of the hoe are past. The virtues of mulch have been discussed at length in the previous chapters. It is a most useful material for the entire landscape and the vegetable bed is no exception. However, interestingly enough, it has only been in the last twenty years that the value of mulching vegetable plants has been accepted. Use mulch to keep down weeds. There should be no bare soil visible anywhere in the vegetable bed! Cover all soil surfaces between plants with a two- to four-inch layer of organic mulch (the most common are chopped leaves, hay, or straw). Spread among and between seedlings that are taller than three or four inches, it will smother almost all weeds. The few that do appear are easily pulled as their roots are loosely held in the layer of mulch.

Mulch offers the same important benefits to vegetable plants that it offers to trees, shrubs, and flowers. In the summer it tends to cool the soil by as much as six to eight degrees. This is important to plant health in July and August when soil temperatures approach 85°F. Most plants slow or even stop growth when the soil temperature exceeds 85°F. They don't get sick, they just stop growing. If a vegetable or flower bed is mulched, the soil around the plants doesn't get as warm as fast, and the plants keep growing in the heat of summer. Organic mulch decomposes very slowly as it does its mulching thing, slowly enriching the soil with humus and providing nutrients for the plants. At the end of the season either dig the partially decomposed mulch into the soil where it will decompose entirely by next spring or place the material in a compost pile.

DRIP IRRIGATION

There are several choices of equipment for watering a vegetable bed. A hand-held sprinkler device on a hose may be sufficient for a small raised bed. Also, an oscillating sprinkler set on the lawn nearby is just fine. However, the best watering device for a vegetable bed is a drip irrigation system. Once installed, it requires less work of the homeowner and delivers water better and more efficiently than other watering techniques.

Drip irrigation devices introduce water into the soil very slowly which is the best way to provide water to plants. While some systems feature emitters or valves spaced every twelve inches along a narrow hose, other systems consist of porous hose that drips along its entire length. Both types are effective; the porous hose system is best for most situations. Made of recycled, chopped-up automobile tires, these hoses are designed to be buried unobtrusively under the soil surface, where they will last for many years. Their billions of little holes leak water in small amounts that are efficiently absorbed by the soil.

Why is slow watering important? Water sprinkled from above, such as from hand-held or oscillating sprinklers, or rain itself, is often wasted. Evaporation and runoff may result in the loss of as much as 30 percent of the water. Water from above settles on foliage and may promote fungal disease in plants that are prone to this problem. Water from drip systems is delivered directly to plant roots, which saves water and improves plant health.

A porous hose system suitable for a ninety-six-square-foot vegetable bed costs about $25. It is important to purchase a pressure-reducing device too. This is screwed onto the irrigation line back at the hose faucet and prevents water from coming out of the house too quickly and shortening the life of the hose. Most porous hose systems will last six to eight years. It is very important to cover the porous hose with soil or mulch as exposure to sunlight causes a slow breakdown of the material.

The absolutely best arrangement for saving time is to have the drip system controlled by some kind of timing device. Most of the mechanical watering timers on the market don't work very well with drip systems because of their lower pressures, but all of the computer-type timers work just fine. They are not cheap, but they can be programmed much like a VCR and will turn on and turn off the drip irrigation system automatically. They can be set to run it every other day for twenty or thirty minutes. Some of these computer devices even have the capability to detect rain and to skip days when it rains. These systems work equally well around shrubs and trees and in flower beds.

While the manufacturers of porous hose drip systems say that they moisten the soil out

Leaky-hose-type of drip irrigation is positioned on this boxed raised bed before young seedlings are planted or mulch, either black plastic or chopped leaves, is added. At about two feet apart these lines will "sweat" moisture to gradually and uniformly soak the soil, minimizing water loss through evaporation or runoff.

to twelve inches on either side of the hose, that distance varies, depending on the type of soil in the vegetable bed. Clay soil allows water from a drip hose to permeate the soil out to twelve to fifteen inches on either side of the hose. Sandy soil may limit the water absorption to only eight inches on either side. Regardless of the type of soil, however, the water does

penetrate down far enough to reach plant roots if the system runs for a long enough time. Three lengths of porous hose running the length of a four-foot-wide bed will provide adequate coverage. If the bed is only three feet wide, then two lengths of hose will do the job.

Regardless of the system used to water, keeping a small vegetable bed properly watered is quite simple. The general rule of thumb in most books is that all plants like about one inch of water per week. So, if it has not rained in a few days, the job is to water the vegetables enough to make up the difference between the one-inch requirement and how much it rained recently. Set an open can or pail out in the bed to catch the water from the sprinkler or hose, or slip it under a section of the drip hose to catch some of the incoming water. When it is one inch full, that means the bed has received about an inch of water. In the spring and fall it will probably be necessary to water once a week if it has not rained. In the summer, twice-a-week watering is usually needed if it hasn't rained in three or four days.

Light sprinkling for just five or ten minutes does not do the job. Water must soak seven to twelve inches down in the soil where plant roots are. Usually, twenty to thirty minutes of overhead watering and forty to fifty minutes of drip irrigation watering will accomplish this.

A small, basic one hundred-square-foot vegetable bed will produce lots of tasty, fresh produce from late June through to the first frost in the fall in September or October. Using raised beds, possibly boxing them, mulching, and installing drip irrigation will assure optimum plant growth and production with a minimum of maintenance. This is an ideal way to experiment with growing some food in the yard. If the experience is satisfying and it seems like it would be a good idea to undertake a slightly larger effort next season, consider expanding the planting space vertically.

ADDING A VERTICAL GROWING AREA

One of the ways to increase the productivity of a vegetable bed without making it any larger is to add trellis devices that allow more efficient use of the vertical space above it. Encouraging plants to grow up rather than out over the soil exploits the air space above the soil and significantly increases production. Many kinds of vegetables are perfectly willing to climb; in fact, many have varieties that are purposely bred as vines.

Pole-type bean plants, for example, produce more beans per square foot of growing area than do bush-type beans. The only reason there are bush bean plants is that they couldn't invent a machine to pick pole beans, so, instead, they invented a bush bean that could be picked by machine.

Plants that grow vertically produce more vegetables per square foot than those that grow as bushes. Adding a seven-foot-tall trellis along

SOME VEGETABLES THAT GROW VERTICALLY

Cantaloupe

Cucumbers

Green beans

Lima beans

Muskmelon

Peas

Squash, acorn and butternut

Sweet potatoes (some varieties)

Tomatoes

Watermelon

one side of a 4-foot-by-24-foot bed increases the growing area to almost 275 square feet. The bed still only takes up about 100 square feet of the backyard but its productivity has been increased about 30 percent.

Tomatoes or beans grown vertically are healthier because they have better air circulation and receive more light. Tomato plants normally sprawl over three or four feet of area in a vegetable bed, but trained to grow up and flat on a trellis, they take up only a square foot or so of soil area. They are also much easier to pick this way.

The more vegetables grown vertically, the more yard space saved for other uses. Here at left the beans growing on the trellises will produce several pounds of beans for every linear foot of trellis.

Vegetables grown vertically have several other advantages as well. The plants are less susceptible to insect attack since most pest insects hover near the soil surface. Because they have better ventilation, vertical plants also have fewer disease problems. The fruits don't sit on the ground and thus are cleaner and better-looking. And finally, for those folks who know that plants grow better if you talk to them, you don't have to bend over to talk to plants that are growing on a trellis.

The problem with vertical growing has always been trying to find or fashion a simple, yet sturdy support for these plants. When they mature and begin to bear, they can get very heavy. Traditionally gardeners have used various trellises, tepees, or poles, all with dubious success. Most vertical structures recommended in gardening books are difficult to set up and tend to become unstable as the season wears on. Often poles fall over and tepees collapse

from the weight of the produce or from gusty summer storms.

The most reliable vertical support for plants is a flat trellis, such as the one pictured below. The key to its stability is its support as part of a boxed bed. The planks used to box in the bed also provide the foundation for the vertical plant supports. It is easy to set up, stable, and attractive.

Making the Trellis

As the illustration shows, twelve-inch pieces of PVC pipe (1½-inch diameter) bracketed to the inside of the planks at four-foot intervals serve as the foundation, or holders, for the trellis poles. The poles may be either 2-by-2-inch wood, or one-inch diameter PVC pipe, which are conveniently available in 8-foot lengths, just fine for this job. Once the bottoms of the poles are sunk into the supporting pipes, the poles are seven feet tall. Any taller and it would be difficult to pick peas, beans, or tomatoes at the top. For shorter people, a six-foot trellis would work just as well.

Construct the actual trellis panel from two 1-by-2-inch wood slats that are four feet long, the distance from one pole to the next. Use a staple gun to attach them to seven-foot lengths of commercial trellis netting, available at most good garden centers. Notice that the trellis netting has a wide four-inch mesh which facilitates the picking of such vegetables as tomatoes and cucumbers through the netting.

Vegetables for Vertical Growing

It is possible to grow vegetables on trellises virtually all season long. Start off with snap peas in the early spring and harvest tomatoes after the first frost in the fall. It is not difficult to grow many of the most common vegetables on trellises.

Peas. There are basically three kinds of peas: traditional green or garden peas, snap peas, and snow peas. Green peas are the familiar ones sold either canned or frozen in grocery stores. They are always removed from their pods, which are too tough to eat. Snow peas are commonly called sugar peas or "Chinese" peas since they are often part of Chinese cuisine, a common ingredient in stir-fry dishes. They have distinctive flat pods through which the tiny, immature peas can be seen. They are served and eaten as is, the pods being very tender. Snap peas were introduced only in the last ten years. They offer the best of both worlds; tasty full-size peas and edible pods. What's even better is that they taste as good raw as cooked.

All the types of peas like cool weather, so they are among the first vegetables in the bed. They are not available as seedlings, so purchase seeds and follow the instructions for planting on the package label. These various types of peas have differing growing habits and heights, but they all need support to grow successfully. Their strong clinging tendrils grasp netting very well as long as they make contact. Some-

---

SOME RECOMMENDED PEA VARIETIES

GREEN PEAS: 'Green Arrow', 'Maestro', 'Petite Provencal' (petit pois), 'Wando'

SNOW PEAS: 'Blizzard', 'Dwarf Gray Sugar', 'Oregon Sugar Pod II', 'Snowbird'

SNAP PEAS: 'Bush Snapper' (does not need trellis), 'Snappy', 'SugarBon', 'Sugar Daddy', 'Sugar Snap', 'Super SugarMel'

---

times young plants must be gently trained at first. When they grow tall enough to reach the trellis, weave their tendrils through the netting to give them the idea. In lieu of a trellis, rig a temporary pea fence using two-foot-wide chicken wire and some stakes. Attach the wire to the stakes and run it along the back edge of the vegetable bed.

Beans. Bean plants that climb and need support are called "pole beans." Pole varieties include the traditional green bean, the wax bean, lima bean, and the roma bean (a wide bean found in Italian cuisine). Young bean seedlings grab on to the trellis by themselves and usually eventually grow over the top of the trellis, hanging down on the other side as they reach the ten or twelve feet in height that many of them are capable of. Most pole beans ripen a bit later in the season than their bush-style counterparts. However, unlike bush beans, which last only two or three weeks, pole beans produce all season long. To encourage this habit, it is important to keep picking them, often a boon to neighbors who receive the surplus. As soon as mature beans on the vines begin to toughen and dry out, the plant will stop producing more beans. Consistent picking works like deadheading flowers—the idea is to prevent the plant from thinking it has set seed and that it can quit producing.

An alternate way to support pole beans is with a tepee rigged with three poles eight to ten feet long. Sink the poles into the ground a few inches and bind their tops together, forming what looks like the framework for an Indian tepee. Plant the bean seeds in a circle just outside the base of the tepee and the seedlings will climb and twirl up the poles. Picking the beans at the top of the structure can be a challenge, but this structure has worked for hundreds of years.

Tomatoes. Tomato seedlings are normally planted at least twenty-four inches apart, but it they are to climb a trellis, space them more closely—twelve to eighteen inches apart. Tomatoes do not automatically attach themselves to the trellis, so have some materials ready with which to tie the growing stems onto the netting. Use the wire Twist-ems that come in a big roll from the garden center or strips of fabric. Be careful not to tie the stems too tightly, or plant growth will suffer.

Remember, determinate tomato plants will not grow much higher than three or four feet and they may not need a high trellis. The indeterminate tomatoes, on the other hand, may grow as high as twenty feet if permitted. It makes sense to clip off the top of the main stem when it hits the seven-foot top of the trellis. This will encourage some subsidiary branching. Mature plants loaded with fruit weigh a tremendous amount, sometimes causing even the most stable trellis to bend over somewhat. It may be necessary to maintain the stability of the trellis by tying a supporting rope on the wooden trellis poles and staking it to the ground or a neighboring bed or structure.

The best way to support tomato plants in

beds that are not equipped with trellises is to use tomato cages, sold in most garden centers. Plant the tomato seedling in the middle of the cage and then encourage it to climb up, out, and around the cage. When it bears tomatoes, they do not touch the ground. The bushlike determinate tomatoes are best suited for this situation.

Cucumbers. There are varieties of bush cucumbers, but vine cucumbers on a trellis produce twice as much food per square foot as bush ones do. One of the reasons for this increase is that cucumbers grown on a trellis will produce fruit up to five weeks longer than the same variety on the ground. Vertically grown cucumbers are also less vulnerable to disease than cucumbers grown on the ground.

While cucumbers have fairly strong tendrils, the vine stems sometimes need extra support, as tomatoes do, when they are heavy with fruit. Tie them to the trellis netting periodically, if it appears that they are being strained. As with pole beans, it is very important to keep picking the cucumbers as they ripen. As soon as a cucumber grows big and fat and yellow, the plant thinks it has produced the seed it needs to survive next year and stops producing flowers. So if vacation arrives in the middle of the cucumber harvest, be sure to have a neighbor keep the vines picked. Cucumbers are very easy to grow and do not mind the heat at all.

The vertical growing of these and other kinds of vegetables represents a slightly more advanced level of food growing than tucking

Some Recommended Climbing Cucumber Varieties

'Burpless' hybrid, 'Early Pride Hybrid', 'Green Knight' hybrid ("burpless"), 'Marketmore', 'Palace King Hybrid' (oriental type), 'Straight Eight', 'Sweet Success' hybrid

plants in among the landscape ornamentals or in a simple bed. With trellises, a simple raised bed becomes more sophisticated and productive with very little additional effort. For homeowners who want to experiment with growing some vegetables in a small area in the backyard, this system is ideal. Once the bed is constructed and, perhaps, trellises are added, it takes very little time to grow vegetables. The plants do most of the work, and if they are mulched and watered with a drip system, the homeowner's main responsibility is primarily to supervise and then gather the harvest.

It remains only to consider the possibility of taking one more step in sophistication and attempting to extend the growing season so that it is possible to have two full "seasons" in the vegetable bed. By adding growing time onto the beginning of the season and, again, at the end of the season, a homeowner can increase the productivity of the little raised bed dramatically, without having to increase the number of beds and the area of the yard devoted to growing vegetables. The next section is for those who might like to try this.

EXTENDING THE GROWING SEASON

Perhaps the most challenging aspect of raising homegrown vegetables is trying to outflank Mother Nature by starting vegetable plants in the very early spring and/or keeping them going into the very late fall. This involves gambling with the frost, since plants are encouraged to grow before the last frost in the spring and beyond the first frost in the fall. To extend the growing season in this way, growers must depend on technology to protect the plants. Gardeners routinely gamble on growing plants outdoors four—and even six—weeks before the last frost or after the first frost and they win only three or four times in every five years. Many of them feel it is worth the attempt and homeowners who are interested in backyard food production can benefit from their experience.

How Cold Affects Plants

Extending the season means putting plants at risk of cold and frost. Most vegetables are essentially annuals and are not cold hardy. However, many can adjust to cold if they are properly acclimated or "hardened." This process takes place in two stages. Cold first slows, and then stops, the growth of plants that are used to a hothouse. Instinctively, however, in response to cold, plants produce natural sugars within their leaf structures which depress the freezing point of the water within their foliage. This protects the leaves from frost damage which normally will cause the plant cells to burst.

Some vegetables have this sugar-producing capacity and can protect themselves from some frost exposure, surviving very cold temperatures. They can even endure a short period of

---

VEGETABLES THAT TOLERATE COLD WEATHER IN SPRING/FALL

Broccoli	Lettuce
Brussels sprouts	Onions
Cabbage	Peas
Cauliflower	Radishes
Chinese cabbage	Spinach
Kale	Swiss Chard
Kohlrabi	

freezing temperatures. They are called cold weather vegetables, and because of this endurance, they can be planted early in the season when the danger of frost still persists. If they can be protected, they will survive and get a jump start on the growing season.

Season Extending Devices

Additional equipment is necessary to grow things when there is a danger of frost and low temperatures. Fortunately there is no dearth of devices, products, and gadgets to protect early season crops. Inevitably, there are among them many home inventions, but the following discussion will address those devices which are readily available in garden centers and mail-order catalogs.

Black plastic mulch. For an early or late season vegetable bed, black plastic mulch is almost a necessity. Readily available in hardware stores and garden centers, black plastic mulch heats up the soil sooner in the spring and keeps it warmer through cold spells. Spread a sheet of the mulch over soil in the part of the bed designated for early crops. Hold it down at the corners with dirt or bricks or something. Because it absorbs the heat of the sun, black plastic mulch raises the temperature in the soil under it six to eight degrees higher than that of unmulched soil. Since plants grow in response to warmer soil temperature, this mulch allows plants to begin growing at least two weeks prior to those in beds without the mulch.

When planting seedlings, cut holes in the plastic by making an X with a sharp knife, then dig the hole in the soil below with a trowel and set the seedling in. Fill in the soil around it and position the flaps of black plastic around it. Be sure the black plastic mulch has some holes in it to permit rainwater to soak into the soil below. You leave the black plastic on the garden for the entire growing season, discarding it in the fall when you put the garden to bed for the winter. In May or June, the black plastic mulch should be covered with two to three inches of organic mulch (e.g., chopped leaves or straw) which serve to cool the soil under the plastic.

Cloches. A cloche is a tentlike device designed to cover an individual plant, such as a cabbage or cauliflower seedling, and protect it from the cold. It acts like a minigreenhouse. Cloches can be made of a variety of materials, such as plastic gallon milk jugs with the bottoms cut off, gallon mayonnaise jars, and informal tents fashioned from clear plastic or agricultural fleece. A particularly effective commercial version of a cloche is Wall O' Water (see illustration). The sides of this plastic tepee are filled with water which provides insulation from the cold to the plant inside. These walls of water protect broccoli, cabbage, and other cool-weather plants in temperatures as low as 20°F. The plants not only survive, but they grow. With Walls O' Water, cool-weather

This young tomato plant is protected from late spring frost by the Wall O' Water. The water-filled sides of this plastic cloche provide insulation so that tomato seedlings can be put out in the yard several weeks earlier than normal.

A blanket of this white, spun polyester material, called floating row cover or Reemay, makes an ideal temporary shelter for cool-weather crops threatened by hard frost. Here lettuce seedlings are shielded from frost, but enjoy sunlight and water, both of which permeate this fleece material.

seedlings can be planted out in the vegetable bed as much as six weeks before the last frost. When the danger of frost is past, simply remove the Wall O' Water or other type of cloche and the plant continues its growth, already twice the size of those set out at the usual time.

Agricultural fleece. Another way to protect early crops is to drape agricultural fleece,

sometimes called "floating row cover" material, over the plants. This white, polyspun material is available in several forms, all of which are extremely lightweight and versatile. The fleece lets light, air, and water into the seedlings it covers. Lay it right over the bed after planting spinach, peas, and lettuce or any other early season crop. As the plants sprout and grow, they lift the material up as it gently rests on

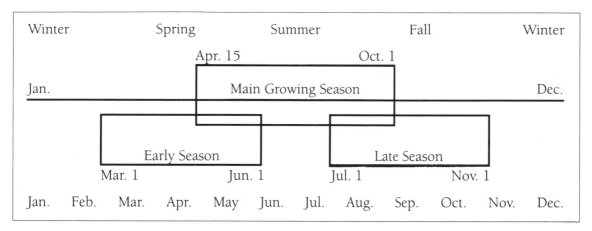

Winter	Spring	Summer	Fall	Winter

Apr. 15		Oct. 1

Jan. | Main Growing Season | Dec.

Early Season | Late Season

Mar. 1		Jun. 1	Jul. 1		Nov. 1

Jan.	Feb.	Mar.	Apr.	May	Jun.	Jul.	Aug.	Sep.	Oct.	Nov.	Dec.

Using products such as cloches and black plastic mulch makes it possible to extend the growing season at each end. Add weeks at the beginning in the spring and at the end in the fall by putting out cool-weather vegetables in prewarmed soil and insulated protectors.

them, protecting plants down to 28°F. It is particularly useful in the fall when frost threatens. Throw it over tender plants in the landscape to protect them at night, and they will continue to flourish during the mild days of Indian summer.

Combinations. The best way to protect early crops in the spring or crops remaining in the garden past first frost in the fall is to use all these devices in combination. If all vegetable plants are mulched with black plastic, are nestled in Walls O' Water or other cloches, and are covered with fleece, they are protected down to about 20° F and will grow almost as fast as if they were in a greenhouse.

The Late Fall Garden

Most vegetable gardeners overlook the benefits of planting a late fall crop in their veggie patch. Most gardens are finished for the season with the first heavy frost, when, with a little planning, the homeowner can be enjoying fresh cool-weather vegetables well into November. Good crops for the late fall include lettuce, broccoli, cabbage, radishes, Chinese cabbage, and parsley.

It is difficult to find seedlings for cold-weather vegetables in the garden center in August, which is when they should be planted for late fall harvest. Here is a case where it may be necessary to start seedlings from seed, either indoors, in a nursery bed elsewhere in the yard for later transplant, or directly in the bed if there is room. Start them about two months before the first frost is expected, following the instructions on the package label. Seedlings are most successfully started in pots or flats filled with soilless mix, the same medium recommended for container plants. It is sterile, light, and drains well. When seedlings are about six to eight inches tall, they can be transferred into the vegetable bed to replace those plants which have petered out.

The trick with fall gardening is to keep an eye on the weather report to avoid exposing your plants directly to early frosts. If you don't have agricultural fleece to protect them, any covering material will work with light frosts, e.g., newspaper cones, bed sheets, etc. In the end the winter weather will win and the garden season will be over, but we've picked fresh lettuce for Thanksgiving dinner and that's a special treat when everything else has turned gray and brown for the winter.

THE COMPLETE VEGETABLE GARDEN

It is obvious that to grow some fresh vegetables and herbs for family use does not require a major commitment of time, energy, and yard space. The project can be undertaken at various levels of involvement and sophistication, so there are several options for prospective food growers. In all aspects of plant care, go slowly. We know more people who have tried growing vegetables and have quit than we do people who are still gardening. In almost every case, the people who have quit tried to do too much too quickly.

It is not an exaggeration to say that a single fully developed vegetable bed, one that is designed to produce fresh vegetables vertically and over an extended season, will not take more than an hour or two a week to maintain once it is built. The system we've outlined here does not require repeated annual digging, because no one walks on it. It does not require constant weeding, because it is mulched. It is easy to water because it has a drip irrigation system, hopefully with a timer. It is easy to feed since a good slow-release fertilizer lasts for a year.

Once built, a boxed raised bed garden with a trellis and extended-season devices takes very little time and effort on the part of the homeowner. Most of the time is spent planting and harvesting produce, the fun part. While vegetable plants experience problems with pest and disease, they are not, in most cases, a major problem. Some of the common pests and diseases and their remedies are outlined in chapter six.

CHAPTER 5
Yard Waste Management

More and more homeowners in America are facing the consequences of state laws prohibiting the dumping of leaves and grass into landfills. This type of yard waste, plus some kitchen waste from residential households, takes up nearly 30 percent of the nation's rapidly diminishing landfill space, and it is obvious that alternatives to dumping must be found and encouraged. Local municipalities, confronting the burden of coping with all the residential yard waste at the local level, are responding by regulating the collection of yard waste in curbside trash pickup. In some cases bags of leaves, grass clippings, and other organic debris are no longer eligible for city pickup. The responsibility for reducing this yard waste problem thus becomes that of the homeowner.

Fortunately, it is quite easy to reduce to zero the amount of yard waste generated by a household. There are several simple techniques and practices that make it possible to utilize grass clippings, leaves, and nonmeat kitchen garbage right on your property, benefitting the plants in the landscape while addressing the national trash problem. In this chapter we will discuss ways to first *reduce* the amount of yard waste generated on your property. Then we will suggest ways to *reuse* most of the leaves and grass clippings that are collected. Finally, we will explain how to *recycle* any yard waste that is left.

Some of the ideas listed in the box take more energy and time than others. Some require special equipment and some require learning new skills. Nevertheless, if the goal is to reduce yard waste output in the trash stream to zero, following the steps listed in the box will do the job and take relatively little time, once the system is put in place.

REDUCING YARD WASTE

Obviously, the easiest way to tackle the problem is to reduce the amount of yard waste generated in the first place. It is not necessary

REDUCE yard waste—Reduce yard waste
by 45 percent
  Leave grass clippings
  Reduce size of lawn
  Change fertilizing strategy
  Use plant-growth inhibitors
  Use slow-growth grasses

REUSE yard waste—Reduce yard waste
by 35 percent
  Mulching
    chopped leaves
    grass clippings
  Woodchip paths

RECYCLE yard waste—reduce yard waste
by 25 percent
  Composting

to cut down all the trees and turn the lawn into a cement patio to significantly cut down on the amount of grass and leaves formerly disposed of in the trash.

Leave Grass Clippings

Most homeowners routinely collect the grass clippings each time they mow the lawn. Grass clippings represented nearly 45 percent of the yard waste that was being placed in landfills prior to the recent rush of restrictive legislation. The average lawn of four thousand square feet might produce two to three bags of grass with each mowing, adding up to over fifty bags of grass in a year's time. As we pointed out in

chapter one, disposing of grass clippings not only clogs landfills, but it denies the lawn a valuable source of nitrogen.

Leaving the grass clippings on the lawn, or "grasscycling," is an easy way to get rid of them. Those clippings quickly decompose, adding valuable organic material to the soil. This amounts to the equivalent of 50 pounds of fertilizer for each 1,000 square feet of the lawn. Remember, research has proven conclusively that leaving grass clippings on the lawn has nothing to do with the creation of thatch. See pages 21–23 in chapter one for all the details on the best ways to leave the clippings so they do not sit on top of the turf. In that section we tell you about "mulching" mowers and their benefits in grasscycling. By this one change in lawn-care practice, up to 20 perent of a typical household's yard waste problem is solved.

Reduce Size of Lawn

In chapter one various ways to reduce the size of the lawn were detailed. When grass clippings are collected rather than grasscycled, reducing the size of the lawn will surely reduce the volume of clippings that accumulate for disposal. So will cutting back on lawn fertilization. Grass that is healthy will do just fine on just one application of slow-release fertilizer in the fall. Eliminating the periodic surges of growth that occur with repeated fertilization during the growing season also reduces the

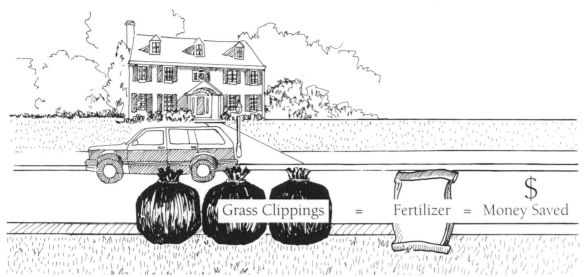

Homeowners who routinely bag their grass clippings and put them out for the trash are throwing away a natural source of nitrogen equivalent to significant amounts of commercial fertilizer.

amount of grass to be cut. The slower the rate of growth of the grass, the fewer clippings that are produced.

Finally, homeowners who insist on collecting grass clippings will want to look carefully at the new varieties of grass that are just now coming on the market. These new mixes of hard fescue, tall turf-type fescue, and rye-grasses are designed to grow very slowly. Some advertise that they cut mowing frequency in half. Fewer mowings mean fewer clippings which means less yard waste.

REUSING YARD WASTE—MULCHING

Homeowners can reuse virtually all the yard waste produced on their property. After all,

leaves, grass, clippings, and even nonmeat kitchen garbage are basically plant material and will decompose over time just as they do in nature. Just as in nature, in woods or fields, they provide a source of nutrition and protection for existing plants. Some materials will require some breaking up or shredding to aid in decomposition, but in the end, any waste produced by the lawn, trees, shrubs, and gardens can be effectively reused around those same trees, shrubs, and gardens. This is what mulching is all about. What's even more interesting is that reusing all this material will not take much more time than putting that yard waste in bags and placing them out on the sidewalk for municipal pickup.

Perhaps the most beneficial, and most overlooked, yard-care practice is using mulch, especially organic mulch. Its virtues—as a soil enhancer, a source of nutrition for plants, a weed discourager, and a water saver—have been discussed in earlier chapters. A mulch of shredded leaves and woodchips is also an ideal way to utilize yard waste products on the property. Leaves alone represent about 30 percent of the yard waste going into America's landfills. Trimmings, limbs, and brush make up another 5 percent. If most homeowners reused them as mulch around trees and shrubs in their yards instead of putting them out for trash pickup, their yards would benefit enormously.

One of the most important things a home-owner can do to protect and preserve plants in the yard is to mulch them. It is a simple matter to spread a few inches of chopped leaves, woodchips, or something similar on the soil over the root systems of young trees, shrubs, vegetables, and flowers. Professional landscapers routinely mulch all new plantings because they know how important this practice is to the health and appearance of the landscape. Rather than purchasing various types of bark nuggets and shredded bark, why not use the organic materials available on your own property, and save money and solve the trash problem at the same time?

MULCH TO CONSERVE SOIL MOISTURE. There should not be any bare soil anyplace on the entire property. Soil exposed to the harsh effects of sun, air, and wind in any season dries out rapidly. Even with frequent watering, plants in bare soil don't seem to get the mois-

ture they need. Mulch is such an obvious solution that many homeowners never think of it. By covering the soil surface and blocking it from wind and sun, an organic mulch can reduce the rate of moisture evaporation by as much as 50 percent, depending on the material used. A porous, spongy layer of chopped leaves or woodchips also discourages loss of water from runoff when rain or the sprinkler delivers more than the soil can quickly absorb. Mulch may make the difference between plants surviving a drought in the middle of August or burning up.

MULCH TO CONTROL WEEDS. Homeowners who mulch flower or vegetable beds spend little time weeding. If the mulch is thick enough (at least two inches, preferably three inches), it will prevent most annual weeds from growing. Those few that do get through are easily pulled up since the soil under the mulch, if it has been properly prepared, never gets hard and compacted. A good mulch virtually eliminates the onerous task of weeding around ornamental plantings.

MULCH TO PROTECT TREES. The danger of allowing turfgrass to grow up close to tree trunks was pointed out in chapter two. A two- or three-inch layer of chopped leaves or woodchips spread on the soil under each tree in a four- to six-foot radius creates a buffer zone against lawn mowers and weed trimmers which cause injury to tree and shrub stems. It also eliminates the competition for soil nutrients from lawn grass and provides cover for surface roots.

MULCH TO PROTECT THE SOIL. Nutrients in the soil are sometimes leached down out of reach of the roots by hard rain directly hitting the soil. This can render soil infertile. Because mulch slows down the rate at which rain enters the soil, it gives the soil a chance to absorb the water, rather than letting it drain off the soil surface or flow down into the subsoil past the roots. A mulch also encourages microorganisms to work nearer the surface of the soil since the soil there stays moist and friable.

Furthermore, organic mulch itself is always slowly decomposing, creating an ongoing nutrient supplement to the soil. The microorganisms in the soil begin almost immediately to break down the mulching material into basic chemicals such as nitrogen, phosphorus, potassium, and many others. Worms and other micro-pals also help to move the decomposed mulch down into the soil where it is available, when mixed with water, to be taken up as food by plant roots. Some people worry about the fact that the decomposing mulch is known to tie up nitrogen in the top few inches of the soil, and that sounds like it might be bad. Well, it is not an issue. The nitrogren lost from decomposing mulch is negligible to the total amount of nitrogen available in a healthy soil.

A generous layer of organic mulch greatly reduces soil compaction. Bare soil tends to be come compacted over time from the beating of the rain and the drying out of the soil particles in the blazing sun. Any mulch protects the surface of the soil from compression by rain by cushioning the impact of the raindrops. Less compaction means healthier plant roots and a more active microlife below the surface of the soil.

MULCH PROTECTS IN THE WINTER. A winter mulch around newly planted trees, shrubs, and perennial flowers and over bulb beds helps stabilize the winter temperature of the soil. It is not intended to prevent freezing, which is not in itself harmful to hardy plants. A layer of mulch does, however, insulate the soil against the extreme temperature fluctuations that occur in unprotected soil during the winter. Alternating freezing and thawing can cause the soil to heave up bulbs, perennials, and small shrubs, disturbing their roots. Also, frequent rapid fluctuations in soil temperature are more harmful to soil microorganisms than a steady cold period. While soil bacteria and fungi invariably come back each spring, their return can be speeded up by insulating the soil from the cold with a layer of mulch.

Lay a thick mulch of several inches of chopped leaves, or lay evergreen boughs over bulb beds in the fall after the heavy frost has frozen the top two inches of ground. (A three-inch layer of mulch may also prevent squirrels from raiding bulb beds in the early spring.) When green shoots begin to emerge, pull the

Mulching around trees and shrubs not only reduces the amount of lawn to be tended, but it provides significant benefits to the plants. A three- or four-inch layer of mulch supresses weeds, prevents evaporation and runoff of water, and organic mulches enrich the soil as they break down.

mulch aside to allow the soil to warm up for the emergence of the bulbs and other perennials. It is not necessary to do this for trees and shrubs.

Yard Waste Becomes Mulch

The best organic mulch is easy to work with, allows air to pass through it, is relatively windproof, holds some moisture, is inexpensive, and is attractive. Fortunately, chopped leaves and grass clippings, major components of the yard-waste problem, meet these criteria. If a shredder is available, even shredded hedge trimmings and tree branches will make an excellent mulch.

Chopped leaves. The deciduous trees and shrubs, those that drop their leaves every fall, provide leaves for wonderful mulch. Those leaves from large shade trees, like sycamore, many maples, and oak, must be shredded or chopped to be effective as mulch. Whole leaves tend to mat when they get wet and can then obstruct uniform drainage of water into the soil. Even smaller leaves from ornamental fruit trees, flowering shrubs, and hedges should be chopped, if possible.

There are a number of ways to chop leaves for mulch. The easiest way is to use the lawn mower with the bag attached. As the leaves fall, simply mow the lawn and chop the leaves at the same time. Another technique is to leave the bag off the mower and chop the leaves while mowing the grass, controlling the pattern of mowing so that the leaves and grass clippings are repeatedly blown onto the uncut grass to be collected later. That way the leaves go through a few times and end up well shredded. This technique works as long as the falling leaves do not pile up too thickly on the lawn; during the period of greatest fall, it may be necessary to "mow" every couple of days, even though the grass is no longer growing at a significant pace.

Another option is to use a shredder designed for handling leaves. Be careful, though, some shredders work well with dry leaves but will jam when the leaves are wet. Some people have had success shredding leaves with a snow blower set in "slow-slow" drive. Another way to shred leaves is to put them in a large garbage can and use a string trimmer. This shreds dry leaves very finely, but it doesn't work too well with wet leaves.

Grass clippings. Grass clippings, either combined with leaves or by themselves, make an excellent organic mulch. Because they tend to decompose and become putrid if they are left in thick piles, spread them in thin layers—no more than an inch thick—over the bare soil. As each layer dries, add another, building up to an effective mulch. Clippings from lawns that have been recently treated with chemical herbicides or pesticides should not be used for this purpose.

Shredded branches and bark. Shredded bark or woodchips spread at least two inches thick around shrubs and trees give the landscape a neat, attractive appearance. While freshly shredded material is pale and does not blend into the landscape at first, it rapidly ages, becoming darker in color, and blends in quite nicely. Woodchip mulches decompose more slowly than leaves and do not need renewing as frequently. They last from two to three years before they need to be renewed.

SELECTING A SHREDDER

Since organic materials, such as leaves and twigs, make better mulch if they are chopped or shredded, homeowners who choose to reuse their yard waste as mulch must consider what equipment they will use.

LAWN MOWER AS SHREDDER. As described above, lawn mowers are useful in chopping leaves, especially the mulching type of mowers which cut the grass and leaves into small pieces. A bagging attachment, while not really essential, facilitates the collection of the chopped leaves.

SHREDDER/VACUUMS/BLOWERS. Leaf blowers have been on the market for some years, but recently their manufacturers have added a valuable feature to some of these devices. The machines vacuum or pull up yard debris and store it in a bag of some sort. Some of these machines now have a shredding knife that simultaneously shreds the leaves as they are blown into the storage bag. Ranging in price from $70 to $150, these machines are effective in reducing the volume of leaves while at the same time creating a wonderful mulching material.

LEAF SHREDDERS. There are now available in garden centers and by mail order machines designed to shred leaves. These leaf shredders usually use the same mechanism as a string weeding tool. Electrically powered, they spin a tough plastic filament at high speed which shreds the leaves into small pieces that fall down through variable-size holes in the bottom of the device. These leaf shredders can shred large volumes of leaves in a short period of time. They perform much better when the leaves are dry, although they can handle wet leaves if they are fed in more slowly.

SHREDDERS/GRINDERS/CHIPPERS. These machines are designed to shred all yard waste materials, though some deal with certain ma-

This electric-powered leaf shredder efficiently shreds leaves by means of a replaceable nylon filament cutting head. Lightweight, it is made of high-density polypropylene and will easily fit over a trash can.

A combination chipper/shredder such as this gasoline-powered one will handle small branches up to two inches in diameter. It will also shred leaves, vines, and small twigs.

terials better than others. They use either a hammering or a knifelike cutting mechanism to process leaves, sticks, vines, chunks of turf, branches, and even limbs up to two or three inches thick. Some of the smaller machines are electric, while most are driven by gasoline engines from 3.5 to 8 horsepower. We make a distinction between the smaller "chipper/grinders" and the larger "general-purpose shredders."

Chipper/Grinders. These machines, either electric or gasoline engine-driven, are designed for homeowners with small yards and gardens.

They range in price from $200 to $500 and are advertised to handle all forms of yard waste. Our experience with these small machines is that they handle sticks, small branches, and pruning trimmings up to one inch in diameter very well. They do not, however, handle leaves in sufficient enough volume to make them useful in shredding leaves. They also do not handle wet materials in most cases as well as a larger all-purpose shredder.

All-purpose shredders. These shredders are larger and are almost always powered by gasoline engines from 3.5 to 8 horsepower. Designed for use on large properties, farms, and commercial gardens, they handle all materials with ease and some can handle sticks up to three inches in diameter. They range in price from $500 to $1,500. Although these general-purpose shredders are very valuable machines, they are priced above what most homeowners are willing to spend for yard waste handling. As more and more families attempt to reuse yard waste, however, a cooperative arrangement among several neighbors becomes an attractive possibility. With participation of four or five families, the cost of a top-notch all-purpose shredder is manageable. Unlike a lawn mower which is used quite frequently, a shredder is usually needed only three or four times a year, so a group of families can share a single shredder with very little inconvenience in scheduling.

SHREDDER SAFETY

Shredders are powerful tools that must be chosen with an eye to safety and used with intelligence and respect. When selecting a shredder, check the machine for general sturdiness. It should be balanced enough so that it will not tip over when it is used in areas where the ground is not perfectly level. The hopper, or feeding area of the machine, should be equipped with some kind of safety guard that will prevent shredded material from flying back up out of the shredding chamber. Ideally, it should have a baffle or guard to prevent hands from inadvertently getting into the shredding chamber, but that is not always feasible. No matter how good the machine, any

---

Tools to Handle Total Yard Waste

SMALL YARD (LESS THAN ONE-EIGHTH ACRE):
Lawn mower or leaf shredder (leaves)
Sticks into trash

AVERAGE YARD (ONE-QUARTER ACRE):
Lawn mower or leaf shredder (leaves)
Chipper/grinder (sticks)

LARGER YARD (MORE THAN ONE-QUARTER ACRE):
All-purpose shredder (all yard waste)

---

shredder is going to become clogged or jammed, so ease of unclogging becomes an important feature.

Most shredders are noisy, so it is important to wear earplugs or protectors while operating them for more than a few minutes. Always wear gloves and safety glasses when operating shredders or chippers.

Annual Landscape Mulching Cycle

Here is a general annual routine to consider for transforming yard waste into mulch. When the leaves drop in the fall, shred them with a lawn mower or shredder and immediately spread them around trees, shrubs, and hedges and on any garden beds in the yard as a winter mulch. Use about four to six inches of chopped leaves, which will settle down to about two inches by spring. The final settled layer should never be deeper than three inches or it will block the roots' access to oxygen. Store any extra chopped leaves in plastic bags for the compost pile or for a summer mulch next year.

In early spring remove the leaf mulch from the beds of bulbs so the soil can warm up for the emergence of the bulbs. Leave the mulch around the trees, shrubs, and hedges year-round, but pull mulch back from the crowns of all perennial plants. To augment the decomposing winter layer, use grass clippings and any extra chopped leaves. By the following fall the mulch around the trees, shrubs, and on the garden beds may be pretty decomposed, so spread a fresh layer of newly chopped leaves for the coming winter. Spread woodchips as soon as they are available any time of year when there is no snow on the ground.

OTHER MULCHING MATERIALS
In some situations, homeowners may find that their yard-waste materials do not provide enough mulch for all the plants on the property. Canadian sphagnum peat moss, chopped straw or hay, compost, aged sawdust, pine needles, seaweed, and even stones and gravel make excellent mulching materials.

Commercially prepared mulches, such as woodchips, shredded pine bark, or nugget pine bark, are available from the local garden center. For appearance, the shredded pine bark is a good choice because it's the most natural-looking. Nugget pine bark is the most expensive of these materials, but it has the advantage of being available in many different sizes. The larger sizes are very long-lasting. Woodchips are the least expensive of the three. Tree trimming companies will often give away entire truckloads of fresh shredded woodchips if they are working in the neighborhood.

WOODCHIP PATHS AND DRIVEWAYS
Homeowners with all-purpose shredders are able to process a lot of the branches and brush into woodchips that can be reused on the property in other ways. In sufficient quantity they are ideal for paths and even driveways. Woodchips make great permanent paths in a raised bed vegetable garden, an inch or two each year eliminating any problems with weeds and mud. They also work as paths in heavily traveled areas of lawns that seem to sport dirt paths where no grass will grow. Instead of trying and retrying to plant grass in an area where no variety of grass will grow, spread a two- to three-inch layer of woodchips to make an attractive path that eliminates the mud that follows every rainfall.

Consider using woodchips on parking areas and driveways rather than paving them over. Woodchips permit rain to soak into the ground where it can be available to the water table, rather than run off down the sewer where it may contribute to flooding problems and be wasted.

RECYCLING YARD WASTE—COMPOSTING

A significant proportion of the yard waste produced in residential yards and gardens can be reduced and reused. Any that remains can probably be recycled. In the home landscape, recycling means composting. Placed in some kind of container and sheltered from the weather, leaves, grass, weeds, twigs, vines, and nonmeat kitchen waste will decompose into valuable humus that can then be returned to the lawn or garden soil.

Compost is the by-product of the decomposition of the organic materials making up your yard and (certain) kitchen waste. Properly made, it looks just like the rich, dark humus found in the woods just under the layer of leaves on the forest floor. Put through a shredder, it looks and feels much like the potting soil mix from the local gardening store, and it has little odor.

Recycling yard and kitchen waste into compost is its own reward. It is nearly impossible to overstate the value of compost to residential landscapes. Most experienced gardeners are well aware of its benefits; they usually make as much compost as they can to build good garden soil. Until the recent state legislation against dumping yard waste in landfills, though, nongardening homeowners had little incentive to learn about this wonderful product. The good news is that composting not only reduces the yard waste problem, it pro-

duces a desirable product. This is truly a win-win situation.

How Compost is Created

Compost is the product of a decomposition process that involves enormous numbers of microorganisms. Bacteria, fungi, and actinomycetes (microscopic plants that decompose organic matter) are the most important composting organisms. They eat the carbon, converting it to carbon dioxide, water, and humus (the portion they can't digest). Nitrogen is the other major microbial nutrient consumed by these billions of garbage disposers. In the process of dining on the garbage, the microbes grow and reproduce. All this activity makes the pile heat up, killing weed seeds and organisms that are harmful to plants and animals.

The natural decomposition of organic materials into compost actually takes place in four steps. First, the organic materials undergo chemical oxidation from their exposure to air and water as they lie on the ground. Then the insects and worms go to work, and their activity gradually reduces the particle size of the materials. This can be speeded up by chopping or shredding yard waste before it goes into the pile. Once in the pile, the materials are subject to the activity of the aerobic, or oxygen-loving, microorganisms mentioned above which further break down the organic materials. Finally, as the air in and around the particles of material is depleted, the anaerobic organisms, those bacteria that exist in an environment without oxygen, take over and complete the decomposition process.

The humic by-products resulting from the digestion of one type of organism becomes the food source for another type. This chain of succession of different types of microbes continues until most of the biodegradable material has been consumed. At this point, what's left is called compost. It's made up largely of microbial cells, microbial skeletons, partially decomposed particles of organic matter, and inorganic particles (glass, sand, rock).

Benefits of Compost

Soils having a high percentage (3 to 5 percent) of organic materials in them produce healthier plants. Therefore, any soil that has compost added is better than any soil not having this beneficial amendment. Compost, once it is worked into the soil by people or earthworms, improves texture and structure. It enables soil to drain excess water from around plant roots more effectively, while simultaneously improving its water-holding capacity. Not technically a fertilizer, compost does break down over time into the basic nutrients used by plants to make food.

Research indicates that soil treated with compost tends to have fewer insect and disease problems. The theory is that the compost encourages a more active and numerous population of beneficial mircoorganisms which in

turn keep the bad guys in control. In short, compost helps save water and fertilizer and improves the health of any plant that grows in that soil.

Materials for Composting

It is possible to make compost with almost any kind of organic material, including straw, hay, woodchips, sawdust, and nonmeat food wastes from restaurants. However, home compost systems use the normal yard waste produced from the average home landscape—leaves, grass clippings, weeds, plant trimmings—and nonmeat kitchen waste.

Leaves. Leaves will compost more quickly if they are chopped or shredded before being piled into a bin. Whole leaves will decompose in time, but they take up more space and almost twice the time chopped leaves do to turn into finished compost. Any kind of leaves can be composted. All leaves, no matter whether they are acidic or alkaline when they start out, will decompose into compost that has an almost neutral pH (6.8 to 7.2). While pine needles, oak leaves, and coffee grounds are naturally acidic and make ideal mulch for acid-loving plants, such as blueberries, azaleas, and rhododendrons, or for inclusion in soil that tends to be alkaline, composting makes them essentially neutral. Pine needles take longer than leaves to fully decompose.

Grass clippings. Grass clippings are good for

composting *only* if they are mixed with leaves or some other dried material, such as straw or hay. If grass clippings alone are piled in a compost bin, the pile will rapidly become anaerobic (without oxygen) and begin to smell very, very bad. In cases where large amounts of grass clippings are available for composting, take time to dry them first. Spread freshly cut grass over a paved driveway or similar surface to bake in the sun for at least a day. When it dries and begins to turn pale and strawlike, grass can be dumped in a compost bin without danger of putrifying and smelling bad. Sod makes good compost if it is first run through a general-purpose shredder to break it up. Also, do not compost any grass clippings that may still have residues of herbicide on them. Wait to mow until after a good rain that will wash away herbicide residue.

Weeds. Most weeds will compost easily, although the same rules apply as with grass clippings. Large amounts of freshly pulled green weeds represent an overload of nitrogen-rich material that can settle into a tight anaerobic mass that smells pretty bad. Mix fresh weeds with some dry material, such as chopped leaves, to forestall the possibility of odor.

Kitchen waste. The people who keep track of this sort of thing say that the average American household produces over two hundred pounds of kitchen waste, or garbage, per year. Most of it can be composted. However, meat or meat products (juices, grease, gravies, bones) or any

WHAT NOT TO COMPOST

diseased garden plants

dog manure

grass or foliage recently treated with chemical herbicides or pesticides

meat products

used cat litter

weeds with ripening seeds

WHAT TO COMPOST

bark	leaves
chunks of turf	paper towels
coffee grounds	peanut shells
corncobs	perennial weeds
cornhusks	pine cones
eggshells	shredded branches
fruit rinds	tea bags
grass	twigs
grass clippings	vegetable peelings
hay or straw	vines

dairy products (cheese, whole eggs) are *not* compostable. While they will decay eventually, they smell bad in the process. Worse, they attract pest animals such as rats. Any leftovers or peelings of vegetables and fruit are just fine, as are eggshells. Common garbage items such as coffee grounds, tea bags, and soggy paper napkins are also fine. As with the grass clippings and weeds, large amounts of kitchen waste should be mixed with some kind of dry material, such as chopped leaves, brush, or woodchips to avoid any odor problems.

Woody plant materials (wood chips, pine cones, brush), even when shredded, take a long time to decompose. Consider using them as a mulch or composting them separately so that they can rot completely without tying up the regular compost pile. Stiff materials such as peanut hulls, cotton burrs, corncobs, and cornstalks won't take quite as long as woodchips, but they'll outlast the softer stuff. Homeowners with heavy-duty shredders can shred sticks and limbs finely enough so that they can be incorporated into a regular compost pile. The compost may have a slightly coarser texture, but it will be fine for use in all situations. Keep sticks and limbs that are not shredded out of the compost pile.

What about pesticide residues? Homeowners worry about putting grass clippings that have been treated with some kind of pesticide on their compost pile. Avoid using any grass in a compost pile that has had any pesticide on it and has not yet been rained on. Usually a steady rain washes all pesticide residues down into the soil around the grass roots and leaves the blades free of pesticide material. If pesticide-treated grass is inadvertently in-cluded in a compost pile, it is not likely to present any problems. Several studies on the subject suggest that most pesticides used in the home landscape break down during composting. Those that do show up are generally at the low end of the range one would expect to find in typical suburban soil, which often contains pesticide residues.

Selecting a Composting Site

Traditionally compost bins have been located out of sight at the back of the property. Certainly a compost bin is not the kind of thing most gardeners and homeowners would want by the back door. Or is it? Maybe the convenience of proximity to the back door will mean the compost bin is used more often. In the wake of the new state laws, manufacturers have made efforts to produce compost bins that are attractive and unobtrusive. There are now many choices in design for homeowners who are gearing up to process their own yard waste.

The most important thing is to select a spot that is shaded and has good drainage. While a sunny location does not impede the composting process, it may cause the pile to dry out a bit faster. The heat of the sun is not necessary to the composting process. Bins situated under trees sometimes cause tree roots to gravitate upward to the surface of the soil under the compost to take advantage of the nutrients being produced by the pile. Move the bin a few feet periodically when finished compost is removed to discourage the permanent surfacing of roots in one area.

Selecting a Compost Bin

If the goal is simply to recycle yard waste by storing organic materials in an unobtrusive bin until they decompose, however long that takes, the container may be very simple in design. This decomposition process is "passive," requiring no special activity by the homeowner, so a simple bin with a cover is sufficient. If the goal is to produce compost as efficiently and quickly as possible, a container with certain other features is desirable. In this case the decomposition process is "active," requiring active participation by the homeowner. A compost bin for this purpose must be designed to permit easy periodic turning of the pile of accumulated organic waste. Turning a pile introduces more oxygen into the materials, which accelerates the decomposition process, resulting in finished compost sooner.

Nongardening homeowners, those people who are primarily interested in storing and recycling yard waste, are most likely to prefer the passive composting system. Any one of a number of bin designs are suitable for this purpose, many of which can be homemade.

The ideal compost bin is between three feet and four feet high, wide, and deep. A bin that is four feet wide, four feet high, and four feet deep is supposed to be the optimum size, accommodating the critical mass of yard waste

This is a standard 4 × 4 × 4-foot compost bin that is homemade. It is ideal for passive composting in the backyard. The removable side slats permit easy access to the finished compost with a shovel or yard fork.

which heats up inside the bin and produces the most rapid decomposition. Piles that are 3 × 3 × 3 feet are almost as good. Even smaller bins allow organic yard waste to decompose, but the process takes longer. The contents of a bin larger than 5 × 5 × 5 will also decompose more slowly because it is more difficult for oxygen to get into the center of the pile. Whatever the size, do not allow the bin to be more than two times higher than it is wide to assure maximum decomposition. A compost bin of

Commercially made backyard compost bins are designed to be easy to assemble and to look attractive. This thermal composter features heavy-duty green plastic panels lined with insulation to concentrate the heat generated by the pile to speed the decomposition process.

proper proportions will decompose a year's yard waste from an average yard before the leaves fall the next year.

A properly designed bin permits oxygen to access the pile, so it should have some sort of openings on the sides. These may be slits cut or holes drilled into its sides, or just spaces between boards or wire sides. An airtight container causes organic yard waste to decay without the benefit of much air, thus creating odor. If possible a compost bin should be covered, either by a lid constructed as part of the design, or by a tarp or plastic sheet. While a certain amount of moisture in the yard waste products is desirable, periodic soaking by heavy rains and snows retards the decomposition process.

Spurred by the new yard waste legislation in so many states, manufacturers have rushed to offer a wide variety of compost bin designs

in a range of prices. Many homeowners, however, may prefer to build their own. First we'll discuss some bins that are available commercially, and then we'll talk about building do-it-yourself designs.

Commercial compost bins. Most commercial compost bins are best suited to the passive composting method. They are easy to fill, but do not facilitate active turning of a pile, though their advertising may allege otherwise. The biggest variable in commercial compost bins is price. Bins are available from $20 through $150, the difference determined mostly by design and type of materials used in their construction. The least-expensive types are uncovered wire boxes, or those made from slats of waste lumber. The most expensive are likely to be made of molded resin or plastic materials which feature air vents, lids, and sometimes special liners to improve their efficiency. While the size of commercial bins varies a bit, most of them are within the $3 \times 3 \times 3$-foot range.

Some demonstrably "active" composting devices are available commercially. They are called *compost tumblers*. Generally cylindrical in shape, they usually have some mechanism for rotating the barrel or cylinder. This effectively turns the pile, allowing oxygen to get into it, speeding the rate of decomposition. At any given time these tumblers have less storage capacity for yard waste than the bin type of design. However, for those who want compost

This compost tumbler is particularly attractive for composting kitchen waste using a carbon base of chopped leaves or peat moss. One load of chopped leaves can handle up to six months' worth of kitchen waste with no odors, no rodents, and no insect problems.

make perfectly good compost bins. Approximately eleven feet of snow fence will make a container three feet in diameter and four feet tall. Wire bins are attractive because they are so light and easy to move around and allow maximum oxygen into the pile. Although some wire bins need support, turkey wire is stiff enough to stand by itself. The ends of the wires on one edge are bent over to engage the other edge, creating a cylinder that is four feet high and four feet in diameter. These wire cylinders are best for "passive" composting, although it is easy enough to turn the pile by lifting the wire off the pile of organic materials, moving the cage to a new location and then throwing the materials back in.

Wooden bins are easy to build if a few woodworking tools are available. Bins made of regular or scrap wood often last at least five years or more. Bins made from pressure-treated lumber, especially the kind rated for contact with soil, should be good for several decades. Both of the following bin designs permit easy access for those homeowners who decide to use the "active" composting method.

as fast as possible, the annual capacity of tumblers for producing compost is probably superior to the bin or box design.

BUILDING YOUR OWN COMPOST BIN

As the illustrations indicate, many materials are suitable for compost bins. Bricks and cement blocks left over from a construction job

Making Compost

The microorganisms that manufacture compost require a specific environment in which to multiply and continue the breakdown process. If that environment exists, they produce beautiful compost. If that environment doesn't exist, they can't thrive and therefore can't produce compost. Fortunately these microorganisms aren't that fussy, and there is a great deal of leeway in how to build a compost pile. The main requirements for good compost are some carbon-containing materials (such as dried leaves), oxygen, and moisture. These alone will create compost, though it may take two years for the final product to be ready. To have compost a bit sooner, mix some nitrogen-containing materials (such as fresh grass clippings or kitchen garbage) with the carbon materials, oxygen, and moisture.

The speed of the composting process depends on the ratio of the nitrogen materials to the carbon materials that are dumped into the pile and on whether the management of the pile is active or passive.

UNDERSTANDING THE CARBON/NITROGEN RATIO

To understand how to achieve an appropriate balance of carbon and nitrogen materials in a pile, it's helpful to think of the carbon materials as the food and the nitrogen materials as the digestive enzymes. The bulk of the organic matter in the pile should be high-carbon food with just enough nitrogen to stimulate the decomposition process. When there is little nitrogen, like in a pile of leaves, the composting process is fairly slow. When there is too much nitrogen material, like in a pile of grass clippings, the excess will be released as ammonia gas and the pile will begin to smell.

Research tells us that a good ratio of carbon to nitrogen in a compost pile is thirty parts carbon to one part nitrogen (measured in dry weight). Because it is difficult for homeowners to determine the true carbon or nitrogen content of composting materials, the scientific thirty to one is not very useful. A more convenient measure of proportions is in bags of leaves and grass.

While a bag of just leaves will eventually decompose, if they are chopped there are more surfaces for composting microorganisms to work on, so the process is speeded up. If grass clippings or fresh weeds are added to chopped leaves, it is speeded up even more. A ratio of five bags of chopped leaves to one bag of grass clippings will produce compost in about one year. A ratio of one bag of chopped leaves to one bag of grass clippings will produce compost in four to six months. Of course, if there are more bags of grass clippings than leaves, the pile will become anaerobic (without oxygen) and will start to smell bad. Obviously, the formula for carbon to nitrogen is not terribly precise. It is a guideline. The actual ratio of materials in any pile is primarily a function of what excess yard waste is available on the property at any given time.

Passive Low-Maintenance Compost Systems

The basic difference between a passive and an active compost pile is the role of the home-

Methods for Speeding Up Passive Compost Piles

CONTENTS OF PILE	RATE OF DECOMPOSITION
Whole leaves, little nitrogen material	2 years
Chopped leaves, little nitrogen	1.5 years
Chopped leaves, 30% grass clippings	1 year
To above, add bioactivators	6 to 10 months
To above, add composting worms	2 to 4 months
To above, add liquid garbage	2 to 3 months

owner. Passive piles are passively managed. A pile is built and allowed to sit until compost is produced, no matter how long it may take. All the homeowner has to do is collect the materials, throw them in the bin, and wait. Additional yard waste materials are thrown on the top as they accumulate, and they gradually decompose over time. The pile never gets very hot inside because the microbial activity is less feverish. Passively managed piles produce compost in four months to two years, depending on the materials and how they are prepared for the pile.

Active piles are consciously built and require the ongoing participation of the homeowner in the composting process. Often the yard waste materials are added in layers to promote a high level of microbial activity which causes the center of the pile to heat up dramatically. By turning the materials period-

ically to introduce fresh supplies of oxygen into the pile, a homeowner can assure that a high rate of decomposition is sustained. Sometimes he adds more nitrogen materials too, to accelerate the composting process. Actively managed piles produce compost in three weeks to six months, also depending on the materials and how they are prepared for the pile. The ensuing discussion will focus primarily on the passive system of composting, on the assumption that most homeowners will find this to be a satisfactory method for recycling yard waste with a minimum amount of effort.

In its simplest form, a passive compost pile is a pile of whole leaves left to decompose as nature sees fit. As the table above indicates, taking a few more steps fine-tunes the process and accelerates the decomposition. Enclosing the pile in a bin and sheltering it somewhat from the rain helps. Chopping the leaves first with a lawn mower or shredder helps even more. Bagging grass clippings and leaves with the mower goes one step better, providing an ideal mix for a passive pile.

Fill the bin to the top and fill five or six bags with any leftover combined grass and leaves. As the material in the bin settles, add the stuff stored in the bags. A $4 \times 4 \times 4$-foot bin can hold the equivalent of over one hundred bags of whole leaves after the bin has settled and been refilled a few times. Once the bin is filled, make sure it is covered to keep the rain from making the pile soggy. While water is necessary for the decomposition process, it is easy to have too much of a good thing. The material in the pile should feel damp but not moist, like a sponge that has been thoroughly soaked and then wrung out. A mix of chopped leaves and grass clippings should turn into usable compost by the next July or August, well ahead of the next leaf fall when the cycle begins all over again.

Speeding up with bioactivators. A few handfuls of garden soil, tossed among the layers of chopped leaves and grass clippings will introduce soil organisms to the pile. This composting microlife, including many kinds of bacteria, fungi, actinomycetes, and enzymes, does the actual work. They break down the organic materials in the soil and will do the same thing for the materials in the compost pile. Commercial equivalents of this handful of soil, although in much more concentrated form, are now available at garden centers. Called compost starters or bioactivators, these products contain billions of microorganisms designed to spur the composting process in a backyard bin. These products will definitely speed up the composting process. The material needed for one $3 \times 3 \times 3$-foot pile will cost three to five dollars. If it is important to process yard waste quickly, these composting products may be well worth the investment.

Speeding up with composting worms. Another way to hurry compost production in a passive system is to add earthworms to the pile. Earthworms love chopped leaves and in a compost pile they function as mini yard-waste processors. In addition to the common earthworm, there are other breeds of worms called "composting worms" or "red worms" that are available from certain mail-order sources. These composting worms reproduce much faster than normal earthworms and live only in composting materials; they will die if put out into the garden soil. Composting worms also usually die if left in the pile over the winter in the North. Overwinter composting worms in a cool garage or basement in a box with dried leaves or shredded newspaper so that they are ready to start composting when spring rolls around. One thousand composting worms will cost about $10 and will definitely speed up the passive compost pile.

Composting worms are so voracious and efficient they often literally eat themselves out of house and home. Once they digest most of

Adding worms to a compost pile accelerates the decomposition process. Use earthworms from the garden such as these, or purchase red worms specifically for this purpose.

the leaves in the pile, they are in danger of starving to death. They should be transferred to a fresh pile of yard waste promptly. The big advantage to using composting worms in a passive compost pile is that they tend to work only on the periphery of the pile, penetrating no deeper than twelve inches from any side. Since the center of the pile is the area of most intense microbial activity, these outer areas normally do not heat up and decompose as efficiently. With the worms processing the out-

side of the pile and the composting microorganisms working the center, you've got a nicely balanced composting operation. With this passive system, only the homeowner is passive!

Speeding up with blended garbage. Most passive compost piles are not appropriate for composting nonmeat kitchen waste generated by the household each week. Garbage such as fruit and vegetable trimmings usually accumulates on the top of the pile where it is tossed. Because it is mostly nitrogen-type material, it may begin to smell. However, some homeowners who want to have passive compost piles that will also handle their kitchen wastes can use food processors or blenders to liquefy their garbage first. Daily, place all nonmeat kitchen waste and some water into a blender or food processor and liquefy it. Then pour this liquid garbage into the pile through holes scooped out by hand in the top of the passive pile. A quick fluffing of the top of the pile covers the hole with chopped leaves.

Pouring the liquefied garbage in different holes every day or so distributes it throughout the pile and achieves the benefit of added nitrogen without having to be turned. The added nitrogen speeds up the decomposition process while simultaneously handling kitchen wastes with no smells and relatively little bother. There are a fair number of gardeners across the country who have been liquefying their garbage for years, but instead of adding the material to a compost pile, they pour the material directly on to their garden beds, usually under some mulch. They report that the technique eliminates the need for any fertilizer in these locations.

For homeowners interested in recycling garbage, there is now a garbage-disposal unit on the market that becomes a composting aid. The Garden Aid (Everest International, 5465 Dodds Avenue, Buena Park, CA 90621; $149.50 plus $5 shipping) catches and spin-dries chopped vegetable wastes so they can be immediately mixed into the soil or added to a compost pile.

Garbage with composting worms. One of the problems with composting is that in the dead of winter, the decomposition process virtually stops. However, some homeowners continue to compost kitchen wastes while also wintering over some composting worms. About two thousand composting worms (two pounds) can process seven pounds of kitchen garbage in a week. Keep the worms in a box with bedding material made of chopped leaves or shredded newspaper. Add garbage to the box in various places as it is generated and cover it with the bedding material. Because it is spread around and because the worms are working on it all the time, the garbage never develops any odors. For folks heavily into the recycling movement, this is a good way to handle kitchen waste and to always have an unusual topic of conversation.

The question of time. It is normally not necessary to add lime to compost piles to improve the breakdown of most yard wastes. Finished compost is usually neutral to slightly alkaline. With added lime, it is likely to be too alkaline for general use when completed. Even if a pile contains large amounts of acidic materials, such as pine needles or fruit wastes, add no more than one cup of lime per twenty-five cubic feet of material. This extra step is optional, usually only complicating what is essentially a simple process. Excessive lime causes loss of nitrogen from the compost pile.

Active Composting Systems

The active method of composting is used by people interested in making compost as quickly as possible. Usually gardeners, these people have a lot of material to compost and lots of gardens and landscape plants to use the compost on. With the ideal mix of carbon material (chopped leaves), nitrogen material (grass clippings), air, and moisture, the decomposition process accelerates so that within a day or two the internal temperature of the pile reaches 140° or 160°F. The heat is an indication of the furious activity of the microorganisms. The rapid decomposition that results from this activity lasts for only a few days, slowing as available oxygen is used up. Sometimes lack of moisture or too much moisture, when the pile is soaked by rain, slows the activity as well.

To heat up the pile again it is necessary to turn the pile and that's where the "active" part comes in. You can turn a pile by moving it from one place to another or by taking it out of its bin and putting it back in, forkful by forkful. This process introduces new oxygen into the pile. If the pile seems to be dried out, add moisture as the materials are put back in. Some people take the trouble to add more green material (nitrogen) while turning the pile to keep the carbon/nitrogen ratio as close to ideal as possible for quick decomposition. This can be accomplished by adding a few handfuls of common lawn fertilizer, which is high in nitrogen, to the pile during the rebuilding. In short order, the newly turned pile will heat up again to about 150°F and stay hot for a few days before things begin to cool down again.

The primary benefit of having a pile heat up to such high temperatures is that weed seeds and many disease pathogens are destroyed at those temperatures. Compost made the slower passive way will not have internal temperatures high enough to kill those weed seeds and pathogens. However, our experience has been that if you are careful not to put weeds just ready to pop their seeds into the passive pile, you will have few problems with weeds or disease as a result of using a passive method.

A pile that is turned once a week and has some nitrogen material added to it each time will decompose into finished compost in about a month. If the material in the pile is put through a shredder each time it is turned, it will become finished compost in three weeks.

People interested in active composting often

This three-bin composter is ideal for an active composting operation. Accumulated materials are chopped and stored in the first bin. When it is time to turn the pile, they are instead transferred into the second bin and the first is left free to store more materials. The original pile is moved to the third bin when it is time to turn it again and the second pile moves over a bin to free up the first space. The material in the third bin becomes finished compost after just a few weeks.

use a series of three or four adjacent bins. They build a pile in bin one. In a week they move that pile to bin two and build a new pile in bin one. Then by the time the pile has gotten to bin three or four it is finished compost and is ready to put out into the landscape.

BUILDING AN ACTIVE PILE

There are a number of techniques in building an active compost pile which assure maximum efficiency. Again, as with passive compost piles, they are optional. It is possible to get perfectly good compost by simply using the right materials and turning the pile periodically. A garden fork, or what is sometimes called a manure fork, is the best tool for turning compost. Shovels are not very effective tools for this job.

Unlike a passive pile that is built over time as materials become available, an active pile is built all at once, so it is necessary to accumulate sufficient carbon and nitrogen materials to build a pile that approximates the ideal size of $3 \times 3 \times 3$ feet or $4 \times 4 \times 4$ feet. Anything smaller will not heat up very well and a pile that is larger is difficult to handle.

Using Compost Tumblers

Compost tumblers represent an alternative to the conventional compost pile. On the market for several years now, they offer some of the advantages of an active composting system, without quite so much effort. Even the largest of the tumblers, however, does not process the volume of yard waste that a pile does. Choose the largest size possible, so that it will hold enough volume of waste materials to generate the required heat to get decomposition going. Tumblers are particularly good for composting kitchen wastes. Load the tumbler with chopped leaves in the fall to provide a basic supply of carbon, and then routinely dump nonmeat kitchen garbage into the tumbler every few days and give the tumbler four or five turns. It all decomposes nicely and never smells bad. In about six months, retrieve the finished compost for use around the yard, add another batch of chopped leaves, and start the process all over again. It is a very convenient way to handle kitchen garbage with no odors or rodent problems.

How Much Compost?

When organic materials are composted, whether by the passive or active method, they are reduced significantly in volume. That is why composting is such an ideal way to recycle yard waste. A pile that starts in a $4 \times 4 \times 4$-foot bin will produce a finished pile of compost that is about $1 \times 4 \times 4$ feet; the four-foot high pile is reduced to a pile that is only one foot high. Finished compost comprises about twenty-five percent of the volume of the original material. A $1 \times 4 \times 4$-foot pile gives you sixteen cubic feet of finished compost; that is enough to spread a quarter-inch layer over eight hundred square feet of lawn or garden. Even a small suburban property can accommodate this amount of compost every year.

Troubleshooting Compost Problems

It is possible you might have a few problems with your compost pile, especially in the beginning of the adventure. When compost piles aren't working properly there are some obvious clues as to why and most problems are easily solved. One way to monitor active piles is to take their temperature. Compost thermometers, available in garden centers and mail-order catalogs, resemble oven thermometers. They are dials mounted on long spikes which reach eight or ten inches down into a pile and register the amount of heat being generated by the decomposition process. The higher the temperature, the better. Other ways to check the temperature of an active pile is to simply stick a hand into the middle of it to check its warmth, or to stick a metal pipe of some kind down into the center of the pile and then to feel its surface immediately after withdrawing it to determine heat levels within the pile. Passive compost piles are normally relatively cool, because the decomposition process is very slow, so a low temperature there is expected. An active pile that has no internal heat is becoming inactive for some reason. The bacteria may need more nitrogen or air or moisture to get going again. Turn the pile, add green stuff, and check the level of moisture.

Another sign that there is a problem with a compost pile is odor. A properly functioning pile should not smell bad. There are usually two possibilities if a compost pile, active or passive, begins to produce bad odors (often a sulfur smell)—either the pile is too wet or it contains too much nitrogen material. Over-watering tends to compact a pile, preventing air from getting into it. This encourages anaerobic bacterial activity that results in fermentation of the yard waste materials, which in turn emit unpleasant odors. Turn the pile so it dries a bit and aerates properly, perhaps adding some more chopped leaves or aged sawdust to absorb some of the moisture. Cover the pile to protect it from rain.

A pile made solely of grass clippings putrifies and smells in just a few days. This is because there is too much nitrogen and not enough carbon to create the ideal decomposition environment. To correct this situation, simply rebuild the pile, adding lots of carbon materials to get a better carbon/nitrogen ratio.

It is possible, though unusual, to have a smelly pile because the leaves and grass are too compacted. If there is not enough oxygen because the materials are too finely chopped and are compressed down in the pile, then odors can occur. Simply loosen the pile by fluffing or agitating the yard waste materials, and maybe add some more bulky materials, such as straw or hay. Don't tamp down a compost pile when building it. Let it settle by itself.

Pile is frozen. Since microbes become inactive below 40°F, small home compost piles can freeze in winter and then start slowly again in the spring. To maintain an active pile over the winter, be sure that it is 4 × 4 × 4 feet and that it has sufficient nitrogen materials and moisture to keep the process cooking. When turning it, fold the outside of the pile into the center of the pile. Do not turn the pile quite so often in the winter to maintain the heat in the center as long as possible.

Insects in pile. Many beneficial critters, such as sow bugs, centipedes, and earthworms, inhabit compost piles. They help with the breaking down of the organic yard waste materials. These are not a problem and should be encouraged. Houseflies and fruitflies, on the other hand, are not desirable, and should not be part of a properly built pile. Always cover kitchen waste with a layer of carbon materials, such as chopped leaves, when adding it to a pile. Turning the pile can usually solve the fly problem. *Do not* apply any pesticides to a compost pile.

Pests in the pile. Some homeowners have reported problems with dogs, cats, raccoons, opossums, and even rats hanging around their compost pile. These animals are not a problem if the pile is built and maintained properly. Again, if kitchen garbage is just thrown on top of the pile, and the pile is not covered, those animal pests may well be attracted to it. However, a properly built pile will never attract pest animals, including rats.

Using Compost

Using compost around the property recycles yard waste completely. Through a natural process that parallels the ongoing decomposition of living things in nature, composting turns inconvenient yard waste into a useful product. There are as many ways to use compost as there are to make it. Spread a layer across the surface of vegetable or flower beds in the fall or the spring. Worked into the soil by hand or with a rotary tiller, or just left to soak in over time, it will enrich the soil with water-holding humus. Likewise, spread a thin layer on the lawn in the spring or fall. Either annual aeration or the worms and microorganisms in the soil below will carry it down near plant roots. Finally, use compost to improve the soil around individual shrubs, trees, flowers, or vegetable plants by spreading it in a circle over their roots at any time during the growing season.

YARD WASTE MANAGEMENT— A SUMMARY

The necessity for individual communities and the homeowners within them to take responsibility for the organic trash that they generate is obvious. Not only are yard waste products such as leaves and grass clippings clogging landfills, but by discarding these valuable raw materials homeowners are missing out on an opportunity to improve the health and appearance of their landscapes. By reducing the amount of yard waste that is produced, and by reusing a significant portion of it as mulch, and then by recycling the remainder into compost, homeowners will be adopting an ethic that must prevail in the next century.

CHAPTER 6
Dealing with Pests

Perhaps the most frustrating aspect of caring for residential yards is dealing with the health problems that plants develop from time to time. Plants in a home landscape occasionally fall victim to various ailments or pests in their environment. It becomes obvious when the lawn turns brown in spots, or a tree starts dropping its leaves in the middle of the growing season. Or perhaps the lilacs become coated with a gray substance or the foliage on the hosta has big holes in it. The average homeowner has few resources for dealing with these developments and the garden center has too many. How can you pick from the rows and rows of products designed to kill diseases and insects?

In the earlier chapters we have outlined various problems encountered by lawns, trees and shrubs, flowers, and vegetables that are a function of poor environmental conditions. Lack of water, insufficient light, compacted soil, plant injury, overcrowding, and poor nutrition

are cultural conditions that can weaken plants and cause them to show symptoms of illness. In fact, cultural problems are most often the causes of pest and disease problems. If plants are stressed by poor growing conditions, they are much more vulnerable to bugs and diseases. The opportunistic bugs and diseases are really secondary causes. Following the suggestions outlined in the foregoing chapters for the care of all landscape plants will go a long way toward keeping them vigorous and healthy and eliminate the stress on plants due to environmental deficiencies. Proper care is the best prevention measure there is.

However, pest problems—those problems caused by bugs, animals, and disease—do occur, even in the healthiest landscape. This chapter is designed to help homeowners develop an ongoing strategy for dealing with these problems. A better understanding of exactly what is lurking out in the yard, why an insect or fungal spore population suddenly explodes, how to detect their presence on a plant, and how to thwart them will make it easier for you to handle the few problems that do develop. The strategy we're going to outline is based on a holistic approach to the yard as a balanced ecosystem and involves the following steps: prevention, observation, targeted treatment, and analysis.

When a plant, a tree, or the lawn looks sick, it is most probably a victim of either disease, or insect or animal attack. Like humans, plants get an assortment of viral, bacterial, and fungal diseases. They may be afflicted by insects or various wormlike pests which attack them on their leaves and flowers or underground at their roots. They are also injured by the activity of animals—rodents, dogs, rabbits, sometimes birds, and others. Some pests work at night, others in broad daylight.

However, as complicated as all this seems, pest and disease problems are not that difficult to handle. There are only a few chronic offenders among the hundreds of kinds of bugs and diseases that are likely to be in a yard at any given season in any given region of the country. Furthermore, there are usually only a few plants in your yard that are particularly vulnerable to those few insects or diseases. By narrowing down the number of possible pest insects and by identifying the few problem trees or shrubs existing in the yard, you can more easily become familiar with them and their habits. Dealing with pest problems will then become a less difficult and more manageable task.

The strategy this chapter suggests is called

Backyard Pest Management or *BPM*. This involves a comprehensive approach to thinking about the yard. BPM involves the prevention and control of plant health problems through an understanding of the pest or disease and the use of modern pesticide products that are safe and effective. It involves learning to anticipate problems, to recognize the particular cause whether it be bug or disease, and then to use a control that is designed for that particular problem.

PEST CONTROL TECHNIQUES ARE CHANGING

The traditional approach to pest management, both on the farm and in the yard, involved waiting until an outbreak of insect or disease pests became apparent, selecting a powerful broad-spectrum pesticide, and then covering the entire area with that material to be sure of killing every pest insect or disease spore possible. In fact, ironically, this approach may have created more pest problems than it solved. Because broad-spectrum pesticides kill a wide variety of bugs and insects indiscriminately, they unavoidably eliminate the normal population of beneficial insects that reside in the area, along with the pest insects they feed on. Only 2 or 3 percent of the insects on a property are likely to be pests or problems, and then only if their population explodes for some reason. All the rest are either harmless to plants or are "beneficial" because they kill pest insects. Most of the time the beneficial insects keep the pest insects under control. If vast numbers of beneficials are killed by pesticide, the balance of the ecosystem is upset for the long term.

With few resident predators, pest insects can easily gain an upper hand again, requiring the use of even more pesticides. Soon a terrible cycle is begun: one pest insect or another constantly gains predominance in the yard, requiring the homeowner to spend more and more time and money reacting to each in turn. The conventional practice of spraying a broad-spectrum pesticide caused more problems than it cured. Routinely applying any pesticide to a lawn or to any other group of plants on the property every year only addresses the immediate problem. The visible bug or disease is often actually only a symptom of some more fundamental problem in the ecosystem and spraying does nothing to remedy that underlying problem.

While it may seem a bit counterproductive, we really want to have some of the bad guys, pest insects and disease spores, on our property. Without any bad guys to eat, the beneficial insects and microbes either die or go somewhere else. It is the presence of the beneficial insects and microbes that usually prevents major outbreaks of any pest insect or disease. The balanced system doesn't exist if all the bad guys are eradicated, so don't panic when you see one Japanese beetle or a few aphids. It is when there are a lot of Japanese

beetles or aphids that some concern is definitely appropriate.

Lessons from commercial agriculture on how to restore and maintain the ecological balance of an area apply very well to the home landscape. They've inspired the backyard pest management strategy that is presented here in which the emphasis is on working with the natural ecological system already in place. Where possible it is better to enlist natural allies to police the yard. Notice that using pesticides doesn't show up until the third step.

BACKYARD PEST MANAGEMENT STRATEGY

1. *Prevention.* Maintain a healthy landscape
2. *Observation.* Monitor plants to spot symptoms promptly
3. *Treatment.* Choose pesticides for safety and effectiveness
4. *Analysis.* Identify the ecological cause

Prevention: Maintain a Healthy Landscape

A homeowner can forestall many pest problems in the yard by taking the broad view of the landscape as a vibrant ecosystem where both "bad" and "good" organisms live and interact in balanced populations. It is also im-

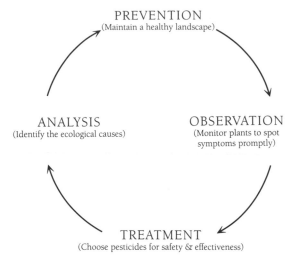

PREVENTION
(Maintain a healthy landscape)

ANALYSIS
(Identify the ecological causes)

OBSERVATION
(Monitor plants to spot
symptoms promptly)

TREATMENT
(Choose pesticides for safety & effectiveness)

The steps for dealing with pest problems in the yard form a continuous loop designed to lead to eliminating the true cause of a pest or disease problem so that it does not return again the next year.

portant to take the long view, and understand that prevention of pest problems in the yard by addressing the underlying causes requires time, perhaps a few years. However, by addressing the underlying causes of plant health problems, and taking steps to establish a sound ecosystem in the yard, prevention of many pest and insect problems is assured. We offer four prevention steps that are easy to incorporate into a yard-care routine and that involve working with nature to promote a balanced, healthy landscape. Each step will make a difference, and all four collectively will definitely reduce pest problems in the yard in the long run.

ESTABLISH PLANT DIVERSITY IN THE YARD.
The more varied the types of plants that grow in the landscape the more varied will be the

population of insects and disease pathogens. It is important to have several kinds of trees and shrubs, and to have both deciduous and evergreen types. A property with only one variety of tree, such as sugar maples, set in a huge lawn with only one variety of grass plant will be much more vulnerable to pest problems than will a home surrounded by lots of different kinds of plants. This is because different plants host, or attract, different insects, both good and bad. The greater the variety of insects in the yard, the more likely there will be a balance struck between the number of pest ones and beneficial ones. This makes it less likely that any one insect will populate out of control.

Flowers are not only an aesthetic addition to a landscape, they have a role in maintaining a balanced ecosystem. This is because they are

The more diverse the plantings in a yard, the healthier the ecosystem will be. The presence of a wide variety of trees, shrubs, flowers, and other plants will assure that beneficial insects feel welcome. These natural predators routinely feed on pest insects, controlling their populations.

a source of food for most of the beneficial insects. Certain flowers, especially those with daisylike blossoms, are favorite hosts for these tiny predators. Because of this, there are now on the market several wildflower seed mixtures that have been formulated to include particular flower favorites of beneficial insects. They, and many other annual and perennial flowers, attract the desirable beneficial insects to the yard where they actively prey on pest insects. These products (for example Border Patrol and Haven) offer plants such as daisies, Queen Anne's lace, black-eyed Susans, buckwheat, and yarrow which attract ladybugs, lacewings, and many of the parasitic wasps. Collectively these beneficials kill thousands of pest insects, such as aphids and caterpillars. Therefore, by planting flowers, a homeowner can recruit natural allies in the fight against pest insects.

Of course, immediately undertaking a large-scale change in plantings in the yard is neither practical nor necessary. Introduction of new and varied plants can be done over time. Knowing that plant diversity in the home ecosystem helps reduce pest problems should be a factor in your future decisions. When it is time to add or replace a tree or a shrub, choose a type that is different from those already growing on the property. When decorating the yard with flowers, select several kinds of flowering plants, rather than have all impatiens or all petunias. One of the benefits of planting ground covers around trees and shrubs, besides protecting those plants from lawn-mower damage, is that most ground covers have very

Friendly Predators Found in Residential Yards

Daddy longlegs

Dragonflies (they don't sting or bite; catch pest insects in flight)

Spiders (webs trap billions of insects)

Lizards

Salamanders/newts

Praying mantis

Owls (go after rodents)

Skunks (go after grubs)

Toads

Ground beetles

Firefly larvae

Ants (some types, like fire ants)

Hornets, yellow jackets, paper wasps

small blossoms which are attractive to many beneficial insects. Ground covers also add variety to a yard previously covered only with lawn grass.

Enriching the diversity of the yard will contribute to a well-balanced ecosystem. While choices of individual plants should be made primarily on the basis of their ornamental contribution to the yard, incorporating the prin-

they are able to withstand infection or attack. When they are weak because of injury or some environmental stress, their resistance is reduced and they become extremely vulnerable to a host of pest problems. Some farmers have found that when a pest insect problem appears, the most effective response is to correct a nutrient deficiency or a watering problem rather than to spray with a pesticide. These experiences suggest that treating the source of stress in the environment and restoring the plant's health and capacity to resist insect attack may be the very best ways to solve the pest insect problem.

So while it may seem like an obvious step, it turns out that by simply taking pains to maintain healthy plants homeowners can significantly reduce pest problems. From this perspective, an insect or disease problem on a particular plant may suggest that the plant was not in top health in the first place. Perhaps there is a soil problem, maybe the plant has

ciple of diversity at the same time is very easy. Over time this will result in an ecologically balanced as well as a beautiful landscape.

MAINTAIN A HEALTHY LANDSCAPE. Research has indicated for years that pest insects and diseases are essentially opportunistic. They tend to zero in on plants that are weak or injured first. If gypsy moths attack a grove of oak trees, they will start on the foliage of the weakest tree and not get to the healthiest trees until last or maybe not at all. It seems that all plants, be they trees, shrubs, flowers, or vegetables, have built-in pest-resistance mechanisms. When they are healthy and vigorous,

Flowers that have flat heads with tight clusters of tiny flowers are favorites of beneficial insects. This Queen Anne's lace blossom attracts tiny wasps that feed on aphids.

ABOVE: *This low-maintenance, attractive land-scape features different textures of evergreen shrubs that decorate the facade of the home and screen the neighboring yard from view. In the spring the azalea and rhododendron toward the foreground provide a burst of color. The tall shade tree cools the home in the summer. Pachysandra reduces the size of the lawn and mulches the tree and shrubs. Containers of geraniums on the doorstep provide a bright focal point at the end of the welcoming path.*

LEFT: *A flowering quince defines this sunny dooryard in the spring. Pachysandra provides winter protection for the daffodil bulbs and will mask their dying foliage after they finish blooming. This ground cover and the evergreen shrubs, which have been properly pruned to an informal, but neat shape, provide color all winter.*

ABOVE: *Because impatiens can handle some shade, it is an ideal plant for mulching trees. The characteristic drooping branches of the live oak have been pruned to raise the canopy so that sufficient light reaches the plants and the ivy beneath.*

TOP RIGHT: *Flowering dogwood and evergreen azaleas mark this driveway entrance. They anchor a low-maintenance, sloping front yard that features many tall trees in a woodland type of setting. A ground cover of ivy mulches all the trees and shrubs and totally eliminates the need to mow grass.*

BOTTOM RIGHT: *The lawn here draws the pedestrian around from the front to the backyard. Because of this foot traffic, it is aerated frequently and is planted with tall turf-type fescue. The spring-flowering plants enjoy sufficient sunlight because the leaves on the large sycamore trees are typically late to emerge. In the winter and early spring their interesting bark shows to best advantage.*

TOP: *These wax begonias fill the spaces between the shrubs to brighten the front of the house, picking up the color of the shutters. Although they will die when cold weather arrives, they are easily replaced in the spring. Notice the shredded bark mulch around the shrubs.*

MIDDLE: *This decorative mixed border of bulbs and shrubs welcomes visitors as they approach the front porch. The smaller grape hyacinths are at the top of the bed, the taller tulips toward the back. When their foliage dies back, the bed will be planted with brightly colored annuals.*

BOTTOM: *City homes often have front yards that are measured in inches. Here the small space in front of the sidewalk is planted in a happy jumble of annuals. Candytuft, petunias, ageratum, geraniums, impatiens, and the occasional perennial hosta crowd the evergreen azaleas in a profusion of color.*

ABOVE: *A shady area in summer makes a wonderful setting for houseplants that need some fresh air. This clivia shares the protection of the Eastern red cedar canopy with hostas and ivy. The bark of the trees and the flower blossom make a striking focal point.*

RIGHT: *Many landscape plants such as this firethorn continue to decorate the yard through the fall and into winter. These berries are effective both in the daylight and at night in the light of the front lamp. They also provide food for birds.*

ABOVE: *Planted with a succession of vegetable plants over a growing season extended a bit into the early spring and late fall, these two boxed beds can produce over 300 pounds of fresh vegetables. This picture shows the landscape in the spring. The paths are permanent and are covered with woodchips to eliminate mud and weed problems. The 500-square-foot area shown in this photograph accommodates vegetables, herbs, mixed flower and shrub borders and beds, apple trees espaliered to form a fence, and a water garden. The utility area screened by the apple fence is a yard waste area where leaves are stored for composting. The birdhouse invites birds to visit the yard and patrol for pest insects.*

LEFT: *These climbing cucumber plants do not take up much space and are both ornamental and productive. Vegetables that grow on trellises benefit from good air circulation and as a result are less vulnerable to disease and pest problems. They are also easier to pick.*

TOP: *Creative use of mulches and shrubs can turn a backyard that is entirely rock into a stunning low-maintenance landscape. This New England site features coarse and fine bark nugget mulches and a variety of evergreens. Junipers that grow as carpets soften the harsh stone surfaces. Both needled and broad-leaved shrubs provide color and texture year-round.*

MIDDLE: *This naturalized planting of daffodils contributes to the sense of comfortable informality of this site. Bulbs planted in this way decorate the untamed areas of a property as they multiply year after year.*

BOTTOM: *Plants in containers and outdoor art turn this utility area into a charming back entrance to the house. The variegated ivy and geraniums prefer the sunnier areas of the porch, whereas the ferns and young marigolds like more indirect light.*

ABOVE: *Plant a low-lying, boggy area in the yard with water-loving plants such as cattails. Maintaining its natural character while adding stands of self-reliant daylilies and self-seeding annual forget-me-nots creates an attractive corner that takes care of itself.*

LEFT: *Ornamental grasses are a favorite plant around pools. Clumps of tall, graceful blades screen the area from public view and soften the look of the paving. The low-growing evergreens—a dwarf red pine, rose daphne, and thyme—mulched with attractive stone reduce maintenance to nearly zero.*

TOP: *Many kinds of flowers thrive in containers. When these hybrid tulips have passed their peak of bloom, the bulbs will be removed and replaced with an assortment of brightly colored annuals. They will brighten the sidewalk along the side of this city house until frost.*

MIDDLE: *An informal collection of flowering plants spills down the steps of this suburban home. The colorful geraniums, dahlias, vinca, and marigolds incorporate the drainpipe into the design while at the same time obscuring its outlet and the discolored pavement beneath it.*

BOTTOM: *Attractive trees and shrubs also enhance a residential landscape through the winter. Evergreens soften architectural lines, add color to the yard, and provide food and shelter for overwintering birds, while the rough bark and stark silhouettes of deciduous trees contribute dramatic interest.*

insufficient water, maybe a rodent has been chewing at its roots, maybe a dog has urinated on it. While it may be important to address the immediate pest problem, try to figure out what the real, or underlying, cause of the pest attack is. What has undermined that target plant's health and made it vulnerable to pest attack?

The early chapters of this book describe simple but important plant care tasks, such as watering, feeding, mulching, and pruning, for the various types of plants in your yard. By taking the trouble to properly care for the lawn, trees, shrubs, and flowers, you not only maximize their ornamental value, but you simultaneously reduce the potential for pest insect and disease problems throughout the property.

ATTRACT BIRDS TO THE YARD. Birds, especially songbirds, represent an ideal natural pesticide for the yard. Even the lowly English sparrow and the starling are wonderful pest insect fighters. Most people don't realize that while most songbirds are basically seed eaters, they must feed insects to their young as baby birds cannot digest seeds. Consequently, the ubiquitous sparrows with their two or three broods each season must collect an enormous number of insects from around their territory. House wrens are similarly celebrated for the number of insects they harvest for their offspring. If their territory happens to be the backyard, they will significantly reduce the insect population there.

Birds prey on pest insects in various ways. Some, such as swallows, kingbirds, phoebes, flycatchers, redstarts, peewees, mockingbirds, and catbirds, feed while they are in flight. They go after a variety of moths, as well as aphids, leafhoppers, horseflies, winged ants, and beetles. Other birds find their prey on the surfaces of plant foliage. Warblers, nuthatches, chickadees, robins, thrushes, orioles, and many others devour aphids, caterpillars, and other wormlike pests while they are in the act of eating plants. Other familiar birds glean insects from the bark of trees and other woody plants. Woodpeckers, nuthatches, creepers, chickadees, wrens, and others bore into stems or pick from bark surfaces insects that are wintering over on plants. They also find various borer pests, timber ants, and plant lice. Finally, some birds are ground feeders. Robins, bluebirds, blackbirds, chipping sparrows, wrens, warblers, meadowlarks, flickers, thrushes, and others peck at the soil to uncover various bee-

Birds are allies in the backyard battle against pest insects. Even seed eaters such as this house finch search out insects in the summer when they must feed their young.

tles, slugs, rootworms, aphids, maggots, grass-hoppers, grubs, and other soil-dwelling pests.

As all this ferocious activity suggests, there is no doubt that a varied and abundant bird population can perform a valuable pest-control service if they will stay in the area. The challenge, then, is to find ways to increase the bird population in and around the yard. There are several ways to do that. Birds need water, shelter, and food. With a little planning homeowners can provide all three.

A varied landscape with lots of different kinds of trees provides many possibilities for bird nesting sites. Many birds particularly like the needled evergreens which provide shelter in storms as well as cones to eat. In yards where there are few trees and shrubs, put up birdhouses to attract bird families. In the absence of a natural source of water on the property or nearby, such as a stream or pond, set up a birdbath. It is extremely important to offer water to birds in both summer and winter.

A certain number of songbirds always take up residence in a yard without a special invitation. The familiar local species, such as cardinals, robins, chickadees, and sparrows, all establish territories that their experience suggests will afford sufficient food for their families. These territories are likely to overlap somewhat and to include your property. For effective insect control, though, the goal is to encourage more than the normal number to move into a given area, which means persuading them to live closer to their neighbors than normal.

The only way to encourage birds to narrow their territory and live more closely together is to increase their food supply. For those that live in the region year-round, that means making sure there is sufficient food year-round to support a more concentrated population. One way to do this is to deliberately plant trees, shrubs, flowers, and perhaps some vegetables that provide a source of food for adult birds and their babies. These plants will inevitably offer them, among other things, a population of pest insects to feed on. Since the winter is normally the time of deprivation, also choose plantings that produce seeds, berries, and small nuts or cones throughout the cold months. Choose both low growing and tall plants to accommodate those bird species which are high feeders and those that are ground feeders. These trees and shrubs will also provide shelter during storms.

Of course, the most reliable way to ensure enough food for a more concentrated bird population is to put seed out in feeders. Many homeowners routinely feed songbirds during the winter, but most do not continue the practice during the summer. In fact, many books recommend not feeding birds in the summer for fear of making them dependent. Close observation by ornithologists, however, confirms that birds always supplement their diet from the surrounding landscape and are not in danger of dependency if they also visit a feeder in the summer.

A good system for feeding birds is to offer seed daily in the winter, if possible, putting

Landscape Food Sources For Birds

SHADE/EVERGREEN TREES

Alder (*Alnus*)

Ash, white (*Fraxinus americana*)

Beech (*Fagus*)

Birch, white (*Betula papyrifera*)

Box elder (*Acer negundo*)

Butternut (*Juglans cinerea*)

Eastern red cedar (*Juniperus virginiana*)

Elm, American (*Ulmus americana*)

Fir, balsam and white (*Abies balsamea, A. concolor*)

Hemlock, eastern (*Tsuga canadensis*)

Holly family (*Ilex*)

Magnolia family (*Magnolia*)

Maple, sugar and silver (*Acer saccharinum, A. saccharum*)

Mulberry, red (*Morus rubra*)

Oak family (*Quercus*)

Pine, eastern white (*Pinus strobus*)

Sassafras (*Sassafras albidum*)

Serviceberry (*Amelanchier*)

Spruce family (*Picea*)

Sweet gum, American (*Liquidambar styraciflua*)

Tulip tree (*Liriodendron tulipifera*)

Tupelo, black (*Nyssa sylvatica*)

Walnut, black (*Juglans nigra*)

ORNAMENTAL TREES

Bayberry (*Myrica cerifera*)

Cherry, flowering (*Prunis serrulata*)

Crab apple (*Malus*)

Dogwood, Japanese (*Cornus kousa*)

Hawthorn (*Crataegus*)

Mountain ash (*Sorbus*)

Winterberry (*Ilex verticillata*)

SHRUBS

Barberry (*Berberis*)

Blueberry (*Vaccinium*)

Buckthorn (*Rhamnus cathartica*)

Euonymus (*Euonymus*)

Firethorn (*Pyracantha*)

Gooseberry (*Ribes uva-crispa*)

Landscape Food Sources For Birds

SHRUBS

Coralberry (*Symphoricarpos × chenaultii*)

Cotoneaster (*Cotoneaster*)

Dogwood family (*Cornus*)

Elderberry (*Sambucus*)

Privet (*Ligustrum*)

Spicebush (*Lindera benzoin*)

Sumac (*Rhus*)

Viburnum family (*Viburnum*)

Wild roses (*Rosa*)

VINES

Grapes (*Vitis*)

Honeysuckle (*Lonicera*)

Scarlet runner bean (*Phaseolus coccineus*)

Virginia creeper (*Parthenocissus quinquefolia*)

Bittersweet (*Celastrus*)

FLOWERS
(do not deadhead, allow flowers to go to seed)

Aster (*Aster*)

Bachelor's buttons (*Centaurea cyanis*)

Basket flower (*Centaurea americana*)

Bellflower (*Campanula*)

China aster (*Callistephus chinensis*)

Chrysanthemum (*Chrysanthemum*)

Coneflower (*Echinacea*)

Cosmos (*Cosmos*)

Dusty miller (*Centaurea cineraria*)

Four-o'clock (*Mirabilis*)

Foxglove (*Digitalis*)

Hollyhock (*Alcea*)

Larkspur (*Delphinium*)

Lupine (*Lupinus*)

Marigolds (*Tagetes*)

Phlox (*Phlox*)

Poppy (*Papaver*)

Pot marigold (*Calendula*)

Portulaca (*Portulaca*)

Snapdragon (*Antirrhinum*)

Landscape Food Sources For Birds

FLOWERS

Sunflower (*Helianthus*)	Tickseed (*Coreopsis*)
Sweet William (*Dianthus barbatus*)	Verbena (*Verbena*)
Thistle (*Echinops*)	Zinnia (*Zinnia*)

WEEDS

Dandelion (*Taraxacum officinale*)	Pokeweed (*Phytolacca americana*)
Pigweed (*Chenopodium album*)	Ragweed (*Ambrosia*)
Plantain (*Plantago major*)	Sedges (*Carex*)

WILDFLOWERS

Bunchberry (*Cornus canadensis*)	Jetbead (*Rhodotypos scandens*)
Butterfly weed (*Asclepias tuberosa*)	Joe-pye weed (*Eupatorium maculatum*)
Cardinal flower (*Lobelia cardinalis*)	Milkweed (*Asclepias syriaca*)
False Solomon's seal (*Smilacina racemosa*)	Nightshade (*Solanum dulcamara*)
Goldenrod (*Solidago*)	Skunk cabbage (*Symplocarpus foetidus*)
Ironweed (*Veronia*)	Solomon's seal (*Polygonatum*)
Jack-in-the-pulpit (*Arisaema triphyllum*)	Violets (*Viola*)

out just enough for a day at a time to ensure that the seed does not rot and cause illness. Then, in the spring when natural food becomes more abundant, shift to a biweekly feeder schedule. Busy parents will be tracking down insects for their babies, but they will appreciate being able to stop off at the feeder once in a while. Seed in the feeder supplements their diet from the yard, but does not replace it.

If a yard has a healthy population of all kinds of birds—even so-called "trash" birds—it will have fewer pest insect problems than if there were no effort made to attract these pest-control allies. It is worth the investment in time and money to make the landscape attractive to birds, to look out and see lots of birds in the yard feverishly working all over the plants, gleaning insects as they go. *A final, important note*: It is extremely important to avoid the use of the insecticide Diazinon in granular form (commonly used to control grubs in lawns) on the property. Songbirds will die if they eat those granules.

YARD CLEANUP. Spring and fall yard cleanup is not yet an institution among homeowners, although many folks find themselves routinely raking leaves in the fall and pruning and sprucing up the landscape in the spring. For those interested in preventing pest problems in the yard, however, thorough yard cleanup is a critical step. It is important to collect and discard the weeds, sticks, and droppings from trees that accumulate on the property over each season. Not only does it improve the look of the place, but it is a major insect and disease control measure. Many pest insects and fungal disease spores depend on this debris for their existence. Some, like slugs, hide in the dark under boards and fallen bark during the heat of the day during the growing season. Other pests lay eggs in decaying plant tissue and overwinter on the debris that is often left around the yard.

To thwart these pests, clean out from under trees and shrubs and replace the old mulch with freshly chopped leaves in the fall. Pull up and discard all dead or dying annual plants and cut back the dried stems and foliage on perennial plants to the soil surface. Chop all newly raked leaves with a lawn mower or shredder before spreading them around the property as mulch to expose any eggs, larvae, and spores on them to their natural predators. Lightly work the top inch or two of soil around perennials, shrubs, and in the vegetable bed to turn up larvae and eggs which the birds can spot and dispatch. Hold off spreading fresh, winter-weight mulch until the ground freezes so that mice will not be tempted to build nests near plant roots.

In the spring, rake up the twigs and debris that have accumulated over the winter. Be sure to collect all the branches generated by spring pruning. Keeping the yard picked up of garden debris makes an important contribution to the objective of reducing pest insect and disease problems.

LIMITED PREVENTIVE SPRAYING. As a general rule, routine spraying of pesticides in an effort to prevent an insect or weed problem is not advisable. This practice is falling out of favor in commercial agriculture and for very good reason. As we mentioned earlier, the indiscriminate use of sprays is as likely to kill the beneficial helpers necessary to keep the bad guys in line as it is to kill the enemy. A sound pest-control strategy suggests that the most effective response to a pest problem this year is to find and eliminate the cause of the problem next year, rather than simply attacking the symptom year after year with preventive spray. The routine application of herbicide and insecticide on a lawn, year in and year out, is not only a bad practice, it is a waste of money.

There are better ways to solve lawn problems (this is further discussed in chapter one).

However, having made this strong statement against preventive spraying, we must concede that there are some exceptions—important ones. The first is a biological pesticide called milky spore disease (*Bacillus popilliae*) which kills grubs in turfgrass. This compound is actually a bacteria that is harmful only to white grubs. Sprayed on the lawn or soil where grubs are a problem, it gradually spreads throughout the lawn, sickening and killing succeeding generations of grubs. It significantly reduces their population over a three- to five-year period, effectively eliminating grub problems for fifteen to twenty years. Milky spore disease is an acceptable preventive spray because it is absolutely harmless to all other living creatures and plants, killing only grubs. It is a one-time preventive measure that will deal with major grub problems effectively and safely.

Another exception to the no-preventive-spraying rule is oil spray. Because so many insect pests and their eggs overwinter on the twigs, stems, bark, and foliage of trees and shrubs, one way to prevent their emergence in the spring is to kill them as they rest. There are two kinds of oil spray designed for use on trees and shrubs. Dormant oil, also called heavy oil or Volck oil, is suitable for use only on deciduous trees and shrubs after their leaves have fallen. Because it is so viscous, it will harm foliage. A lighter oil, called light oil or "superior" horticultural oil, is suitable for ever-

greens. Because it is thinner, it does not harm needles or the broad leaves of shrubs like rhododendrons. Sprayed on to thoroughly cover all plant surfaces, these oils coat them with an airtight cover, effectively smothering any aphids, scale, whiteflies, mites, or mealybugs. Evergreen euonymus shrubs are notoriously vulnerable to scale attack. The light oil spray over the bark and leaf stems of the euonymus plant a month or so before last frost will suffocate most of the scale insects overwintering on that shrub. This preventive step does not harm beneficial insects, most of which overwinter in other places. The oil spray reduces the scale population to a level where scale predators can control them in the spring.

A final exception to the no-preventive-spraying rule is sulfur- or copper-based fungicide. Many plants, roses, lilacs, phlox, and asters among them, are traditionally afflicted with various fungal diseases. These mildews and spots are not necessarily life-threatening, but they badly mar the appearance of these ornamental plants. Periodic preventive sprays of fungicide over their foliage may discourage fungus diseases such as black spot on roses or powdery mildew on lilacs. Of course, the best preventive step in these cases would be to choose disease-resistant types of roses and lilacs, but often the plants are already in place when a homeowner purchases a home. Cultural practices such as changing mulch, spraying foliage with antitranspirant sprays, and avoiding overhead watering also help prevent fungal disease problems. A preventive spray of a sulfur- or copper-based fungicide will supplement these measures.

Individually, these four simple preventive steps are effective in reducing potential pest and disease problems in the yard. Collectively, they represent a firm foundation from which to launch a backyard pest control strategy based on achieving a balanced ecosystem in the landscape. They help minimize the need for pesticides to cope with the insects and diseases that are, in fact, often only symptoms of more fundamental problems in the yard.

Observation: Monitor Plants to Spot Symptoms Promptly

Inevitably pest and disease problems will appear from time to time. Despite efforts at prevention, sometimes unusual weather, the inadvertent introduction of a pest on a new plant, the population cycles of certain insects, and other factors foster an outbreak of aphids, beetles, or whatever. In that case remedial action for the short term may be necessary to save the plant or the crop. So a most important step is prompt diagnosis. Pest and disease problems are most easily controlled when they are caught early on.

It is important to be observant in the yard. Take a few minutes to walk around and enjoy the view every week and check nearby plantings and the lawn while mulching or mowing or doing other routine maintenance chores. Insect and disease problems usually first be-

come apparent when a homeowner notices that a certain plant does not "look right." Closer inspection reveals that foliage is limp, chewed, curled, or discolored, or plant stems are drooping or dying.

For the average homeowner the hardest part is identifying the disease or insect culprit. It may seem from books on plant problems as if there are hundreds of possible harmful insects or diseases that could be at fault, but this is not really the case. While there may be hundreds of insects that are pests in some places in certain situations, there are seldom more than five or ten insects in a particular yard that could cause problems from time to time. That's not a large number, and they rarely strike at the same time, much less during the same year. In addition, you will find that of all the many different plants growing in the landscape, it is only a few, maybe five to ten, that seem to be more vulnerable to pest attack. Learning to identify five to ten insects that seem to hit the five to ten plants in the yard over time is not a terribly difficult task.

IDENTIFYING INSECTS

One of the most helpful facts about insect life is that each species has characteristic ways of working and follows a specific timetable in the landscape year after year. For instance, if Japanese beetles appear in the yard around July 3 one year, chances are they will show up at this time every year. Slugs are equally predictable. So are aphids and whiteflies. This predictability makes it much easier to anticipate their arrival and to be on the lookout for them. Examine a plant that doesn't look right in early July, and chances are the first of the season's Japanese beetles will be eating its foliage. This is the signal to undertake control measures, such as putting out traps. This is not, however, the signal to start spraying the entire yard. If the early arrivals are spotted and traps are set out properly, it's highly likely that the beetle problem can be controlled. Pesticide spray may never be needed.

Monitoring the arrival of the few familiar pest insects that are likely to be in the yard enables homeowners to prevent their growing in numbers large enough to do serious damage. There are a variety of devices and tools on the market that help with monitoring. Most of them are traps of some kind. Traps, for the most part, are not used to actually control the population of a pest insect. Rather, they are used to confirm that the aphid or the thrip or, in the case of California in recent years, the medfly has emerged or arrived. Forewarned, it is much easier to prevent an insect population from getting out of hand. As we noted earlier, there will always be a few harmful insects on the property—that's part of the normal balance of things. They provide food for the beneficial insects and encourage them to stay in the area. In small numbers they do not do serious enough damage to need any particular attention. At the same time, once aware that they have arrived, homeowners know to keep an eye on the tender new foliage on the lilacs or peonies.

Since many pest insects are attracted to the color yellow, a yellow piece of plastic or cardboard covered with a sticky substance such as Tanglefoot or used motor oil serves as a perfect early warning device. The earliest whitefly or aphid arrivals will become stuck on the trap and signal their presence.

Over the years monitoring for the pest insects by close observation and use of traps reveals which of the hundreds of potential pests are actually present in the yard. Chances are there will be fewer than five throughout the entire year. Simultaneously, the plants most vulnerable to those few pests will be identified, allowing the homeowner to greatly narrow down what needs to be observed each year. This experience also familiarizes home-

The Ten Most Unwanted Insect Pests

INSECT	DAMAGE	TARGET
Aphid	Curled, puckered leaves	Most plants
Bagworm	Loss of vigor	Evergreen trees and shrubs
Gypsy moth	Defoliation	Oaks, evergreens
Japanese beetle	Holes in leaves and blooms	Roses, raspberries
Lace bug	Leaves pale, mottled	Azaleas, andromedas
Mite	Leaves yellow	Junipers, many others
Scale	Crusty bumps on stems	Euonymus
Slug	Holes chewed in leaves	Hostas
Weevil	Holes in leaf edges	Azaleas
Whitefly	Leaves yellowed, limp	Tomatoes, flowers

owners with the appearance and habits of the pest bug, making identification next year very simple. It does not take long to learn that aphids seem to always congregate under the newest leaves of a plant, mites often make tiny webs in infested plants and look like specks of pepper if they are knocked off a stem into a handkerchief. Slugs chew ragged holes in leaves at night and can be found hiding under nearby rocks during the day, and scale insects encrust plant stems with small bumps.

IDENTIFYING DISEASES

Close observation is also essential in the case of plant disease. A wilted plant or one with spotted or whitish foliage clearly signals a problem. However, identifying diseases is much more difficult than tagging a pest insect. First examine the plant to rule out the possibility that insects may be causing the symptoms. Then try to determine whether the disease is fungal, which can be treated, or bacterial or viral, which cannot. Most diseases in the home landscape are fungal in nature.

A rule of thumb for distinguishing between fungal diseases and the others is that fungal disease usually takes days and even weeks to manifest itself, while the bacterial and viral diseases usually strike very quickly, in just a day or two. They are often carried to the plant by insects and infect it immediately if conditions are favorable. A plant that falls ill seemingly overnight may be infected with a virus or bacteria. A healthy zucchini squash plant can be completely dead in just a few days after getting the bacterial blight spread by the squash beetle. The only recourse in this case is to destroy the plant or shrub promptly, before the disease can spread to nearby plants. Dispose of it in the trash, not the compost pile. Be sure to disinfect any tools, such as shovels and pruning shears, with a spritz of household disinfectant spray or by dipping them in a solution of household bleach and water.

Fungal diseases develop on plants or trees and shrubs gradually, and many of them are more of an aesthetic rather than life-threatening problem. The mildews that cover lilacs and phlox and the leaf spots that mar rose foliage do not kill the plants if they are otherwise healthy. Although it is best, if possible, to identify the disease with the help of a book on the subject or a knowledgeable friend, control measures are similar for them all. Treatment usually involves spraying affected foliage with one of several types of fungicide available by mail order or in garden centers. Sprays must be repeated frequently over the season to achieve control once a fungal disease has become established on a plant.

Most fungal diseases are spread by microscopic spores that float through the air or are bounced up onto the plant from the soil by rain or overhead watering devices. Fungicides

Fungal disease spores are transmitted to a plant by the wind or by water splashed up onto plant foliage from the soil surface by raindrops. Mulch prevents the rain-splashed spores from getting to the plant. A healthy plant is the best defense against wind-carried spores.

can be used as a preventive step on plants such as roses, lilacs, and phlox which are very vulnerable to fungal diseases, or they can be used as a control to stop the spread of the disease and give the plant a chance to overcome the effects of the disease. Two fungicides are listed later in this chapter which are generally effective in controlling the most common fungal diseases found in the home landscape.

SETTING STANDARDS OF DAMAGE

When routine monitoring of the landscape reveals insect pest or disease problems, it is important to decide on a personal tolerance level. How much pest activity is acceptable? At what point is it serious enough to merit the time, energy, and money it will take to treat it? After all, if the goal is a balanced ecosystem in the yard, a certain number of pest insects and a certain incidence of disease will be part of that.

It is impossible and illogical to have zero pest insects. Every property has aphids. Most properties have mites. Lots of properties have slugs. A person who wants a totally pest-free yard should live in a high-rise apartment with an asphalt landscape.

Treatment: Choose Pesticides for Safety and Effectiveness

Homeowners differ on what is an acceptable amount of pest damage. Some are poised to do battle if a few holes appear in the foliage of one or two hosta plants or the green beans. Others are oblivious until the hostas are in shreds and the green bean foliage is lace. It is at some point between these two extremes where a judgment about when to use a pesticide or some other pest-control device must be made. Remember, to keep beneficial insects around, there must be some pest insects available to them for food. If all the bad guys are eliminated, the beneficials move over to the neighbor's yard, leaving your plants more vulnerable to the next pest attack.

Experience is the best guide to the control of pests in the yard. After a few encounters with infestations and observation of how the plant is affected, it is easier to judge when intervention with pesticides is appropriate. In some cases it is not necessary at all. For instance, the best way to deal with aphids on chrysanthemums is to simply pinch off the tender branch tips where they invariably cluster. Mums need to be pinched back several times early in the summer anyway, and the aphid-infested tips can be put in the trash and eliminated. End of problem.

CHOOSING A WEAPON

If it is obvious that a pest infestation is serious enough to merit control action, a pesticide must be selected. This is not a simple task, especially for people who are concerned about safety issues. There are lots of products lining the shelves of the garden center that are labeled by the United States Environmental Protection Agency (EPA) for use on particular insects. The problem is that the average homeowner has no way of evaluating the relative effectiveness and safety of the various products.

Pesticides have been among the hottest topics in the American media over the past few years, and what has resulted from all that attention is much confusion and not just a little hysteria. Finding the facts among all the hype and smoke is next to impossible. This next section offers help in finding the proper pesticide for the pest insect or disease in question—a pesticide that is both safe and effective.

The pesticide product must be safe. Safe for you and safe for the environment. At the same time, the product must be effective in solving the pest problem. It doesn't make much sense to have a very safe product that doesn't kill the pest insect. What is necessary, then, is a product that is simultaneously specific to the pest insect that is the problem (that takes some information), safe for the yard and family, and effective. Here are some tips on how to accomplish all of those objectives.

PESTICIDE SAFETY

The EPA has some very precise and terribly technical definitions of what constitutes safety of a pesticide. In order to meet EPA requirements companies that produce pesticides often invest many years and millions of dollars in testing. They produce copious amounts of technical data also. We have spent many years studying that technical information in an effort to translate it into concepts and principles applicable to our own backyard.

Our operating definition of a safe pesticide is one that kills the target pest insect, disease, or weed efficiently while causing as little harm as possible to the environment. A "safe" pesticide does its job and then biodegrades swiftly. Properly used, it has no toxic effects on people, pets, birds, ground water, and soil life, such as earthworms. Homeowners should be under no illusions, however. Most pesticide products are powerful. They have to be in order to do their job. Therefore it is extremely important that they are used properly. A "safe" pesticide might very well be harmful to a person who drinks a cup of the stuff. It might be harmful to earthworms and other soil life if it is mixed triple strength rather than mixed according to the directions on the label. The discussion in this chapter assumes that the pesticide is used only as it was intended to be used and applied according to the instructions on the label of the product.

IMPACT IN THE ENVIRONMENT. While a pesticide may be relatively safe for humans to use, it may not be acceptable in the home landscape because it has a potential for harming other living things like birds, mammals, fish, earthworms, butterflies, or honeybees. Cats may brush up against a newly sprayed plant and then lick their fur. Birds may peck at pesticide granules or eat slugs that have been poisoned with a pesticide. Dogs may walk on lawns treated with pesticides. It is important to know how each pesticide used will affect the residents of the home landscape.

We do not use or recommend any pesticide that offers any danger to pets, birds, and earthworms. Pesticides dangerous for fish, but in all other respects appearing safe, may be okay to use on properties that are not near ponds or streams. In some cases careful timing can mitigate the dangers of a pesticide. For instance, some of the stronger insecticides kill honeybees and butterflies. If they are used in the late evening when honeybees are in their hives, they will not be harmed. By morning the pesticide, if it is appropriately "safe," should have broken down into its chemical components which would be harmless to those honeybees. Bt (*Bacillus thuringiensis*) kills caterpillars and that includes those that turn into desirable butterflies. The key is to avoid using this biological insecticide on bushes frequented by the butterfly larvae. This is why informed use is so important.

Clearly, the safety of a pesticide has a lot to do with its persistence in the environment. How long does it hang around in its toxic form before breaking down into its basic, less toxic chemical components? The longer it persists in its toxic form, the more danger it represents to innocent passersby of all kinds. One of the reasons DDT was banned was that it retained its toxic power for a long time, long enough to enter the food chain. The faster a pesticide material breaks down, the better. Most of the pesticides recommended in this chapter break down within either hours or just a few days. Those that are more persistent should be used only as a last resort. Even though a product appears to be harmless to all soil organisms, if it persists for more than a few weeks, there is greater opportunity for some unexpected and isolated harmful incident.

POTENTIAL FOR ISOLATED HARM. Finally, there is one indicator of safety that does not lend itself to scientific measurement or that does not fit into a nice neat chart. That is the potential of any particular pesticide for causing some very isolated but harmful impact on a specific person or pet. No matter how carefully any pesticide product is studied, there is always some chance that someone who comes in contact with the substance is going to have a very toxic reaction to the material. The re-

action may be caused by a supersensitivity or allergy to some part of the compound that could not be predicted in the basic research used to test its general impact on people and the environment. Periodically stories appear in the news about someone dying or becoming crippled in some way and a direct or indirect contact with a particular pesticide is suspected. These incidents are very unusual, but they are still disturbing. How can an individual home-owner tell whether she or a member of her family is potentially sensitive to any of the pesticides?

This is a very sensitive area in dealing with the pesticide question. Sometimes these isolated tragedies scare people away from using pesticides that are basically safe, and they suffer economic or environmental loss from a pest problem that could have been easily controlled. It is important to keep these isolated instances in perspective. Many, many more Americans die from honeybee stings than die from exposure or contact with any pesticide. Yet honeybees are not banned, because they are fundamentally valuable environmentally and agriculturally. People who are especially sensitive to them avoid contact with honeybees whenever possible.

In fact, most of the people who are harmed, apparently from a pesticide, are full-time pesticide applicators or are farm workers using the materials for hours and days at a time in a very concentrated fashion. Many of these workers apply pesticides without appropriate protective clothing and without care to the potential danger of using the concentrated materials. The number of pesticide incidents among private homeowners using a product as directed on the label of the bottle or package is very small indeed.

Logic suggests that allergic readers who are particularly sensitive to various foods, pollens, and chemicals may be wise to minimize their contact with the more powerful chemical pesticides as a matter of course. Children, whether they are allergic or not, should not be allowed to play in areas that have been sprayed with any pesticide, no matter how "safe" it is proven to be. The cat and the dog should be kept in the house until all pesticides have dried completely. These are the same kind of common-sense precautions taken when filling a lawn mower with gasoline, when painting in a closed area, or when cleaning the oven.

Most pesticides available to the homeowner from normal retail and mail-order channels are perfectly safe if used and stored properly. There are a few products that are sufficiently toxic and offer enough evidence of potential harm that they should be used only by professionals trained to use pesticides and should not be used in the home landscape. While not enough is known yet about those products to suggest they should be banned from all use, we believe they should not be used in the home landscape. Those products are not mentioned at all in this book. That does not mean that if a product is not mentioned in this book it is harmful. It does mean that only those products that satisfy the criteria mentioned above on

safety for use by homeowners in residential landscapes are included.

PESTICIDE EFFECTIVENESS

Homeowners need safe pesticides but also ones that do the job. A very safe product that is only sometimes effective is not a terribly attractive solution to a pest problem. How is it possible to find out if a product is in fact potentially effective against whichever pest needs to be controlled? It is not easy. The effectiveness of a particular pesticide used to control a particular pest is a function of its appropriateness for that target pest and its proper use in the right environmental conditions. Insecticidal soap is effective in controlling aphids, but it must have direct contact with the aphid. No contact means no effectiveness. It is most effective if it is used on young aphids; old aphids take a few applications. It must be mixed according to instructions. If the mix is too strong it may kill the aphid but also might harm the leaves of the plant.

BASIC MEDICINE KIT FOR LANDSCAPE

In spite of all the confusion about determining what is safe and what is effective, it is possible to recommend to homeowners certain pesticides that are appropriate for residential use. Just as we have the household medicine cabinet in the bathroom that contains standard home health products, every property owner should have a landscape medicine cabinet. The generic products listed on page 194 comprise a basic arsenal for handling the problems that typically develop in yards. Most of these products are made by more than one manufacturer, and wherever possible options are indicated. There is a resource list in the appendix that gives mail-order sources for all these pesticides. Most of them, however, are found in the better garden centers and hardware stores throughout the country.

This selection of products provides the tools necessary to address most of the common insect pest and disease problems homeowners are likely to confront over the years. Obviously, there will be specific situations where additional products will be needed, but for general pest control needs, this collection of pesticides offers a good basic start for handling the most common problems. The chart on page 195 indicates roughly which insecticide is effective with which of the more common insects.

All these products, except Bt, can be stored indefinitely in a dark, dry place not subject to major temperature variations. The Bt contains bacteria and so should probably be replaced each year to assure potency.

LIMIT THE RESPONSE

An important principle in this approach to pest control is to, whenever possible, limit treatment to the immediate area or plant that is infected with a disease or a pest insect. Use spot treatment of insect problems rather than spraying a pesticide, even a safe pesticide all over the yard, "just to be sure." Remember, the natural balance of beneficial insects and pest insects is fairly delicate. Spot applications of a pesticide will seldom upset that balance. Broad, area-wide applications can very well upset that balance and create more pest problems next month.

	HORTICULTURAL OIL	INSECTICIDAL SOAP	PYRETHRUM	Bt
Ants			x	
Aphids	x	x	x	
Bagworms				x
Beetles		x	x	
Caterpillars				x
Flea beetles			x	
Gypsy moths				x
Japanese beetles			x	
Lace bugs			x	
Leaf miners			x	
Leafhoppers			x	
Mealybugs		x	x	
Mites	x	x	x	
Scale	x	x	x	
Thrips			x	
Webworms				x
Weevils			x	
Whiteflies	x	x	x	

Analyze the Cause

Once a pest problem is noticed, the culprit identified, and the pesticide selected, the problem is as good as solved—or is it? Responding to curled leaves on the viburnum by spraying the visible black aphids on the leaf undersides will probably eliminate those pests. However, the "problem" of the curling leaves is not necessarily solved by killing the aphids. The aphids are really only a symptom of a larger problem, just like a cough is only a symptom of a cold. The plant has aphids for some reason that needs to be understood in order to truly solve the "problem."

Spraying pest insects or diseases with a pes-

When a pest problem requires the use of a pesticide, the pesticide should be used only on the affected plant. Every effort should be made to avoid broadly spraying any pesticide around the landscape.

ticide sets them back for the short term, but over the long term they are likely to return unless the viburnum's underlying problem is addressed. Ultimately, the most important pest-control step is the one that follows the spraying, namely, analyzing the underlying cause of the pest insect or disease problem. By identifying the cause of the shrub's vulnerability to aphids, it may be possible to avoid a return of the problem.

This is not always easy, and sometimes it is just not possible. But what are some of the possibilities?

The primary cause of insect and disease outbreaks on individual plants is that they are located in the wrong place. This is also true of houseplants. A troubled plant may be vulnerable because it gets too much sun, or not enough sun. It may be in soil that is too wet, or is exposed to too much wind. So the first diagnostic question to ask is, is this plant vulnerable because it is struggling with undesirable growing conditions?

Next, ask whether it is an inappropriate plant for the region where it is growing. Perhaps this variety is chronically susceptible to aphids in certain climates. Maybe there is a better variety of this plant that is bred to be resistant to aphids. After that, evaluate the care that the vulnerable plant has received. Is it fertilized properly? Is it possible that the soil pH has changed over the years? Is the soil around the roots compacted? Does it get sufficient water? These and the other variables, which have been discussed in the previous chapters on basic plant care, directly affect plant vigor. The bottom line is a plant that is not healthy and happy will not be able to fend off pest attacks successfully.

In the end, it is not necessary to diagnose the underlying cause of pest problems in individual plants every time. But if a holly on the property develops scale year in and year out, then it's a good bet that something is fundamentally wrong within its environment. It may be time to look further for ways to correct the situation, maybe by calling in a gardener neighbor, the extension agent, or a professional horticulturist. Simply fighting the scale does nothing to truly make that plant healthier.

Discovering that the pH of the soil is alkaline and the holly wants acid may very well eliminate the scale problem for good.

DEALING WITH ANIMAL PESTS

This chapter deals primarily with insect pests and diseases; however, pest animals can drive a caring homeowner to distraction. The prevention principles outlined at the beginning of this chapter apply to preventing animal as well as insect pests. The steps for controlling the problems, however, are not necessarily identical.

With animals, be they squirrels, moles, deer, or something else, the big question is how much damage to tolerate before taking action. A few holes in the flower bed probably do not merit a declaration of war on the total local squirrel population. On the other hand, if entire shrubs are disappearing, the deer problem may deserve immediate serious attention.

At the back of this book is a list of supplemental tip sheets dealing with the most common animal pests. Each tip sheet provides detailed descriptions of the options available for gaining control of pest animals, such as deer, moles, rabbits, squirrels, and others.

POSSIBLE PEST VISITORS TO THE YARD

Of all the hundreds of potential culprits, a pest visitor in the yard is most likely to be one of about twenty common types of insects. Below is a list of these familiar pests and a brief discussion of each.

ANT

Description: Ants may be black, brown, or red, either with or without wings. True insects, they have six jointed legs and segmented bodies with enlarged abdomens. They may be from one-sixth to one-quarter inch long.

Symptoms: More a nuisance than a danger, ants cause damage to ornamental plants indirectly. Their mounds and tunnels mar lawns, disturbing grass roots. Their presence on the tender new growth of plants usually signals the presence of aphids which they herd in order to feed on the "honeydew" that aphids excrete. Carpenter ants tunnel in the heartwood of tree trunks, weakening them and making them vulnerable to other pests and storm damage.

Control: Control ants in lawns by pouring insecticidal soap, pyrethrum, carbaryl, malathion, chlorpyrifos, or boiling water into their nests. Encourage birds such as woodpeckers, juncos, mockingbirds, flickers, nuthatches, orioles, and chipping sparrows to visit the yard.

APHIDS

Description: Aphids are soft-bodied, pear-shaped insects a little bigger than the head of a pin. They may be yellow, black, brown, or green, and cluster on stems and under leaves to suck juices from tender, young plant tissues.

Symptoms: Foliage infested with aphids curls, puckers, and turns yellow. Ants, attracted by the aphids' honeydew secretions, are often

Although there seems to be a type of aphid for just about every plant, they are not always a problem in the yard. Typically, aphids will cluster at the tips of tender new shoots to suck juices and are quite visible to the observant homeowner.

visible on affected plants. Check leaf undersides for small groups of aphids. Various species of aphids attack a wide variety of ornamental and vegetable plants.

Control: Pinch off stem tips that are covered with aphids and discard them in a plastic bag. Spray heavier infestations with insecticidal soap every two to three days. Spray stubborn infestations with pyrethrum, carbaryl, or malathion. Spray late in the day to minimize danger to nearby beneficial insects.

BAGWORMS
Description: Bagworms are dark-brown caterpillars with white or yellow heads. They hide in cocoons, or bags, made of silk and bits of leaves or needles attached to the outside in which they feed and reproduce. Eventually they emerge as moths. A fully developed bag

is about two inches long and protects up to one thousand eggs over the winter, which hatch the following spring. Bagworms feed on shrubs and trees and are capable of killing them if left uncontrolled.

Symptoms: Small spindle-shaped bags hanging from the branches of trees and shrubs indicate the presence of bagworms.

Control: During the winter handpick the visible bags and burn them. In the late spring and early summer, after the caterpillars emerge and begin eating, spray the foliage with Bt (*Bacillus thuringiensis*) at ten-day intervals through mid-July. When they ingest it, Bt sickens and kills the caterpillars.

BORERS
Description: There are many kinds of borers that feed on ornamental and vegetable plants. They are the larvae of moths and beetles. The stalk borer is brownish with white stripes. Its head may be black or yellow. The iris borer is a slender green worm that becomes fat and smoothly pink with black spots on its side as it matures. The European corn borer is a grayish pink caterpillar with spots on each of its segments and a black head. The lilac borer is pale yellow with numerous black spots.

Symptoms: These wormlike larvae typically burrow into plant stems to feed. They usually overwinter as eggs either in grasses or foliage near the host plant, on bark surfaces, or in stems. The larvae burrow into plant tissues, carving out galleries and tunnels in branches and stems. Borer attacks cause rough knotlike swellings on the trunks and older limbs of woody plants like lilacs. Infested branches often wilt, and are frequently so weakened by the boring that they break. Sawdust hangs at the openings made by the borers. In flowers and vegetables, they chew on foliage and burrow into stems, weakening them and often killing the plant. They often open the way for other pests and diseases to attack the host. Lilacs, rhododendrons, corn, irises, dahlias, delphiniums, bee balm, chrysanthemums, phlox, salvia, asters, columbines, and birch trees are favorite borer targets. Newly transplanted trees are quite vulnerable to borer infestation.

Control: It is difficult to control borers once they have entered plant stems. Start early in the season to catch them before they begin the season's work. Thoroughly inspect trees and shrubs before the spring season arrives and cut and burn any dying stems and twigs below visible borer holes. In June, crush any eggs on bark surfaces. Clean up all garden debris such as grasses and dead leaves and weeds that may harbor overwintering eggs. During the summer season, check to see if fine boring dust is being pushed from small borer holes. Probe tunnels which are fairly straight with a flexible wire to crush any borers inside. Wrap the trunks and major limbs of newly transplanted trees with Tree Wrap, burlap, or wrapping paper, overlapping it to block access by borers while the tree is vulnerable. Spray Bt (*Bacillus thuringiensis*) on the foliage of plants while borers are feeding on them. Sometimes splitting the stalks of infested flower and vegetable plants, removing the borer and binding the stalk back up with tape is effective. Beneficial insects such as ladybugs and ground beetles are effective against the stalk borer.

CATERPILLARS

Description. Caterpillars are the larvae of various moths and butterflies that frequent the yard. They are usually about two inches long at maturity and sport as varied decoration as their flying parents. Tomato hornworms are green with seven or eight white stripes and a black horn projecting from their rear segment. Parsley worms are green with white-spotted black bands on each body segment. Eastern tent caterpillars are hairy and black with white stripes and narrow brown and yellow lines and a row of blue spots on their sides. Rose budworms are green with elongated black spots or whitish orange markings on their backs. These and other caterpillars all share a fondness for plant foliage. While in this larval stage they have enormous appetites and will eat voraciously.

Symptoms: Chewed leaves and/or buds, and telltale webs or nests among the foliage indicate the presence of a caterpillar of some kind. Leaves may be chewed around the edges or fully skeletonized in a matter of hours.

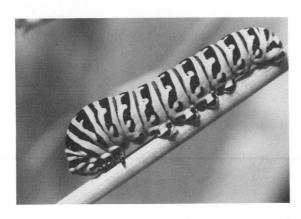

This caterpillar favors the foliage of celery, parsley, and carrots. Because it eventually turns into the beautiful swallowtail butterfly many homeowners are inclined to tolerate its presence.

Control: Pick off all visible caterpillars within reach. Cut out and destroy the infested buds, leaves, and webbed tents. Spray or dust the foliage or infested plants with Bt (*Bacillus thuringiensis*) during the period that the caterpillars are feeding. They will ingest the bacterium, sicken and die. Repeat the Bt sprays after rains and every ten to fourteen days until the symptoms and the caterpillars disappear. If the caterpillar infestation is so overwhelming as to threaten the life of the tree or shrub, spray its leaves, top and bottom, with pyrethrum, carbaryl, or malathion. Be sure the spray contacts the pests. Usually two applications, three to four days apart, are enough to get the numbers back down so the Bt can keep them in control.

CUCUMBER BEETLES
Description: Cucumber beetles may be spotted or striped. They are yellow or greenish yellow with black heads and black markings.

From a quarter to a half inch long, they have yellowish white or beige larvae.

Symptoms: Adult cucumber beetles chew holes in the leaves, flowers, and fruit of a wide variety of ornamental and vegetable plants. Some introduce brown rot into stone fruits, like peaches and apricots. They especially like corn, tomatoes, eggplant, melons, squash, cucumbers, peas, beans, dahlias, chrysanthemums, daylilies, and coreopsis. Their larvae feed on the roots and stems of plants early in the growing season.

Control: Handpick any visible beetles immediately and drop them into a jar of soapy water to drown. Introduce beneficial nematodes into the soil to attack the grubs. Packaged in powder, they are mixed with water and sprayed on the soil. For long-term control inoculate the soil in the yard with milky spore disease (*Bacillus popilliae*) which will eliminate grubs in a few years. In the spring gently cultivate the soil around the shrubs to expose any beetle eggs or larvae to the weather and to predator birds such as evening grosbeaks, juncos, rufous-sided towhees, nuthatches, brown thrashers, eastern bluebirds, mockingbirds, robins, flickers, Steller's jays, orioles, and chipping sparrows.

FLEA BEETLES
Description: Flea beetles are tiny. Only one-tenth of an inch long, they are shiny black

with curved stripes of yellow or white. They jump like fleas when disturbed.

Symptoms: These adults and their larvae feed on the plant foliage, leaving tiny pinholes and making the leaves look freckled. Broccoli, cabbage, cauliflower, eggplant, and many other vegetable plants are favorite hosts. These insects also transmit plant diseases.

Control: Clean up garden debris to remove overwintering eggs. Because flea beetles thrive in hot, dry conditions, mist plants with water during the hottest part of the day to raise the humidity around them. Cover crops with white polyspun agricultural fleece to protect them from infestation. If plants are attacked, spray foliage with two sprays of pyrethrum, carbaryl, or malathion, three or four days apart. Spray late in the day to minimize damage to nearby beneficial insects.

GRUBS

Description: Grubs are the larval stage of various kinds of beetles, such as those described above. The adult beetles lay eggs in the soil or grass sod in midsummer, and they hatch wormlike larvae that nestle in the soil in a curled position and feed on plant roots through the winter. Grubs are usually three-quarters to one and a half inches long at maturity. Plump and whitish, they have three pairs of legs and brown heads.

Symptoms: Lawn grass that is affected by grubs develops irregular brown patches which appear to be scorched. This sod lifts up easily, its roots having been destroyed. Often grubs are visible in the soil just beneath it in the late spring or early fall. The presence of grubs is often signaled by mole or skunk activity in the yard. These animals seek out and feed on grubs. Ornamental plants that suffer grub attacks wilt and look sickly. Bulbs that have been planted in areas formerly covered with grass are vulnerable to grub attack, as they feed on bulbs and roots.

Control: Control grub population in the soil by attracting predator birds such as starlings or blackbirds. For long-term treatment, inoculate the lawn soil with milky spore disease (*Bacillus popilliae*). The bacterium infests grubs, decimating the population within two or three years. For more immediate effect, introduce beneficial nematodes into the soil. Packaged in powder, they are mixed with water and sprayed on the soil. Dursban also kills grubs on contact.

GYPSY MOTHS

Description: Found in the eastern United States, gypsy moth larvae are caterpillars that grow to about 2½ inches, with five pairs of blue spots and six pairs of red spots along their backs. They climb from hiding places on the ground into the trees and feed all night. They can defoliate a mature tree in two weeks. While they often recover and develop new leaves, infested trees and shrubs may die after repeated defoliation. Adult male moths are light tan to dark brown with wingspans of 1½ inches. They have blackish wavy bands across the forewings. Female moths are larger, nearly white, with 2½-inch wings and feathered antennae. They do not fly. Their egg masses are covered with velvety, buff-colored hairs, and contain four hundred to five hundred eggs. Gypsy moth caterpillars are most active from late April to mid-June. In July, they encase themselves in brown shells to pupate, eventually emerging as moths.

Symptoms: Damage will not be immediately noticeable, since the young larvae feed only around leaf edges. Once an infestation is established and the caterpillars grow, it is possible to see masses of caterpillars feeding and to hear their excrement dropping from branches. Their favorite is oak, but gypsy moth caterpillars will eat a wide range of foliage, including evergreens such as juniper. Gypsy moth larvae are often confused with the eastern tent caterpillar and fall webworm, both of which make silken tents in trees. Gypsy moths do not make tents.

Control: Handpick caterpillars within reach and drop them into a jar of soapy water to drown. Spray affected tree and shrub foliage with Bt (*Bacillus thuringiensis*) just as the new caterpillars emerge and begin to feed. When they ingest it, the bacteria will kill them in a matter of days. Spray two or three times more

at five-day intervals, repeating after a rainfall. Wrap the trunks of large trees with bands of sticky tape available at garden centers to trap the caterpillars as they climb up to feed at night. Crush any egg masses found on tree trunks during the winter.

JAPANESE BEETLES

Description: Adult Japanese beetles are a half inch long, with shiny metallic green and copper brown wing covers. Their larvae (grubs) are grayish white worms, with dark brown heads. Fully grown grubs are plump, three quarters to one inch long, and lie in the soil in the distinctive arc-shaped resting posture and feed on plant roots (see Grubs on page 201).

Symptoms: Japanese beetles emerge from the soil or lawn at the end of June or early July and promptly seek out plant leaves and/or flowers. They feed in groups, often piled on one another and are visible from several feet. They chew large holes in petals and foliage, often completely skeletonizing leaves. They crowd onto rosebuds and devour them before they have an opportunity to open. The number one insect pest of roses in many parts of the United States, they also like apple trees, cherry trees, grapes, raspberries, rhubarb, green beans, lindens, elms, maples, birches, black walnuts, mountain ash, and many other plants.

Control: To control Japanese beetles, set up pheromone beetle traps a week before expected emergence in your area, making sure traps are no closer than fifty feet from the rose bed or any other plant vulnerable to beetle attack, such as raspberries. (Some beetles are attracted to but miss the trap, so having the trap too close to a target plant can make the situation worse instead of better.) Several times a day, if possible, handpick accessible ones as they feed and drop them into a jar of soapy water to drown. If they appear in overwhelming numbers, spray them with insecticidal soap that is combined with pyrethrum, carbaryl, or malathion.

Using the Japanese beetle traps for three to five years will significantly reduce the beetle population on your property, especially if they are put out the minute the first beetle is spotted. Be tolerant of starlings in the yard because they will eat Japanese beetles. In cases of serious chronic infestations, consider inoculating the lawn with milky spore disease (*Bacillus popilliae*). This disease attacks beetle grubs. It takes a year or two to be effective, but then it lasts for many years.

LACE BUGS
Description: Adult lace bugs are small square-shaped bugs, three-sixteenths of an inch long or less, with elaborately reticulated wings that resemble lacework. Eggs hatch in May, then young bugs begin to feed on leaf undersides.

Symptoms: These bugs feed by sucking juices from foliage tissues. Leaves of affected plants turn pale, their upper surfaces mottled with whitish dots, their undersides covered with tiny bugs, accompanied by numerous brown specks of their excrement. From a distance affected plants appear to be off-color, the foliage dull and stained. Favorites of lace bugs are rhododendrons and azaleas, chrysanthemums, oaks, asters, sedums, snapdragons, verbena, and others.

Control: These pests are effectively controlled by spraying them with malathion or carbaryl. Follow the directions on the product label carefully. Spray late in the day to avoid harming nearby beneficial insects.

LEAFHOPPERS
Description: There are lots of different kinds of leafhoppers which injure trees, shrubs, flowers, and vegetables. Most are greenish yellow to brown and blunt-profiled, and they range from one-eighth to one-third inches long. They are slender and wedge-shaped, and hold their wings in a rooflike position above their bodies. They're very active, moving sideways or hopping suddenly when disturbed. Both nymphs and adults suck juices from plant leaves, buds, and stems. Eggs hatch in May and young insects feed on leaf undersides.

Symptoms: Infested foliage becomes stippled and distorted. The leaves eventually shrivel and drop off. Honeydew from the insects' feeding may give foliage a glazed appearance and foster growth of sooty mold. Because certain leafhoppers transmit disease to host plants,

Leaf miner pests damage plant leaves by tunneling into their cells and sucking the juices found there. They leave behind pale, dry tissues that trace their progress and mar the appearance of the foliage. Columbine, pictured here, is a favorite host of leaf miners.

affected plants often become stunted and deformed. Among the plants pestered occasionally by leafhoppers are beans, celery, rhubarb, potatoes, beets, eggplant, asters, coreopsis, dahlias, lobelia, phlox, poppies, black-eyed Susans, dianthus, roses, salvia, some maples, hawthorns, poplars, and willows.

Control: For chronic leafhopper problems, devise a protective cover for target plants from agricultural fleece. Put this over the plants in the early spring to prevent access by leafhoppers when they hatch. Spray bugs on infested plants with insecticidal soap laced with isopropyl alcohol (mix 1 tablespoon alcohol to 1 quart of commercial soap spray). Encourage chickadees, purple finches, sparrows, swallows, and wrens to visit the yard. Several beneficial insects such as lacewings and trichogramma wasps prey on leafhoppers.

LEAF MINERS

Description: Leaf miners are larvae of various insects such as beetles, sawflies, moths, and small black flies. They hatch from eggs laid on the undersides of plant leaves into small yellowish white, greenish, or black maggots, about an eighth of an inch long. They burrow inside leaf tissues for about a week. As they feed, they carve out tunnels and blotches that show on leaf surfaces as brown or white winding lines. Some leaf miner species produce five or six generations a year.

Symptoms: Leaves of affected plants develop telltale winding trails or blotches on their surfaces. Some leaves may be so infested that they develop a blistered appearance, while some turn white and die. Often the leaves persist on the plant all season. Favorite hosts of leaf miners are holly, columbines, beans, blackberries, cabbage, potatoes, peppers, spinach, chrysanthemums, delphiniums, verbena, coralbells, baby's breath, and primroses.

Control: Remove and trash (do not compost) all affected leaves. If necessary, prune back branches until healthy growth remains. Remove severely damaged bushes. Clean up all weeds and garden debris to control overwintering eggs. Larvae can sometimes be repelled by spraying shrubs or trees with an insecticidal soap solution in late June or early July. Cover plants that have chronic problems with leaf miners with agricultural fleece to prevent the flies from laying eggs on plant leaves. Malathion spray, begun two weeks before female flies are active (mid-May in Ohio) and repeated every three to six days for a month or six weeks will kill the leaf miners.

MEALYBUGS

Description: More of a problem in the South, mealybugs are a fifth to a third of an inch long, with oval, flattened bodies. They are adorned with short, soft spines along the edges of their bodies and covered with white, waxy powder. These pests gather in cottony white masses on plant roots, and along stems, branches, and the veins of leaves, sucking sap and reducing plant vigor. They produce two or three generations a year.

Symptoms: Mealybugs are visible as clusters of white cottony fuzz on stems and leaf veins. Infested plants wilt, and may eventually be-

come stunted. They are unsightly and do not grow well. Honeydew secretions from the insects' feeding encourage mold growth on the foliage and attract ants. Various mealybug species attack holly, citrus, columbines, grapes, violets, chrysanthemums, sunflowers, primroses, salvia, verbena, and many greenhouse plants in the North.

Control: Control mealybugs by spraying them with an alcohol-insecticidal soap spray every two to three days until the pests disappear (mix 1 tablespoon of isopropyl alcohol with one pint of insecticidal soap mix). Malathion is also an effective control. Spray foliage and stems of infested shrubs with a light horticultural oil in March or April, just before new growth starts, to kill overwintering eggs.

MITES

Description: Mites are spiderlike insects, about one-fiftieth of an inch long, or the size of a grain of pepper. They may be yellow, green, red, or brown and are always found on the undersides of leaves. They flourish in hot, dry conditions, and in situations where the use of pesticides has eliminated their competition and natural predators. Always a problem in greenhouses, in many outdoor areas they are now a major pest of ornamental plants.

Symptoms: Two-spotted spider mites and the red spider mite stipple and discolor leaves as they suck the juices from them. As the infestation proceeds, leaves become spotted red, yellow, or brown, curl, and drop off. Flowers fade or become distorted, and plants may become stunted. Mites spin telltale webs across leaf surfaces and on new growth. Few ornamental plants are truly immune from mite attack if conditions are favorable. Common targets are roses, columbines, daylilies, dahlias, delphiniums, irises, phlox, verbena, salvia, pansies, and chrysanthemums, as well as many evergreen shrubs, like holly, and shade trees.

Control: Start control measures as soon as stippling on foliage is noticed. Spray infested bushes in the early morning with a forceful water spray to knock the mites from leaf undersides. Repeat the water spray daily for three days. If that doesn't do the job, spray the mites with insecticidal soap every three to five days for two weeks. Avoid overuse of insecticides in the yard. Keep foliage of affected plants moist during dry periods. A spray of light horticultural oil, applied in March or April before new growth starts, destroys many overwintering mites on trees and shrubs.

NEMATODES

Description: Nematodes are slender, unsegmented roundworms. Most are soil dwellers, less than a twentieth of an inch long, and are invisible to the unaided eye. While certain species are beneficial, many others are harmful to plants because they attack roots underground, feeding on tissue and sometimes introducing disease.

Symptoms: Shrubs infested with nematodes look sickly, wilted, or stunted, with yellowed or bronzed foliage. They decline slowly and die. Root systems are poorly developed, even partially decayed. They may smell badly from secondary infections introduced by the nematodes. Roots have knots or galls on them. Effects of nematode activity are most apparent in hot weather, when plants fail to recover promptly from the heat. Root knot nematodes are rose pests. They also attack abelias, barberries, clematis, citrus trees, dahlias, delphiniums, forsythias, gladioli, hydrangeas, Japanese holly, lawn grass, pachysandra, peonies, poppies, geraniums, mock oranges, marigolds, vinca, verbena, weigela, and many other plants.

Control: If it is available, add lots of compost (especially leaf mold) to the soil around plants to encourage the growth of beneficial fungi that attack nematodes. Fertilize with fish emulsion diluted with water, drenching the soil around each affected bush. Dig out and remove any plants that have died from nematodes with the soil that surrounds the infected root systems. Discard them in the trash.

SCALE

Description: Scale insects are tiny insects that spend most of their lives protected by small, round waxy shells. These shells may be hard and reddish brown, or soft pale bumps. They appear on plant leaves or clustered in the crotches of twigs and along branches and where leaves are attached to stems. Scale insects suck plant juices, sometimes introducing toxins into the host plant at the same time.

Symptoms: The first sign of a scale attack is often discoloration of the upper leaf surface, followed by wilting. This is followed by leaf drop, reduced growth, and stunted plants. Heavy infestations of this pest kill plants. Some species excrete honeydew, which coats foliage and encourages ants and sooty mold growth. White, cottony, or woolly masses appear on twigs, usually in the crotches or close to the buds of plants. Various types of scale affect many plants, among them peonies, bee balm, sunflowers, verbena, phlox, ash, black locust, elms, euonymus, grapes, citrus trees, and fruit and nut trees.

Control: Scrape scale bumps off plant surfaces with a fingernail or a cotton swab dipped in isopropyl (rubbing) alcohol. Spray heavily infested plants with a mixture of alcohol and insecticidal soap every three days for two weeks (mix 1 tablespoon of isopropyl alcohol to a pint of the premixed commercial soap spray to help the soap penetrate the protective shells). For chronic scale problems, spray affected plants with horticultural oil during the winter to smother overwintering scale eggs.

Use light or superior type oil on evergreens, heavy or dormant oil on deciduous trees and shrubs. Clean up yard and garden debris.

SLUGS

Description: Slugs are essentially snails without shells. Most are one to two inches long, but some have been known to reach a length of eight inches. They may be white, gray, yellow, or brown-black with various pale markings. Moist, well-mulched gardens with acidic soil present the ideal environment for these pests; they love rainy days. They feed on plant foliage at night, and hide during the day under leaves, boards, and other yard debris.

Symptoms: Plants attacked by slugs show large, ragged holes in their foliage. Sometimes whole seedlings are devoured. Often a telltale shiny trail of mucous indicates that slugs have traveled in the area. They begin feeding at the bottom of a plant and work their way up. Favorites of slugs are tomatoes, hostas, hollyhocks, sedums, primroses, delphiniums, pansies, bellfowers, daylilies, irises, begonias, lettuce, strawberries, roses, snapdragons, and rhododendrons.

Control: The best way to control slugs and snails is to trap them with either homemade or commercial traps. Fill a pie plate or some other shallow container with beer. Slugs will be attracted to the yeast and drown. Refill the pan after rainfall. Use these traps early in the season to catch newcomers and discourage a population explosion in the yard. Two cultivars of hosta, 'Invincible' and 'Sum and Substance', are resistant to slug attack.

THRIPS
Description: Adult thrips are tiny, slender insects, one-twenty-fifth of an inch long, variously colored pale yellow, black, or brown. They have four long, narrow wings fringed with long hairs and very short legs. New generations of thrips appear every two or three weeks. They tend to concentrate in clusters on plants where they rasp plant tissues, then suck the juices that leak out. Thrips deposit copious amounts of excrement at feeding sites which causes additional damage to plants. Thrips populations sometimes swarm in fields and are carried on the wind to new areas. Thrips also may carry viral diseases to plants.

Symptoms: Plants attacked by thrips have leaves and petals that are dried out and silvery in appearance. Sometimes leaves blacken from dying tissue, and flowers and buds are distorted or streaked. Dirty spots of excrement may be visible, even though the thrips usually are not. A favorite target of thrips are roses, especially red, white, yellow, and other light-colored varieties. Thrips disfigure buds and petals. The buds become deformed and fail to open properly, while the damaged petals turn brown and dry. New growth also may be damaged in the same way. Various thrips species attack citrus trees, grapes, peach trees, dahlias, bellflowers, foxgloves, hollyhocks, onions, peonies, daylilies, verbena, irises, gladioli, chrysanthemums, laurels, and privet.

Control: Since thrips burrow deeply between flower petals, early identification and control is important. Set out yellow sticky traps around roses or other hosts about four weeks after the last frost as early warning devices. As soon as thrips show on the trap, spray buds with insecticidal soap with an equal amount of pyrethrum added every three days for two weeks. Commercially available predatory mites, lacewings, ladybugs, and beneficial nematodes are effective backups to the soap spray. Thrips prefer a dry environment, so make sure plants are adequately misted and/or watered. Since thrips are equally at home on weeds, keep the yard clear of weeds and plant debris.

WEEVILS
Description: Weevils are about a quarter inch long, varying from light to dark brown, with fine, parallel impressed lines on their wing covers. They are sometimes called snout beetles because their heads are elongated into long, slender, downward-curved snouts. They commonly live under tree bark or in other plant tissues and feed mostly on foliage. Weevils emerge from the soil to feed by midsummer, concentrated in a fairly limited area because they don't have functional wings. Some types feed in the daytime, others only at night. They

chew large notched holes along the edges of leaves, but some types of weevils drill holes in flower buds, fruits, and vegetables, and scar seedpods. As grubs they often attack plant roots as well.

Symptoms: Ornamental plants victimized by weevils usually show ragged foliage, and closer examination reveals the classic notched leaf edges. In advanced cases the whole leaf may be devoured except for the midribs and large veins. Weevils of various kinds may be found on rhododendrons, columbines, daylilies, sunflowers, potentillas, coralbells, lilies-of-the-valley, veronica, chrysanthemums, lupines, peonies, roses, primroses, hollyhocks, fruit trees, beans, peas, cabbage, carrots, lettuce, potatoes, radishes, tomatoes, turnips, arborvitae, Douglas firs, cedars, willows, pines, poplars, and privet.

Control: Many weevil species "play dead" when disturbed, folding their legs and dropping off plants to the ground. Gently beat the branches of the infested bush and catch the startled insects when they fall in a cloth spread beneath the shrub. Apply Tanglefoot to the trunks of shrubs to prevent the adults from climbing up and eating the leaves. As soon as weevils appear, begin spraying weekly with pyrethrum, carbaryl, or malathion mixed with a small amount of isopropyl alcohol which improves the pesticide's penetration. Cover all leaf surfaces to get any weevils that have not dropped to the ground. For some weevil infestations, sabadilla dusted on the shrub is a better solution. Introduce predatory nematodes (they're available commercially) into the soil around the shrub to attack the feeding grubs.

WHITEFLIES

Description: Adult whiteflies, their presence clearly visible on leaf undersides, are white-winged, mothlike insects about one-sixteenth inch long. Their bodies and double sets of wings are coated with white wax. In their pupal stage they are oval and greenish white. It is not uncommon for several whiteflies in several stages of growth to be on the same leaf, including a circle of eggs. Adults suck juices from plant tissues, producing copious amounts of honeydew as they feed. Bump or brush branches of an infested plant or shrub and they will suddenly fly up, looking like airborne dandruff.

Symptoms: Plants infested with whiteflies have gradually yellowing foliage, the leaf surfaces being covered with yellowish mottling where the juices have been sucked out. Eventually sticky honeydew coats the leaves, which in turn encourages the development of sooty mold. The mold darkens the leaves and blocks the light from them, causing stunting of the affected plant. A major pest in greenhouses, whiteflies may also be found outdoors on a wide variety of vegetable plants, especially tomatoes, as well as shrubs and flowers such as salvia, verbena, chrysanthemums, black-eyed Susans, fuchsias, lantana, coleus, and others.

Control: Hang yellow sticky traps near plants where whiteflies are suspected. Encourage common songbirds to visit the yard. Spray infestations of whiteflies with insecticidal soap spray every three to five days for two weeks. If that doesn't work, spray the whiteflies with pyrethrum, carbaryl, or malathion every five days for two weeks as a last resort.

CHAPTER 7
Value of Landscaping

The sum of all its plants—lawn grass, ground covers, trees and shrubs, flowers, and vegetables—plus the sum of all its parts—space, topography, buildings, walkways—equals a home landscape. The previous chapters have addressed the choice, uses, and care of plants in the home landscape, and now it is time to discuss integrating plants with the more permanent features of a property. This chapter looks at the yard as a whole and suggests ways to combine all the elements of a property in a way that works for a busy homeowner.

Landscaping is a process. Whether it is done by a professional or a homeowner, landscaping is adjusting, changing, or even completely remaking the way a yard looks and works. Landscaping can be as minor as adding a shrub to the front yard or as major as regrading and replanting a whole area or adding many trees and shrubs to accent or screen a brand-new swimming pool from public view. Regardless of how extensive the changes are, the home-owner has the central role in the landscaping process. Because you live on the property, you know it best and are in a position to identify its problems and possibilities. You will be involved in the planning phase of landscaping for sure, and, for less complex jobs, may choose to do the actual work as well.

This chapter offers some ways to think about a home landscape. Unlike most other discussions of landscaping which assume that beauty is the primary goal of a landscape design, ours will take a pragmatic, functional viewpoint. Our assumption is that a landscape should first and foremost work for the people who live there. Its elements should be integrated in such a way that it is comfortable, safe, convenient, and easy to care for. While aesthetics are an important consideration, we feel that they are secondary. As a result, this chapter discusses landscape planning from a functional perspective recommending several ways to think about the yard.

First, evaluate the yard in terms of the plants

Functional, safe, comfortable landscapes do not have to be elaborate. Here the lawn area is reduced by large beds of ground cover.

and how they make the yard more comfortable and accessible. Ask yourself, how can plants be added or moved to contribute to the comfort and usefulness of the various parts of the property? Think about the practical parts of the yard, such as utility and recreational areas. Are they situated in such a way as to contribute to the convenience of the yard? Next, think about the value and function of various landscape systems, such as irrigation and lighting. Would their presence make the yard more comfortable and useful? Then, determine what problems exist in the landscape. Are there drainage, soil, or water problems that need to be corrected? Going through this exercise facilitates the planning process, making final decisions much easier.

Whether landscaping is done all at once or spread over several seasons to ease the pain on the pocketbook, it is important to have a coherent plan at the outset. The more thinking done at the beginning, the less problematic and frustrating the experience will be. Landscaping is much like renovating the interior of the house; it entails an inevitable amount of inconvenience, dirt, and disruption. The final result, however, usually makes all the hassle worthwhile.

A PRACTICAL APPROACH TO LANDSCAPE DESIGN

Our practical, functional approach to thinking about the landscape assumes that most homeowners and yardeners know best how they want their yard to work and that, in most cases, it is not necessary to hire a professional designer or architect to come in and do a design. Exceptions, of course, are major projects in which engineering, plumbing, or electricity are involved, or if extensive plantings are to be put in. Certainly in these cases and in situations where the property is unusually large or has significant site problems the services of these professionals are to be devoutly desired. Anytime large amounts of money are to be expended, it is a good idea to get professional advice.

Harkening back to the interior decoration analogy, the object of "redecorating" your property is to have it look lovely, but it is even more essential that it be livable. Think of the outside landscape as a series of rooms. A typical yard has at least five rooms: the front yard, two side yards, the backyard, and the boundary lines. Some rooms are used for play, some for company, some for storage, and some for passage. These rooms should work properly. They should do for the homeowner what he or she wants them to do. A landscape design that focuses on the functionality of the yard will assure that this happens.

A corollary to this principal of functional design is that a good landscape design should reflect environmental and maintenance considerations. Is the yard organized and planted to be least demanding of water? Many parts of the country don't have water shortages yet, but the availability of water is a serious concern to a growing number of regions of America. For that reason a landscape should have the right plants in the right place. As a result they will require less water, food, and attention, reducing maintenance time. Similarly a landscape designed with maintenance in mind features curved lawns that facilitate mowing, sufficient space behind the shrubs along the front of the house to allow for ladders, and trash cans convenient to the kitchen door as well as the street. A properly designed landscape is one that is easy to care for and manage.

Of course, aesthetics must always be considered in a landscape design. However, no matter how beautiful a particular tree or flower might be, if it is not appropriate for the ecosystem in the yard, it will require a lot of extra care and not be practical for that yard.

By following some basic principles, you will insure you have a landscape that is aesthetically appealing. In the most simple terms, a landscape should have balance and proportion. Unless it has a formal design, it should have more curved lines than straight lines. The plantings should feature a variety of colors, sizes, and textures and offer some ornamental interest all year round. In the end, however, if a landscape design is based on careful evaluation of the property and is functional and easily maintained, the aesthetic side of things will fall naturally into place. If the room works and if the right plants are in the right place, the yard will be an attractive place to be.

THINKING ABOUT THE FUNCTIONS OF LANDSCAPE PLANTS

From the functional perspective, plants do more in the landscape than just sit there and look pretty. In fact, most plants have jobs in the yard. They serve a landscape purpose and therefore contribute to its comfort, safety, or convenience. Plants can:

- divide or separate
- screen for privacy
- fill in space
- manage light
- conserve energy
- attract wildlife
- provide food
- decorate

While all these jobs are not necessarily needed in every yard, it is worthwhile to think about

Plants That Make Good Dividers and Screens

EVERGREEN

Heath (*Erica mediterranea*) 'Brightness'*

Lavender cotton (*Santolina incana*)

English lavender (*Lavandula officinalis*) 'Hidcote'*

Osmanthus (*Osmanthus heterophyllus*)*

Leyland cypress (× *Cupressocyparis leylandii*)

Common yew (*Taxus baccata*)

Lawson cypress (*Chamaecyparis lawsoniana*) 'Green Hedger'

English holly (*Ilex aquifolium*)

Common boxwood (*Buxus sempervirens*)

Firethorn (*Pyracantha rogersiana*) 'Flava'*

Hemlock (*Tsuga canadensis*)

Japanese holly (*Ilex crenata*)

Portugal laurel (*Prunus lusitanica*)*

Cherry laurel (*Prunus laurocerasus*)*

Ebbinge's silverberry (*Elaeagnus × ebbingei*)*

Ponticum rhododendron (*Rhododendron ponticum*)*

Rosemary barberry (*Berberis × stenophylla*)

Simon's cotoneaster (*Cotoneaster simonsii*)

DECIDUOUS

Cherry plum (*Prunus cerasifera*)*

Cinquefoil (*Potentilla fruticosa*) 'Katherine Dykes'*

Common hawthorn (*Crataegus monogyna*)

Flowering quince (*Chaenomeles × superba*) 'Rowallane'*

Forsythia (*Forsythia × intermedia*) 'Lynwood' and 'Spectabilis'*

Japanese barberry (*Berberis thunbergii*) 'Aurea' and 'Atropurpurea'

Littleleaf lilac (*Syringa microphylla*) 'Superba'*

Mock orange (*Philadelphus × hybrida*) 'Mantreau d'Hermine'*

Snowberry (*Symphoricarpos × doorenbosii*) 'White Hedge'*

Spirea (*Spiraea × bumalda*) 'Anthony Waterer'*

Winter currant (*Ribes sanguineum*) 'King Edward VII'*

Rugosa rose (*Rosa rugosa*) 'Blanc Double de Coubert'*

bears flowers if not sheared too formally

Vines That Are Suitable for Screens

Black-eyed Susan vine (*Thunbergia alata*) 'Mixed'

Boston ivy (*Parthenocissus tricuspida*) 'Veitchii'

Chinese wisteria (*Wisteria sinensis*)

Clematis (*Clematis montana, C.* × *jackmanii, C.* × *hybrida*)

Climbing hydrangea (*Hydrangea petiolaris*)

Climbing nasturtium (*Tropaeolum majus*) 'Tall Mixed'

Dutchman's pipe (*Aristolochia*)

English ivy (*Hedera helix*)

Everlasting pea (*Lathyrus latifolius*)

Hardy kiwi (*Actinidia kolomikta*)

Honeysuckle (*Lonicera*)

Mile-a-minute vine (*Polygonum baldschuanicum*)

Morning glory (*Ipomoea rubrocaerulea*) 'Heavenly Blue'

Passionflower (*Passaflora caerulea*)

Sweet pea (*Lathyrus odoratus*) 'Winston Churchill'

Trumpet creeper (*Campsis radicans*)

Virginia creeper (*Parthenocissus quinquefolia*)

Winter jasmine (*Jasminum nudiflorum*)

---

them. Are these jobs needed in your yard? Are they presently filled by plants? Are the plants appropriate for the job? The answers to these questions may suggest changes that need to be made in your landscape.

Plants as Dividers or Separators

Using plants to mark the boundaries of the yard is a common practice throughout the country. Many homes are separated from their neighbors by a hedge, a line of shrubs, or by a fence supporting a vine of some kind. Sturdy privet is one of the most frequently used shrubs for this job. Now, there is no question that a privet hedge does a perfectly good job as a separator between property lines, but it is a high-maintenance plant because it requires shearing every month or two during the growing season. There are other plants, such as osmanthus or yew, which have a fairly compact form, do a good dividing job, and yet require only one pruning a year. Many shrubs can be grown in a line but be left unpruned to achieve a natural effect or sheared as a hedge

Trees and shrubs function well as dividers and screens. Here a row of handsome arborvitae assures privacy and provides an evergreen backdrop for plants and yard furniture.

for a more formal look. Some of these are evergreen, others deciduous. Many offer flowers and/or berries that make a boundary row or hedge even more attractive. There are lots of options, and some are listed on page 214.

Some homeowners install chain-link fences around the backyard to keep small children safe or to restrain the family dog. These fences are very functional, require little care, but are not terribly attractive. Here is where a low-maintenance vine such as honeysuckle or sweet pea can be useful, covering the fence without reducing its functional value. Where plants serve as dividers or separators, ask: Are they doing the job? Do they require minimal maintenance? Are they attractive? If the answer to any of these questions is no, then this is an area that may be ripe for change.

Plants as Screens

Shrubs, trees, some flowers, and vines also function effectively as screens. In this role they form a living wall to shield the property from sounds, wind, or public view. They also serve to obscure trash cans, air-conditioner compressors, and other utilities on the property. A row of shrubs around a deck or patio affords privacy to the family, as does a mass of vines twining around and over a pergola or porch. Planted in rows about two or three feet apart, young forsythia, mock orange, or lilac will mature into a shrub screen over five feet tall. While they lose their leaves in the winter, they offer flowers and often berries during those months when their screening job is needed.

Similarly, evergreen shrubs, such as Leyland cypress or Japanese holly, serve as a screen or barrier when planted in a line close enough to touch each other, blocking out highway noise or public view year-round.

Shrubs with thorns, such as barberry or hawthorn, are very effective at discouraging dogs and other four-legged visitors from entering private areas on the property. Sturdy rampant vines such as honeysuckle, mile-a-minute, or trumpet creeper will rapidly cover run-down sheds, rock piles, or other unsightly areas on the property.

Effective Ground Covers for Lawn Areas

Bearberry cotoneaster (*Cotoneaster dammeri*) (sun)

Blue fescue (*Festuca ovina glauca*) (full sun to light shade)

Bugleweed (*Ajuga reptans*) (light to medium shade)

Creeping lilyturf (*Liriope spicata*) (medium sun to medium shade)

Creeping juniper (*Juniperus horizontalis*) 'Glauca' and "Douglasii' (full sun)

Dichondra (*Dichondra micrantha*) (full sun to light shade)

Irish ivy (*Hedera helix*) 'Hibernica' (high indirect light to full shade; full sun once established)

Japanese pachysandra (*Pachysandra terminalis*) (bright shade to dense shade)

Lily-of-the-valley (*Convallaria majalis*) (light shade)

Mondo grass (*Ophiopogon japonicus, O. jaburan*) (light to medium shade)

Myrtle (*Vinca minor*) (light to medium shade)

Sweet woodruff (*Asperula odorata*) (light to full shade)

Wild strawberry (*Fragaria chiloensis*) (light shade)

Wintercreeper (*Euonymus fortunei*) 'Minima' and 'Kewensis' (sun to light shade)

Plants as Fillers

The grass plants that make up your lawn are really nothing more than fillers of open surface area. They fill space, serving primarily to hold the soil and minimize dust. Collectively, as a lawn, they prevent erosion, connect various outdoor rooms such as the front yard and the side yard, and provide color and texture to the landscape. Homeowners typically take this all for granted and rarely entertain the idea of changing the size or shape of the lawn.

Yet, the American lawn is the highest maintenance collection of plants on the average property. It must be constantly mowed and watered, and often fed, aerated, and weeded. It needs frequent repair in worn areas and re-seeding overall. Any serious evaluation of a landscape must include consideration of the role of the existing lawn and whether some other plants might do the same job with a lot less maintenance than grass plants.

There are many, many plants that do a fine job as fillers. Many homeowners find that low-growing, evergreen ground covers such as pachysandra and ivy are just as good as lawn grass, except as a recreational surface. There are a host of ground-cover plants that are suitable as lawn substitutes. Generally speaking, perennial plants are preferable, because they are permanent, but any plant that has a neat, compact shape, low-growing foliage, and a habit of growth which causes it to form a weed-smothering carpet is a good candidate for a filler. The green trailing or vinelike ones are best for filling lawn areas.

Recently it has become fashionable to use wildflower seed mixes or meadow mixes to replace conventional lawn grass. While a properly cultivated wildflower patch makes a wonderful space filler, there are two major drawbacks to its use as a lawn substitute. First, with wildflower mixtures it is difficult to be sure that a given seed mix is, in fact, appropriate for the region and climate where the property is located. Once sown, germination of the wildflower seeds may never occur, or it many occur haphazardly if the flowers are unsuited to the area. Many plants may not survive the heat of summer. Often tall and short plants, annuals and perennials, and some grasses are combined in a mix, so that it has neither uniformity of bloom time nor size, resulting in a yard that looks weedy or scraggly a good part of the season. This informality is more appropriate for use in an undeveloped area at the rear of the yard. It does not present a neat look from the street and some towns (and neighbors) are not prepared to tolerate it.

Second, wildflower plantings are not as easy to grow and maintain over several seasons as it would seem. Done properly, putting in a wildflower patch from seed is tantamount to starting a lawn. Wildflower patches should be seeded in the fall. First, kill the existing ground cover of grass or weeds, or whatever, with a herbicide such as Roundup. Two or three weeks later, mow the dead plants as low as possible. It may be advisable to spot treat any new weeds that have sprouted in the meantime if the fall weather is mild. Then rake the surface of the area to loosen the soil so that the seeds will make good contact with the soil. Wait until at least after Thanksgiving, even until the first of the year, to sow the seed. Most wildflower mixes feature plants that like sun and require minimum water; however, it is important to water the patch well until the seeds have sprouted and seedlings are well-established. It will be necessary to mow any lawn grass around the patch, but the patch itself will not need mowing until the following late fall, after it blooms. Each season it may be necessary to reseed some annuals and to spot weed to get the patch off to a good start. Wildflower meadows can be lovely, but they do take considerable work to install and maintain.

There are some alternatives to the wild-

ORNAMENTAL GROUND COVERS FOR USE AS FILLERS

Baby's tears (*Soleriolia soleirolii*) (shade)

Basket-of-gold (*Alyssum saxatile*) (sun)

Bellflower (*Campanula gargarnica*) (sun)

Bouncing bet (*Saponaria officinalis*) (sun)

Bishop's hat (*Epimedium grandiflorum*) (light shade, some sun)

Crown vetch (*Coronilla varia*) (sun)*

Dead nettle (*Lamium maculatum*) (shade)

Dwarf rosemary (*Rosmarinus officinalis*) (sun)

Evergreen candytuft (*Iberis sempervirens*) (sun)

Heath (*Erica*) (sun)

Japanese knotweed (*Polygonum cuspidatum compactum*) (sun)*

Lamb's ears (*Stachys byzantina*) (sun)

Phlox (*Phlox stolonifera, P. subulata*) (sun)

Silvermound (*Artemisia schmidtiana*) (sun to partial shade)

Snow-in-summer (*Cerastium tomentosum*) (sun)

Spring cinquefoil (*Potentilla verna*) (sun or light shade)

Stonecrop (*Sedum acre, S. album, S. sarmentosum* and others) (sun)

Sweet alyssum (*Lobularia maritima*) (sun)

Sweet violet (*Viloa odorata*) (partial shade)

Thyme (*Thymus serphyllum*) (sun)

Tends to be invasive.

flower seed mixes for those who would like to try wildflowers in a small area. These pre-seeded wildflower products eliminate a lot of the effort described above and are available by mail order. Superlawn, Inc., in California offers a Wildflower Growing Mat that is basically a felt pad imbedded with wildflower seeds and fertilizer. Kill all weeds in the area intended for the wildflowers with herbicide, then loosen the soil surface with a rake. Unroll the mat and lay it flat over the roughened soil, then water. On slopes or hills, cover the mat with a thin layer of peat moss. It is important to keep the mat moist until the seeds germinate and the young plants are well-established.

Wildflower Carpet by Applewood Seed Company is also designed to take the effort out of growing wildflowers. It is essentially wildflower sod, a mat of densely packed, three-inch-tall perennial wildflower plants whose roots are already well-developed. Use it just as you would use lawn sod. Lay it down over weedless, roughened soil and water well. Because the plants are already three months old, they establish themselves rapidly and dependably, providing a real head start. These mats contain sixteen different kinds of plants, purposely selected because they adapt to a wide range of climates. There are no annuals or grasses included. Not only is this wildflower sod ideal for replacing lawn areas, but it is a mini garden in itself. Use it in a bed or border area that is dedicated to flowers.

Many kinds of ground covers can serve as fillers in areas of the yard other than the expanses of lawn. Plant either green or flowering ground-cover carpets around specimen trees and shrubs growing in the lawn as recommended in chapter two. Use these low-growing plants as living mulch to fill in around foundation shrubs near the house and garage, use them between stepping stones, as edging for walks and drives, and for erosion control on slopes. Because ground covers discourage weeds, there is a role for them in among flower and vegetable plantings and along the edges of garden beds. In addition to the lawn fillers listed above, there are literally hundreds of plants of various heights and habit that can do these jobs, and the box on page 219 lists some of the most common.

The few examples in the box above represent only a handful of the plants potentially useful as filler in the landscape. Obviously, a decision to plant ground-cover plants around the yard will require a trip to the local nursery to learn what plants are appropriate for the particular site.

Plants to Adjust Light

Most homeowners are aware that plants, especially the large trees, on their property affect the natural light available in the yard, but few appreciate how plants can be used to actively manipulate light. Ask yourself, how much shade do we want? Are the existing trees too dense? Should there be more trees to relieve the summer heat on the shrubs and the other plantings?

Sometimes, to get more light the plan may be to simply raise the canopy of the trees already on the property. Pruning off all the lower branches up twenty feet along the trunks of mature trees opens up the understory area, permitting the penetration of bright, indirect light that stimulates a wide variety of woodland plants that otherwise would not survive the deep shade. This step alone, or combined with the strategic removal of spindly, undersize trees that may crowd the area and contribute to a severe shade problem, will greatly improve the accessibility of light to the yard.

Some shade is very welcome. In situations where there is constant bright sun, especially common in yards of newly built homes, the landscape plan will undoubtedly include planting trees. Figuring out how a young sapling is going to affect the shade around the house in twenty years is something of a challenge but not impossible. Some research at the local library or arboretum will yield information about the mature height and spread of shade and ornamental trees, as well as their typical rates of growth.

Remember to take into account how the shade pattern of a tree varies over the seasons. During the summer months when all trees have foliage to block it, the sun is high in the sky and during the winter months, when all but the evergreens have lost their foliage, the

Homeowners are becoming increasingly aware of the possibilities for art around their landscapes. Whimsical statuary, wall plaques, and murals are common. Because this wonderful shade tree is pruned high to allow more light into the yard, it also provides an ideal support for this mobile.

sun is low in the sky. Take advantage of these factors to direct the sun where you need it. A deciduous tree in full leaf will protect a flower bed from midday summer heat, yet allows some warmth from a weak winter sun to shine through its bare branches to warm the bulb beds. Trees and shrubs definitely have an important lighting role in residential yards.

Plants to Conserve Energy

Of course, directly related to their role in controlling light outside in the yard is the role of trees and shrubs in climate control within the house. Deciduous trees can make a major contribution to reducing the home's energy bills by functioning as coolers in the summer and heaters in the winter. As indicated in chapter two, large shade trees, planted in the proper locations around your house can reduce air-conditioning costs by 25 percent. After they shade the hot summer sun, they lose their leaves and allow the sun's rays to heat the house a bit during the winter. For their part, evergreen trees serve as shields. They block sun in the summer and winds and driving rain in the winter.

A home sited on the top of a hill or in a flat, exposed area is vulnerable to harsh winter winds. No matter how well insulated such a home is, higher heating bills are inevitable. A line of trees or tall shrubs positioned to create a windbreak for the house will more than make up for their cost in reduced heating bills over the years. Evergreens make the best windbreaks, but because they are slow growers, it is worthwhile to plant a line of faster growing deciduous trees in front of them to do the job until the evergreens are tall enough. At that time the deciduous trees are cut down.

Properly sited, trees and shrubs can reduce household energy costs. In the summer the foliage of a large shade tree near the house will help cool it by blocking the sun. In the winter, its foliage gone, the same tree allows the sun to warm the house. Shrubs and trees also make effective windbreaks.

Plants for Wildlife

Increasingly in this modern world mankind is reminded of the significance of our relationship with the wildlife with which we share this planet. These days more and more homeowners recognize that their home landscape was formerly wild habitat for many species that are now under enormous ecological pressure. Many homeowners are inspired to invite wildlife into their yards and to enjoy the close encounters and the delightful spectacles that ensue. The presence of a rich and diverse wildlife population in the yard offers a lot more than entertainment. It contributes to the health and functioning of the entire residential ecosystem. While not all animals are equally welcome, even those that are a nuisance at times, like squirrels, skunks, and deer, all make a contribution.

Plants, of course, play a pivotal role in this

Trees That Are Effective as Windbreaks

DECIDUOUS

American plum (*Prunus americana*)*

Ash (*Fraxinus americana, F. pennsylvanica lanceolatea*)*

Beech (*Fagus*)

Black haw (*Viburnum prunifolium*)

Black walnut (*Juglans nigra*)*†

Box elder (*Acer negundo*)*

Bur oak (*Quercus macrocarpa*)*

Common hackberry (*Celtis occidentalis*)*

Cornelian cherry (*Cornus mas*)

Dahurian buckthorn (*Rhamnus davurica*)

European hornbeam (*Carpinus betulus*)

Honey locust (*Gleditsia triacanthos*)*†

Japanese tree lilac (*Syringa reticulata*)

Laurel willow (*Salix pentandra*)

Linden (*Tilia*)*

Maple (*Acer ginnala, A. plantanoides, A. rubrum* and others)†

Oak (*Quercus imbricaria, Q. phellos*, and others)

Osage orange (*Maclura pomifera*)*

Poplar (*Populus alba, P. nigra* 'Italica', *P. tremuloides*, and others)*†

Russian olive (*Elaeagnus angustifolia*)*

Siberian crab apple (*Malus baccata*)

Siberian pea tree (*Caragana arborescens*)*

Washington hawthorn (*Crataegus phaenopyrum*)

White willow (*Salix alba*)*

EVERGREEN

Arborvitae (*Thuja*)†

Carolina hemlock (*Tsuga caroliniana*)

Eastern red cedar (*Juniperus virginiana*)*

Juniper (*Juniperus*)

Pine (*Pinus nigra, P. resinosa, P. strobus*)

Ponderosa pine (*Pinus ponderosa*)

Spruce (*Picea abies, P. glauca,* * *P. omorika*)

*low-water demand
†fast-growing

Incorporate amenities for birds into landscape features. This birdbath provides a nice focal point for small shrubs. The gravel mulch is low maintenance and helps reduce lawn size.

natural system. They are the chief beneficiaries of the healthy and balanced ecosystem, and, in return, they function as life supports for wildlife in the yard, just as they do in the wild. Animals, bugs, and birds need three things: shelter, food, and water. During bad weather and when they are raising their young, birds, insects, amphibians, and mammals all need shelter. Homeowners who wish to develop a habitat for diverse wildlife need to plan a landscape that has lots of plants that function as shelter and sources of food. A variety of grasses and ground covers, trees and shrubs, even an intentional brushpile or patch of brambles at the back of the property will offer cover to numerous creatures, and shrubs and trees will provide food.

Large shade trees provide stable nesting support for large birds and squirrels. They are also good sites for bird and bat houses. These creatures will devour enormous numbers of insects in return for their living quarters. Evergreens of all kinds provide excellent winter shelter for birds, while both deciduous and evergreen trees supply cones, nuts, and seeds for birds and small mammals. Their bark often harbors grubs and insects to feed birds and many ornamental trees and shrubs, such as crab apples, hollies, and barberries, provide fruits and berries for all kinds of animals.

In terms of landscape planning to attract wildlife, the more a property resembles a natural woodlands at the edge of a field, the more likely a healthy diversity of wildlife will find a supportive environment. By deliberately choosing plants that will function as sources of food and shelter for wildlife you can increase their population and the health of the yard. For specific help, contact the National Wildlife Federation for information on their "Backyard Wildlife Habitat" program (8925 Leesburg Pike, Vienna, VA 22184).

Plants to Eat

Having plants in the landscape that are edible for humans is certainly not a new idea. Earlier, in chapter four, the idea that food plants can have an ornamental function in the yard was discussed. However, it is also true that some ornamental plants in the yard also function as sources of food. Everyone knows someone who makes jelly from rose hips or cactus flowers. The fruit of the Cornelian cherry (*Cornus mas*) and the Japanese dogwood (*Cornus kousa*)

Excellent Sources of Food and Cover for Backyard Wildlife

Birches (*Betula lenta, B. lutea, B. papyrifera, B. populifolia*)

Black cherry (*Prunus serotina*)

Box elder (*Acer negundo*)

Canada hemlock (*Tsuga canadensis*)

Common hackberry (*Celtis occidentalis*)

Common persimmon (*Diospyros virginiana*)

Dogwoods (*Cornus alternifolia, C. florida*)

Eastern poplar (*Populus deltoides*)

Eastern red cedar (*Juniperus virginiana*)

Firs (*Abies balsamea, A. concolor*)

Hawthorns (*Crataegus phaenopyrum* and others)

Hickories (*Carya cordiformis, C. ovata, C. tomentosa, C. glabra*)

Maples (*Acer nigrum, A. pensylvanicum, A. rubrum, A. saccharum*)

Oaks (*Quercus*)

Pines (*Pinus banksiana, P. flexilis, P. resinosa, P. strobus*)

Serviceberry (*Amelanchier laevis*)

Spruces (*Picea glauca, P. mariana, P. pungens*)

Sumacs (*Rhus copallina, R. glabra, R. typhina*)

Viburnums (*Viburnum lentago, V. prunifolium*)

Willows (*Salix discolor, S. nigra*)

---

are also tasty. While it is not advisable to indiscriminately sample the various berries and leaves on the plants in the yard—in fact, it is potentially dangerous—it is interesting to know that so many plants have several roles. For those who are interested in this aspect of plants in the landscape, there are several books available on edible landscape plants. Check our resources section for recommended titles.

Plants That Decorate

Everyone is aware of the decorative role that plants have in the home landscape. Certainly from the aesthetic view of landscape design this is the paramount issue. In terms of this chapter it is the point where the functional perspective on landscape planning naturally and properly blends into the aesthetic one, because one of the many functions that plants serve in the landscape is to make it beautiful. Perhaps their decorative function is the one that you most appreciate when you think about the plants in your yard.

The contribution flowers make during the growing season is the most obvious one, but it is important not to overlook what other plants have to offer throughout the entire year. A landscape plan should include a wide variety of plants that offer ornamental interest all year long. In addition to flowers, many vines, trees, and shrubs provide bright berries, interesting bark, and dramatic dried pods and seedheads that decorate the bleak winter landscape.

Certain plants are so beautiful that they can be plunked right in the middle of the front lawn by themselves. These are called "specimen" plants. Flowering crab apples, lindens, rhododendrons, and lots of other shade trees and ornamental shrubs are useful as specimen plants. Their function is to serve as a focal point for the front yard, or anywhere on the property for that matter.

The role of both specimen plants and groups of shrubs or trees as focal points is reinforced by the growing popularity of outdoor lighting systems (discussed later in this chapter). Now some families even choose plants because of how they will look at night when they are illuminated. Even at Christmastime deciduous trees, formerly not lighted as the needled evergreens were, are being tastefully decorated with small white lights that showcase their trunk and branch patterns. A close look at the plants in the yard that are serving as specimens is an important part of the overall evaluation of the landscape and plan for change.

Obviously, from a landscape planning perspective, every plant on a property has one or more functions. The questions to ask are two-fold. Are the plants currently in the yard functioning satisfactorily? And are there landscape functions, such as screening, energy conservation, or wildlife attraction, that are not being met by any plants at the moment? The answers to these two questions will provide important information about possible changes in the landscape design.

THINKING ABOUT LANDSCAPE IN TERMS OF AREAS

Of course, there is more to a landscape than plants. Another way to think about a yard is to evaluate it in terms of its functional areas, primarily utility areas and recreational areas. Are they currently functioning well in relation to the house, and in relation to each other? Are there any changes needed to improve the usefulness of these areas? These areas take up space in the landscape and must be considered in planning.

The utility areas found around most American homes are the practical, essential spaces that help households work. Everyone needs a space to store trash cans, a driveway either to park the car or to get the car into the garage, and an area to process yard waste. The goal in landscape design is to assure that their function—storage or access—is carried out effectively and that their appearance is attractive.

Evaluate both the effectiveness of each area in performing its function and how its appearance might be improved. Firewood stored at the back of the yard behind a hedge may look just fine, but it is inconvenient. Perhaps a smaller pile closer to the back door might be a good idea. If the trash area always seems to be cluttered, maybe the area should be expanded to accommodate more cans and a screen of plants should be installed around the spot to eliminate the eyesore.

Driveways are a problem. Even professional landscape designers struggle with how the needs of cars often dominate the people part of a landscape. One way to downplay the intrusiveness of this utility is to use materials

Typical Utility Area in Home Landscapes

Air conditioners/meters	*Paths*	*Yard waste management*
Driveway	*Pet area*	*Trash collection*
Firewood storage	*Tool storage sheds*	

that are more natural to the environment than cement or macadam. Not only do these hard surfaces strain storm sewer systems with rain runoff, but a significant amount of water is lost to the home landscape. The amount of water running off the parking lots of malls in this country is a relative drop in the storm sewer bucket compared to all the water lost to macadam driveways.

To hold the water for the benefit of the landscape, consider using materials that allow it to soak into the soil and the water table below. Low-maintenance, attractive, and functional driveways can be made of gravel, unmortared brick, loose, flat, or round stones, Belgian blocks, or even woodchips. There are new paving materials on the market now suitable for parking lots and driveways which are grids made of steel or cement with spaces in them for growing grass or other attractive ground-cover plants. The driveway looks green from the street, but is strong enough to handle the weight of automobiles.

Walks and paths are another area worth evaluating in terms of function and appearance. Consider something other than concrete, both for the aesthetics and to allow water to percolate into the water table. Gravel comes in all sizes and colors and makes a wonderful path or walk. Brick is attractive. Stone is elegant, though a bit more expensive. Laid over a bed of sand these materials will permit water to reach the soil, but effectively discourage weeds. Informal but attractive paths can be made of woodchips, especially for areas of the lawn that receive so much traffic that lawn grass does not have a chance. When the kids grow up or traffic patterns change, they are easily changed back into lawn. In the meantime, an unsightly area of the yard is made both functional and attractive.

Recreational Areas

Yards where kids live usually have an area that serves a recreational function. The sandbox and swing set are obviously examples. For adults, this might be the deck or patio. So is the swimming pool area or tennis court. Whatever the activity, the design of that area will be based on criteria that are different from those that apply to other landscape areas, such as the front yard. In an area dedicated to play by small children, the safety and comfort of the landscaping is important. The areas under the jungle gym and swing set do not support grass and often develop puddles after rain. It is likely to be a surface on which children fall. Some alternatives to compacted dirt or paving are woodchips, sand, or synthetic pads that will cover the soil and break falls. They are all reasonably attractive, yet very functional.

The appearance of decks, patios, and swimming pools is enhanced by plants grown in containers. These are areas where guests are entertained and appearance may be as important as function on some occasions. Annual flowers in strategically placed urns and pots are easily changed for fresh, bright, seasonal color. Remember, it is important that containers on sunny decks and patios be watered frequently. As part of the landscaping plan, consider purchasing containers with some kind of water reservoir system built in to minimize the watering chores.

Just as looking at plants in terms of their functions is useful in evaluating the landscape, so is looking at utility areas in terms their functions. Are these areas as effective and attractive as can reasonably be expected? Do they require as little maintenance as possible? If the answer to any of these questions is no, then the landscape plan should include some changes in these areas.

THINKING ABOUT THE LANDSCAPE IN TERMS OF SYSTEMS

Another useful way to think about the yard is in terms of its systems. These are the networks or connecting mechanisms that enable the elements of the landscape to perform their various functions. Homeowners are often unaware that these systems are in place and functioning almost daily.

There is probably a system for getting water to the lawn on the property. There is also a system of lights to illuminate parts of the outside, although it may be just the front-door light. There are traffic patterns in the yard, whether they are recognized formally by walkways or informally by worn spots in the lawn.

Landscapes around homes that include children must function for them too. A good landscape plan considers their needs.

Functional landscapes provide spaces for informal outdoor living. Here a deck links the indoor space to the outdoor landscape, extending the area for eating and socializing into the yard where plants are at home.

Lay drip irrigation lines around plants and along beds. Cover them with an inch or two of mulch to protect them from the ultraviolet rays of the sun and to hide them from view. The supply lines (the dotted lines in the drawing), which deliver water from the faucet to the drip hose, are buried four to six inches below the soil.

While some of these systems may already be formally in place, in some cases it may be worthwhile to install or expand others. A well-thought-out landscape design should reflect these plans.

Irrigation Systems to Save Water

Most homes have one, maybe, two faucets connected to the water system for getting water outside. Typically they support a simple hose arrangement for use with a lawn sprinkler or to wash the car. However, since more and more areas of the country are experiencing reduced rainfall and water shortages are more common, using an overhead sprinkler arrangement to water an entire yard is increasingly

regarded as wasteful and expensive. Home-owners with generous yards are turning to more sophisticated water systems such as drip irrigation to keep plants watered while conserving water. Overhead sprinkling is reserved for lawns only.

Most modern drip irrigation systems no longer require professional installation. They feature hoses of various designs that allow water to drip along their length and seep into the soil very slowly, a drip at a time. They work very well on all plants in the landscape except for lawns and can be set up almost any time of the year. Properly installed, most drip systems require that the hoses be covered by soil or mulch, so it is easiest to lay them out in the fall or early spring when the plants are dormant and the soil around them is clear of weeds.

A drip watering system is ideal for any garden bed—flower or vegetable—for groupings of shrubs, for around trees, and for hedges. Used with a computerized timer control device that can be programmed like a VCR (costing about $50) the system will water the entire landscape regularly at predetermined intervals for specified lengths of time and then shut off. Some systems will even override with a delay if it rains. In most areas, homeowners program the system to turn on the water once a week during the spring and the fall. During the summer months more frequent watering may be necessary.

Drip systems use only about 40 percent of the water that overhead types of watering systems use to deliver the same amount of water to the plants. Virtually no water is lost to evaporation and runoff, as happens with overhead sprinklers.

Cover drip lines with mulch to prevent loss of water from evaporation and to protect the lines from ultraviolet light damage from the sun. This way they are hidden from view and do not detract from the appearance of the landscape, even when they are operating. For lawns, the pop-up sprinkler system is still the best automatic watering system in the home landscape. Unlike the drip systems for other plants, this type of sprinkler system for lawns does require professional installation. It must be set deep enough to avoid damage from aerating equipment.

Lights for Convenience, Safety, and Security

An evaluation of the home landscape systems will include a new appreciation for the role of lighting in the yard. Here's a case where the functional role has been expanded as technology has improved upon the simple light by the door. The new low-voltage lighting systems now available offer convenience, safety, and security.

It is relatively simple to link outdoor lights to a special motion detection switch that notes when the car drives into the driveway and turns on the front lights automatically. That is convenient. Fixtures are now available that light up steps in the front walk or stairs to the deck with low-voltage lights to prevent tripping, adding a measure of safety to the landscape. Motion switches located in a few strategic places in the yard to augment bright lighting on the property add improved security to the landscape—any intruder in the yard will turn on the outside lights.

The new low-voltage lighting systems require very little electricity to operate so are not a drain on the electric bill. They are easily installed by the homeowner, but some careful planning is advised prior to the purchase of the parts. Having at least two outside electric outlets facilitates hooking up the outside lighting equipment. It is best to set up the system and let it function for a few weeks before burying the wires to get them out of sight, as it may be necessary to make some refinements in the arrangement.

Outdoor lighting has an aesthetic as well as functional role in the yard. Various types of fixtures make it possible to illuminate in different ways. Accent post fixtures direct a soft glow to downlight walkways, shrubbery, and drives. Garden light fixtures illuminate plants and dramatize foliage textures. Floodlights, properly placed, can uplight specimen trees, doorways, and landscape features, such as trellises, or they can backlight trees and shrubs to dramatize their shapes and textures. Because with lighting, as with so many other things, there is a fine line between tasteful and too much of a good thing, incorporate outdoor lighting into the landscape plan cautiously.

Here is a case where a professional landscape designer may be helpful.

Traffic Patterns

Evaluate whether the established system of walkways reflects the traffic patterns in your yard. Does the front walk bend to the left, but everyone uses the side door which is on the right? Is the mailman wearing a path in the lawn? Does the front walk go straight out to the street, so a shortcut across the lawn is the best way to get to the driveway? Is the shortest way to the trash cans over a strip of lawn? It may be time to change things to accommodate real traffic patterns. Walkways should mark the most direct routes to the utility areas.

Waste Management System/Yard Waste System

In these days of recycling, waste management in and around the home is becoming a serious issue and a functional landscape will reflect this. The outdoor area set aside for storing trash and garbage awaiting municipal pickup is part of the waste management system. So are the compost pile and a brush pile that store yard waste. Consider how well these waste management systems function as they presently exist. Are they convenient, sanitary, and adequate? If the garbage can is close enough to the patio or deck to be detected on warm days, it should be moved. If the compost bin is so far to the back of the yard that it's too much trouble to put stuff in it, maybe it should be moved. If the view that confronts guests pulling into the driveway is a line of trash cans, maybe a line of screening shrubs or a fence is in order.

THINKING ABOUT THE LANDSCAPE IN TERMS OF PROBLEMS

One last way to think about landscape is from the perspective of its problems. Any aspect of the yard that does not function properly, is unsafe, inconvenient, or unattractive is a problem. Addressing them becomes part of the landscaping plan because their solution may have a significant impact on the final landscape plan. As examples, let's look at three primary problems that can affect the landscape design.

Soil Problems

Perhaps the most common problem facing homeowners in America is poor soil, and the solution to that problem represents a very serious challenge. Over the past twenty to thirty years it has become routine for developers to remove and sell the top ten inches of topsoil surrounding a new home site prior to building. Builders then bring in very heavy equipment to remove stumps and grade the site, seriously compacting the entire area. When the home is completed, they typically truck in eight or ten inches of low-quality soil to serve as topsoil. Trying to grow grass or any other kind of plant in that environment would challenge even the most experienced horticulturist.

In the case of even older homes, the soil is likely to be seriously compacted from years and years of people traffic, play, and walking behind lawn mowers for literally thousands of mowings.

The extensive discussion of compaction in the chapter one reflects the pervasiveness of this problem. It may be the underlying factor in a host of other problems. Poor drainage in the yard may be a result of soil compaction. Unsightly surface tree roots may be a result of soil compaction. The failure of shrubs and trees to thrive may also be a result of this problem.

Another potential soil problem may be its chemistry. If plants don't grow well on the property, this may be a signal that the pH of the soil, the measure of its acidity or alkalinity, is so extreme that the soil cannot support them. Rainwater sometimes leaches alkaline material from stucco and mortar, especially around new construction, which causes the soil to become excessively alkaline. Watch for telltale signs, like moss growing on the soil. Consult the sections on soil preparation in the previous chapters on lawns, trees, vegetables, and flowers.

Taking pains to assure that the soil in the yard is good is worth it. All plants will have a much better chance of being healthy and beautiful. If the yard is suffering because of poor soil conditions, then the prescription is hard work to get the soil back in shape. It may be the most important landscaping job of all.

Topographical Problems

Some homeowners have problems because their property has difficult terrain. Steep grades present problems in drainage, access, and especially growing plants. Lawn grass is virtually out of the question because of the difficulty of mowing. Growing ground covers is a good solution to this problem because, once established, they hold the soil, require little maintenance, and look attractive. Another solution to slopes is terracing. This is especially nice in the backyard, where boxed beds of flowers or vegetables function to hold the soil, provide food, and solve a topographical problem.

Properties sometimes have low-lying areas and dips where drainage is a problem. One solution may be to fill them in if not prohibited by local wetland laws. Another may be to make a virtue of necessity and develop a bog area and grow plants that like to have wet feet. Similarly, if a spring or stream is on the property, take advantage of the water and grow water-loving ornamental plants and grasses, or edible plants like watercress. Even huge boulders in yards can be turned to advantage through the judicious use of mulches and shallow-rooted plants. No yards are problem-free. Some homeowners with perfectly flat yards find them to be a problem. Include these factors in the overall evaluation of your property so that the final landscape plan can address them.

Plants Are a Problem

Sometimes it's the plants already in place in the yard that are the problem. Many homeowners really dislike at least one of the trees or shrubs that is in their care. Shrubs get overgrown, coarse, and rangy as they age, and are no longer an asset to the landscape. This is often true of the "foundation" shrubs builders are fond of putting in along the front of the house. Trees get old or damaged and don't look very good. Some people dislike on principle plants with thorns or plants that drip fruit or seeds. When evaluating the landscape, be sure to note these problems.

There is nothing wrong with replacing a tree or shrub that represents a problem. Plan to remove it and replace it with something more desirable. Even if it is so large that professional help is needed, it is worth the money. However, most shrubs and many trees can be removed by homeowners and their neighbors who are not averse to hard work. In cases where a shrub or tree is simply overgrown, the solution may be to renovate it, as discussed in chapter two.

Another type of plant problem is the unwanted rampant weed or vine that insists on a place in the yard. It may be desirable to set aside an area on the property, especially if it is good-sized, that is left basically undeveloped, and natural brambles, vines, and cover grasses can be welcomed there as shelter for wildlife. These same plants have no place, though, in a limited yard. The solution is usually to spray them with an herbicide such as Roundup and kill them off. Woody vines and brambles are stubborn and may require several doses of herbicide applied directly on the ends of pruned stems. Your landscape plan should include this project.

"Better Plants"

Plants, no matter how functional or lovely, also become problems when they are in the wrong place. The importance of having the right plant in the right place has been stressed in several chapters in this book. Such a plant represents what horticulturists call a "better plant." The concept of using "better plants" is so important that it is appropriate to reiterate it as this book comes to a close. People who work with plants have learned that each has particular environmental specifications, a "right place," if it is to grow well. That right place will have the proper light, the appropriate soil conditions, and the kind of weather that the plant requires to thrive. Alter any of these variables, and the plant will not do as well; radically change any of these variables, and the plant will not grow at all. As an extreme example, lilacs grow well in Rochester, New York, and won't grow at all in Atlanta, Georgia.

Applied to the residential landscape, the idea of "better plants" means that it is important to choose plants that are right for your smaller environment. A better plant for a yard is one that not only will be healthy there, but will also not take too much care to remain healthy. By this criteria, hybrid tea roses are not better plants. They are lovely, but it takes enormous effort to keep them that way in the typical yard. Landscape roses, on the other hand, are better plants. They bear lovely flowers, but require very little care and attention.

A better plant is one that, when compared with other plants or even with other varieties of the same plant, has greater value to a particular home landscape. A better plant for that yard is adapted to its climate and soil. If it blooms, it blooms longer than other varieties and has attractive foliage throughout most of the season. A better plant is likely to be quite disease resistant and will have a rather neat growth habit, eliminating the need for much staking and pruning. Better plants are sometimes a bit more expensive than other plants, though that is not always the case.

To discover which are better plants for your yard, study the plants in the neighborhood. There is a natural sorting out that occurs in neighborhoods and communities over time. Plants that do well are recognized by their owners as "better plants" and are grown every year. They are noticed by neighbors who then plant them. Many of the better plants in a local geographic area become what a friend from Mississippi calls "pass-along" plants. These are the ones that are loved because they thrive dependably year after year. They are given to friends as gifts because they can be depended upon to grow well and make their owners happy.

Study the plants in the area and identify those that are appealing. Ask their owners or a neighbor what they are. Remember, any lilac is not a "better plant" just because a lilac thrives in the neighbor's yard and looks beautiful; it is that certain variety of lilac that is the "better plant." The same goes for geraniums, petunias, oak trees, and tomato plants. Searching for better plants that are appealing can be an ongoing activity when traveling in the area. When it is time to replace problem plants, you will have plenty of possibilities in mind.

Putting the Plan on Paper

After thinking about the yard from each of the perspectives suggested above, decisions about changes should be easier to make. At this point it is time to work on paper. Sketch a rough layout of the property showing the existing landscape features. This exercise reveals interrelationships between areas, between systems, and even between plants. It is a good thinking

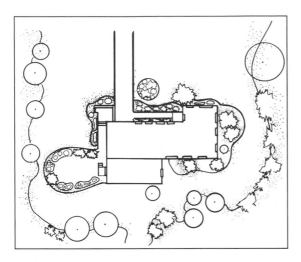

Even if you're not much of an artist, a rough sketch of your landscape helps you to plan changes in plantings, lighting patterns, and drip irrigation layouts. It should be roughly to scale, but precision is not necessary.

discipline. A second sketch with proposed changes roughed in is very helpful in confirming decisions and calculating amounts of supplies needed. Done to scale, a sketch makes it is easier to estimate amounts of peat moss for the lawn or how many feet of electric cable will be needed to rig the outdoor lights.

As the plan takes shape on paper it will also become increasingly apparent whether the job is manageable by a do-it-yourselfer or whether it is time to seek the services of a professional. The issue is not always just about the question of skills; it may also be a question of time or complexity. Then it further becomes a question of which kind of professional to consult: a landscape architect, a landscape designer, or a landscape contractor.

If the job is going to involve significant engineering activity, including earth moving, reinforcement, drainage, plumbing, and construction of buildings, walls, and terraces, then the landscape architect is probably the place to start. Their strength lies in their engineering background and less so in horticultural training, although many firms have partners who specialize in each area. If plants, and the introduction of new plants into the yard, are your primary concern, a landscape designer is probably the best person for the job. Their skills lie in finding the best plants for each situation in your yard and designing pleasing and functional combinations of plants. Some landscape designers are in business for themselves, while others may work at garden centers and nurseries, providing design services for their customers. All of these professionals will recommend designs, but the homeowner has the last word. Have a designer do a consultation and use whichever suggestions seem attractive and feasible. In either case, the architect and designer give recommendations and probably some technical drawings. They do not usually do the actual work.

For help with the landscaping work, a landscape contractor, or landscaper, is the person to call. Most of the small or family-owned landscaping businesses are skilled in planting and maintaining plants and may or may not be qualified to offer anything but the most basic design advice. Many larger landscape contracting firms have available within their company architectural and design professionals—sort of a full-service shop. Be cautious about following the advice of a person not trained in design work. The final decision, of course, comes down to time and money and how much of each is available for the landscaping project.

Once a plan is established, it is not necessary to do everything at once. Many families take four or five years to carry out their plans, thus spreading both the time and financial drain for the job. Sometimes it is most cost-effective to have professionals put in trees and prepare beds, and then undertake the rest of the planting yourself over a season or two. If time is not of the essence, it is much easier to find friends who are willing to pitch in and help from time to time on jobs that normally would be hired out. More and more homeowners are discovering bartering services as a way to save money. Perhaps the electrician will install the outlets for the outdoor lighting in return for help putting in his lawn, or programming his computer, or whatever.

One of the big concerns when contemplating any major landscape change is whether the investment in money is worth the return. In most cases, the return investment is quite good. The popular remodeling magazine *Practical Homeowner* has done a survey of the return on investment for each of the twenty most common home-improvement projects, both inside and outside the home. They found that landscape improvement in the form of new trees and shrubs can add as much, or even a little more, money to the value of the property after five years as the landscaping project costs in the first place; a 100 percent return on your investment isn't bad!

We also measure the return on investment in a landscaping project more abstractly. Where one lives and how one feels about that place has a lot to do with how that person feels about his or her quality of life. If homeowners like the way their yard works and looks, if they feel comfortable and safe in their yard, and if they feel the yard is reasonably easy to care for, then they will be happier people in all aspects of their lives. It is as important for mental health to find your outdoor space agreeable as the indoor space. Fixing up the front yard—taking away the overgrown shrubs, planting some pretty new shrubs, and adding some flowers to spruce everything up —makes everyone feel a little better each time they come home from work or shopping and walk up that front walk. Considering the number of times people come home, liking what they see every time is going to add significantly to their quality of life.

Improving the yard so that it functions well, takes little care, and looks beautiful may take years. Adding "better plants," renovating shrubs, starting ground covers, installing lighting, and other tasks take time. But gradually, eventually, it will reflect the personality and preferences of the yardener who lives there.

APPENDIX A
Safe Pesticides

INSECTICIDES TO USE FIRST—THE FIRST LEVEL OF ATTACK

The following insecticides are considered effective and very safe for most of the pest insect situations commonly found in home landscapes. Their safety lies in their low toxicity for humans and animals, in their rapid breakdown into harmless components, and in their specificity. They are contact insecticides and work only when they touch the target insect or caterpillar either on, or in, its body. They harm only specific groups or types of insects, unlike the general insecticides which indiscriminately kill whatever insects are in the area and persist for days and even weeks in the environment. Those we recommend are most effective if used when pest populations are small and—in the case of caterpillars—when they are young, so it is important to catch infestations early.

Try one of these weapons as an opening shot. If they fail to control the pests successfully, then resort to the more powerful insecticides discussed in the section that follows this one. In all cases read the entire label carefully and follow instructions for use, storage, and disposal of all the products mentioned below.

HORTICULTURAL OILS

There are two grades of horticultural oil—the traditional heavier grade oil, which is often used as a preventive spray on fruit trees in early spring, and the newer light horticultural oil, which is an effective insect control because it can be used on foliage without harming trees even in the summer months.

Traditional heavy horticultural spray oils have a viscosity of 100 to 200. They are sometimes referred to as "dormant" oil, because they are to be used only on deciduous plants that have dropped their leaves and are dormant. Used on plants that have needles or foliage, this thick oil will clog the pores on leaves and buds, cutting off respiration and killing the plant. These dormant oil sprays were designed to be used in late fall through early spring, primarily on fruit trees. Sprayed on bare branches and stems of these and other dormant trees that harbor overwintering insect eggs in their bark, the oil smothers the eggs and helps prevent problems the next season.

The newer type of oil, called "superior" type or light horticultural oil, is lighter and less viscous (60 to 70) than the dormant oil. It evaporates much more quickly from leaves and stems. Any common woody ornamental plant that has foliage can tolerate a spray using a 2-percent solution of this oil, as long as the plant is healthy, soil moisture is adequate, and low relative humidity creates conditions conducive to fairly rapid evaporation of the oil. A 2- to 3-percent solution is very effective against mites and other soft-bodied sucking insects as well as scale, and it has minimal impact on beneficial insects.

Used during the growing season when insects are at work, light horticultural oil works by thinly coating the insect and suffocating it. Use a lower concentration of oil on plants with hairy leaves. If you are uncertain about using the oil on a particular plant, test it on a few leaves. Damage will show up within several days in the form of yellowing leaf tips and margins. Light horticultural oil is effective in controlling aphids, mites, mealybugs, scale, and whiteflies in the spring, summer, or fall.

Horticultural oils are extremely low in toxicity to man, pets, and wildlife, due in part to their lack of residual life on vegetation. They pose little threat to any natural enemies of target pests.

INSECTICIDAL SOAP

Products sold commercially as "insecticidal soap" are effective in controlling a large number of common soft-bodied plant insect pests, including aphids, mealybugs, mites, and whiteflies. Soap is an alternative weapon to light horticultural oil.

Insecticidal soap must be sprayed directly on the pest insect to be effective. It penetrates the insect's body and disrupts the normal functions of both cells and membranes. While they are called "soap," these products are not the same as regular kitchen soap spray. The commercial brands have been especially formulated to be lethal to specific pests, and to avoid damage to plants and beneficial insects. Only commercial soap sprays are recommended for reliable, uniform performance.

The effectiveness of insecticidal soaps in certain circumstances is enhanced by the addition of various other materials to the soap spray. Sometimes product labels indicate that pyrethrum or citrus oil has been added to the formulation. Sometimes homeowners may add alcohol or garlic oil to insecticidal soap sprays to increase their effectiveness.

Insecticidal soap will control the following insects:

With no additives—aphids, mites, mealybugs, whiteflies, leafhoppers, plant bugs, squash bugs, harlequin bugs, and grasshoppers.

With citrus oil added (available commercially)—crickets, earwigs, fungus gnats, lace bugs, leaf-feeding caterpillars and beetles, scale, and thrips.

With pyrethrum added (available commercially)—hard-bodied insects like beetles, in addition to certain caterpillars not controlled by soap alone.

Because insecticidal soap loses its insecticidal properties when it dries, it is best to use it on cloudy days. Spray insects in early morning or late afternoon if possible. Insecticidal soap is normally fast-acting. Once it covers the pest, it starts working. Results can be observed within hours after the application. To determine if significant inroads have been made in the pest insect population, examine the affected plant three days after spraying the soap.

BACILLUS THURINGIENSIS (Bt)

Bt is a naturally occurring bacteria that is lethal to most leaf-eating caterpillars on trees, shrubs, flowers, and vegetables, but is harmless to all other insects, animals, and humans. It comes in powder form to be used as a dust or, when diluted with water, as a foliar spray. It is also sold in liquid form to be made into a spray. It is sprayed or dusted on the leaf surfaces of vulnerable plants so that the caterpillar will eat it. When the caterpillar ingests the Bt, it causes paralysis of the pest's digestive tract. It does not die immediately, but it stops feeding within two hours, which is the ultimate objective. The caterpillar will die within 72 hours.

Because of this lag time between application of the Bt and the death of the caterpillars, homeowners sometimes assume the product did not work. A close inspection of the affected plant should reveal that defoliation has stopped. That is the indicator. Properly applied, Bt should reduce caterpillar populations 70 to 90 percent, leaving the survivors for the birds and other natural predators. It is most effective if it is sprayed on the affected plant when the caterpillars are small and young.

Once dusted on a plant, the powder form of Bt remains potent for three to seven days, as long as it doesn't rain. Repeat the dust at five- to seven-day intervals to catch newly hatching caterpillars. Sprayed on plant foliage, the liquid form of Bt is potent for only twenty-four hours, so be prepared to repeat the spray in three to five days if the problem persists or if it rains.

Bt now comes in several forms, each for a specific purpose:

B.t.k. (*Bacillus thuringiensis* variety *kurstaki*) is the general-purpose material that homeowners buy when package labels have just the words "Bt" or "*Bacillus thuringiensis*" without the variety name attached. This product is suitable for the home landscape.

B.t.t. (*Bacillus thuringiensis* variety San Diego) is a new product that is designed exclusively for controlling Colorado potato beetles and the elm bark beetle.

B.t.i. (*Bacillus thuringiensis* variety *israelensis*) is very effective against mosquito and black fly larvae, and is available in slow-release formulations.

MILKY SPORE DISEASE

Milky spore disease (*Bacillus popilliae*) is actually a bacteria that kills white grubs. It does not harm any other insects or animals and is ideal for long-term, effective protection of the lawn against grubs. Spread on the lawn and/or other soil, the bacteria enter the soil and come in contact with the white grubs that are lying just below the surface. They infect them and then multiply inside the grubs, creating millions more bacteria that spread through the soil and attack other white grubs. It takes three to five years to achieve maximum control of succeeding generations of grubs, but the control then lasts two or three decades. During this time the bacteria go dormant when the grub population is eliminated and wait for another infestation to occur.

Spread this dry powder on newly mown grass and water it in with a hose. Only one treatment is necessary and this can be done anytime, except when the ground is frozen. Use approximately 20 ounces of spore dust for every 5,000 square feet of lawn. Read the product label carefully and follow instructions.

PREDATORY NEMATODES

Commercially packaged predatory nematodes represent a very safe biological insecticide. The product consists of millions of microscopic, non-segmented eellike worms one-tenth to one hundred-twenty-fifth of an inch in length suspended in a powder. Unlike the harmful root-knot nematodes which attack plants, beneficial or predatory nematodes only attack mostly soil-dwelling pest insects. These naturally occurring organisms will control a large number of soil-dwelling grubs and larvae of pest insects and eggs of beetles and weevils. This product, available by mail-order under several brand names, is mixed with water to form a slurry which is then sprayed on the affected plants. Thus activated, the worms seek out and destroy the target pest insects.

Upon entering the soil, beneficial nematodes are attracted to the heat and carbon dioxide emitted by healthy larvae of destructive grubs. The nematodes enter the grubs through natural body openings and release a toxin that is fatal only to the grub. Death occurs within twenty-four to forty-eight hours. The nematode then reproduces, and its many progeny leave the host's body and begin seeking actively for other susceptible insect pest larvae. Beneficial or predatory nematodes can live in the soil and kill insects for many weeks, depending on the soil's moisture and temperature. For best results, be sure the soil is moist and its temperature is above 70°F. Predatory nematodes are effective through the growing season but will not winter over in enough numbers to continue to be helpful the next year.

Predatory nematodes control:

In the lawn—armyworms, Asiatic garden beetles, billbugs, Japanese beetle larvae, June beetles, leatherjackets/crane flies, oriental beetles, sod webworms, white grubs, wireworms. For most of the lawn grubs, especially the Japanese beetle grub, apply nematodes in the late summer or in midspring when the grubs are likely to be most active. Predatory nematodes, as a short-term solution, work well in concert with the more long-term milky spore disease described above.

In the flower garden—black vine weevil, cutworms, European chafers, flea beetles, fungus gnats, iris borers, masked chafers, mole crickets, root maggots, rose chafers, white-fringed beetles.

In the vegetable garden—cabbage root maggots, carrot weevils, citrus weevils, cucumber beetles, cutworms, flea beetles, mole crickets, onion maggots, root maggots, strawberry root weevils. For controlling cutworms, apply nematodes just before setting out transplants.

In trees and shrubs—While the product has not been fully approved for controlling borers, many gardeners around the country have found predatory nematodes useful in controlling borers already embedded in the stems and branches of tress or shrubs. Spray the liquid nematode solution on the affected branches at the site of visible borer holes. They will enter the hole and seek out the borer.

INSECTICIDES FOR USE AS A LAST RESORT—THE BIG BANGERS

The following insecticides are also very effective. They are, however, considerably more toxic to insect populations than the products listed above. This is in large part because they are broad-spectrum or general-use products and kill any insect in the area indiscriminantly. Their effectiveness is a function of their persistence in the environment. It is not necessary to spray the actual pest insect directly with these products. Sprayed on plant surfaces, they will linger, their potency sustained, anywhere from one to four days, depending on the product.

The products listed below have been selected as the safest of their type. They represent a backup weapon against landscape pest problems that do not yield to the products listed above as opening shots. Used properly and with restraint, these more powerful products are safe for use in the home landscape. They are listed below in order of least powerful to most powerful.

Never use any of these products as a general preventive spray all over the yard. They will all kill honeybees (except rotenone), butterflies, and beneficial insects. Use them to spot treat specific insect problems on specific plants to minimize their impact on the ecological balance of the yard. It is not necessary to have all of these products on hand; one or two will be sufficient to handle the rare overwhelming or especially stubborn pest invasion that is not controlled with the first-strike products above.

PYRETHRUM

Pyrethrum is a broad-spectrum natural botanical insecticide that works as a contact or stomach poison. It is an oil derived from the ground dried flowers of the African daisy and is now sold in both natural and synthetic form, both of which are equally effective. It also appears as a second ingredient in formulations of other insecticide products, some of which are more powerful than others. When combined with insecticidal soap it becomes more effective, especially against hard-shelled insects such as Japanese beetles.

Alone, pyrethrum is an effective general-purpose insecticide. It biodegrades in about six hours. Used late in the day, it will do its job and evaporate before the honeybees appear the next morning. It is now also sold in an encapsulated form. This means it is contained in little microscopic bubbles that are delivered in a spray from an aerosol can. What is significant about this technology is that the little bubbles protect the pyrethrum from biodegrading for several days, making it more effective for a longer period of time. However, this form of the product also makes it more dangerous for beneficial insects wandering by. The most powerful form of pyrethrum comes in combination with two other botanical poisons, rotenone and ryania. This material will kill the insect one or two different ways, improving the effectiveness of the product, but also making it more dangerous to the environment.

Pyrethrum, especially in combination with other products or in encapsulated form, will kill virtually any pest insect it comes in contact with. Poured into the soil as a drench, it will control insects a few inches below its surface. Because it does biodegrade within hours or days, it may be necessary to apply it again in five to seven days until most of the pests are accounted for. Pyrethrum quickly loses power when stored in open containers, but retains effectiveness up to three years in closed containers.

MALATHION

Malathion is sold as a wetable powder or an emulsifiable concentrate which mixes into a clear to amber liquid with a garlic odor. It is probably the safest of the widely used synthetic insecticides, somewhat less toxic to humans than rotenone and similar in toxicity to ryania and pyrethrum. Malathion retains its effectiveness on plant surfaces for one to three days. It kills virtually any pest insect it contacts. It is especially useful on vegetables and, because of its short life, is less toxic to beneficials than other synthetic materials.

CARBARYL

Carbaryl, generally sold as "Sevin," kills insects by contact. The insect must touch the material. The carbaryl then enters the insect's body through its outer shell and kills it by disrupting

	HORTICULTURAL OILS	INSECTICIDAL SOAP	BT	MILKY SPORE	NEMATODES	PYRETHRUM
Ants		X				X
Aphids	X	X				X
Bagworms			X			
Borers			X		X	
Caterpillars			X			X
Cucumber beetles				X	X	X
Flea beetles						X
Grubs				X	X	
Gypsy moths			X			
Japanese beetles				X	X	X
Lace bugs						
Leafhoppers		X				X
Leaf miners		X			X	
Mealybugs		X				X
Mites	X	X				X
Nematodes						
Scale	X	X				X
Slugs						
Thrips		X				X
Weevils					X	X
Whiteflies	X	X				X

the nervous system. Death occurs quite quickly. Sevin is usually sold in liquid form, either in a concentrate needing dilution or in a ready-to-use form, usually in a spray container. It will kill virtually any insect that comes into contact with it. If insect problems continue, spray them again within five to ten days of the first application. Sevin is extremely toxic to aquatic life. Do not use it near water or wetlands. When washing out spraying equipment, be very careful not to pour the rinsing water into a waterway or pond.

MALA-THION	CARBARYL	ROTENONE	DURSBAN
X	X		X
X	X	X	
X	X	X	
X	X	X	X
X	X	X	
			X
X	X		
X	X	X	X
X	X		
X	X	X	
X	X		
X	X	X	
X	X	X	
X	X	X	
X	X	X	
X	X	X	X
X	X	X	

ROTENONE

Rotenoids, the rotenone-related products, have been used as crop insecticides since 1848. Rotenoids are produced in the roots of two genera of the legume *Derris* grown in Malaya and the East Indies, and *Lonchocarpus* (also called cube) grown in South America. It is a contact as well as a stomach poison to insects and is sold both as spray concentrate and ready-to-use dust. It kills insects slowly, but causes them to stop their feeding almost immediately. Like all the other botanical insecticides, its life in the sun is short—about one to three days. It is effective in killing almost any insect it contacts.

DURSBAN

Chlorpyrifos is the active ingredient in dursban insecticides. Dursban kills the insect by contact. As the insect touches the material, it enters its body through its outer shell and kills it by disrupting its nervous system. While dursban will kill almost any insect on a residential property, we recommend that it be used only to deal with insects in and under the lawn. Lawn pests are very difficult to control, and dursban is the most effective, safest broad-spectrum product for this propose. Avoid using Diazinon, another common lawn pesticide. It has been banned by the EPA on public golf courses and in public parks because it kills songbirds. Dursban does not kill songbirds.

Dursban is a fairly persistent insecticide, especially if it is used in the soil. However, there is no evidence its prolonged potency in the soil hurts anything other than pest insects during this period. Spread on the lawn in granular form and watered in, Dursban lasts 127 to 287 days. Used as a drench, the better method, it lasts 111 to 187 days. Dursban resists dilution in water because it is strongly "sorbed" to soil particles, meaning it adheres or sticks to those particles. As a result, it is virtually immobile in the soil while it is sitting there. This means that the chances of its spreading into the ground water by runoff and leaching are virtually nil. Dursban will control the following lawn pest insects: ants, armyworms, billbugs, chinch bugs, fall web-worm, fleas, grasshoppers, millipedes, sod web-worms, ticks, white grubs, and wireworms,

HERBICIDES

Herbicides are poisons designed to kill weeds and other undesirable plants. Many are broad spectrum, so the danger with herbicides is that, improperly used, they will also kill the desirable plants nearby, such as lawn grass, flowers, vegetables, and small shrubs. The products listed below are safe products if used according to the instructions on the label. Each product has strengths and weaknesses, and each has a somewhat different purpose in the landscape.

GLYPHOSATE HERBICIDE
Known commercially as "Roundup" or "Kleenup," glyphosate herbicide is a very powerful grass and weed killer. Glyphosate herbicides are nonselective, meaning they will kill most nonwoody plants they come in contact with. When absorbed through the foliage of the plant, glyphosate is carried throughout the plant's system, providing complete kill, even of the roots. It works by blocking the production of certain proteins found only in vegetation, causing the plant to starve. It is necessary for homeowners to plan ahead for major projects and to be patient with this product, as it takes ten days to two weeks to show results.

Glyphosate products are very, very effective. They are excellent for use as step one of renovating a lawn, killing all existing grass and weeds in advance of seeding the new lawn grass. These products are also useful for killing weeds in gravel driveways or paths, along foundations, and in the cracks of concrete sidewalks. Gly-

phosate herbicides also kill some woody plants and vines, such as poison ivy and brambles; however, it usually takes a number of applications to be completely effective.

Because glyphosate herbicide must contact the leaves and stems of plants that are actively growing to be effective, it doesn't work on plants before they emerge from the soil, nor on ones that are dormant in the winter. It is most effective on plants that are partially mature. To avoid killing desirable plants growing in close quarters with unwanted target weeds, protect them with a barrier of paper or other material. It may be necessary to daub the herbicide on the target plant with a brush, to protect nearby ornamental plants. Do not spray glyphosate herbicide on windy days or when the temperature is below 40°F.

These products are harmless to people, pets, birds, earthworms, and the microbiotic life in the soil. They bind with the soil and do not leach into ground water. They are broken down by soil microbes in about four to six months. The product has no residual soil activity.

SOAP-BASED HERBICIDE
A soap-based herbicide sold under the name of "SharpShooter" is a broad-spectrum vegetation killer that destroys plants on contact. It works only on herbaceous, nonwoody plants. It's made of potassium salts of saturated fatty acids, which are soaplike materials. When this herbicide is sprayed on a plant, it causes the plant to desiccate, or lose water rapidly. It causes a visible reaction in target weeds within hours in most cases, and they die within a day or two. This product is particularly good with fleshy annual weeds, such as lamb's quarters, chickweed, and purslane, that have fairly shallow root systems. Perennial weeds, such as dandelion and Cana-

dian thistle, usually require two or three applications over the season to kill them off and are more appropriately treated with glyphosate herbicide if it is on hand. Used for weeds in a lawn, soap-based herbicide will kill nearby grass plants as well. It may be necessary to reseed the bare spot with a turf patch kit.

2,4-D HERBICIDE

Sold under many different product names, 2,4-D is an herbicide designed to kill broad-leaved weeds, especially those in lawns. It does not kill grass. It is effective in controlling dandelions, clover, plantain, and many other broad-leaved lawn weeds. A systemic herbicide, 2,4-D is easily absorbed by the foliage on which it is sprayed and is translocated throughout the treated plant, which dies in seven to fourteen days. In the soil, 2,4-D residues usually dissipate within a month (primarily due to microbial degradation). Do not use this product in warm weather when temperatures exceed 80°F. Use this powerful product only to spot treat small areas of the lawn containing broad-leaved weeds. If the weeds cover more than 50 percent of the turf area, then use a glyphosate herbicide and replant the lawn.

APPENDIX B
Vegetable Seed Planting Guide

If starting vegetables from seed, plant them at the following depths and distances apart. All distances are given in inches unless otherwise indicated.

CROP	PLANTING DEPTH FOR SEEDS	INTENSIVE PLANTING DISTANCE FOR SEEDS/PLANTS
Beans, snap bush	1–2	4
Beans, snap pole	1–1 ½	6
Beans, lima bush	1 ½–2	4–6
Beans, lima pole	1 ½–2	6–8
Broccoli	¼–½	12–14
Cabbage	½	12–16
Cabbage, Chinese	½	10–12
Carrots	¼	2–3
Cucumbers	1	12 when trellised
Eggplant	¼–½	18–24
Lettuce, leaf	¼–½	4–6
Peas, green	2	2–4
Peas, snap	2	2–4
Peppers, hot	¼	2–15
Peppers, bell	¼	12–15
Tomatoes	½	12–18

APPENDIX C

How Much to Plant in the Vegetable Patch?

This chart provides a rough estimate of how much you can expect to harvest from twelve square feet of planting.

CROP	APPROXIMATE YIELD FROM 12 SQ.FT. OF BED (3 × 4 FT.)
Beans, snap	10–15 pounds
Beans, lima	4–5 pounds
Broccoli	8–12 pounds
Cabbage	12–25 pounds
Cabbage, Chinese	10–15 pounds
Carrots	12–20 pounds
Cucumbers	20–35 pounds
Eggplant	20–40 pounds
Lettuce, leaf	12–15 pounds
Peas, green	3–7 pounds
Peas, snap	6–10 pounds
Peppers, hot	50–60 peppers
Peppers, bell	30–40 peppers
Tomatoes	20–30 pounds

APPENDIX D

Container Planting Guide for Vegetables

These instructions give the minimum-size container needed. Anything larger will do just fine. Unlike with flowers and shrubs, use garden soil mixed with some peat moss for the growing medium.

Beans, pole: One plant per twelve-inch-deep container holding at least a half gallon of soil. Rig a six-foot-tall trellis or pole to support the mature plant. Plant three plants in a five-gallon container, first rigging a three-pole tepee and then setting in the plants.

Broccoli: One plant per three-gallon container twenty inches deep.

Cabbage: One plant per one- to two-gallon container twelve inches deep.

Cabbage, Chinese: One plant per three-gallon container twenty inches deep.

Carrots: As many plants as an eight-inch-deep pot can handle. Be sure the container is deep enough; even the shortest carrot varieties must have plenty of space.

Cucumbers: One plant per one- to two-gallon container for bush type.

Eggplant: One plant per five-gallon container at least twelve inches deep. Embed a stake or a cage in the soil to support the plant.

Lettuce, leaf: One plant per pint of soil in a container at least six inches deep.

Peas, snap: One quart of soil for each plant in containers that are least twelve inches deep. Erect a trellis at least four feet tall.

Peppers: One plant per five-gallon container at least twelve inches deep. Provide a stake or a cage to support the plant.

Tomatoes: One plant per five-gallon container at least twelve inches deep. Provide a sturdy stake or a cage to support the plant.

Best Varieties of Vegetables for Container Gardening

Beans, pole	Any	Eggplant	'Dusky', 'Morden Midget'
Broccoli	'Crusader Hybrid'	Lettuce, leaf	Any
Cabbage	'Baby Head', 'Dwarf Morden'	Peas, snap	Any
Cabbage, Chinese	Bok choy, michihli, wong bok	Peppers, hot	Any
Carrots	'Baby finger Nates', 'Gold Nugget', 'Oxheart', 'Short n' Sweet', 'Tiny Sweet'	Peppers, bell	Any
		Tomatoes	Only determinate varieties of regular-size tomatoes such as 'Celebrity' or the small container hybrids or cherry tomatoes such as 'Patio Hybrid', 'Pixie Hybrid II', 'Basket King Hybrid', and 'Tiny Tim'
Cucumbers	'Bush Crop', 'Patio Pic', 'Pot Luck', 'Spacemaster'		

APPENDIX E
Vegetable Growing Guide

This chart indicates which vegetables can handle a little frost. It also shows how long it takes the vegetables to become ripe and how long the harvest period will last. The "T" after some of the numbers indicates the average days of maturity from the date of transplanting. Transplants are likely to be four to six weeks old already.

	FROST TOLERANCE	AVERAGE DAYS TO MATURITY	HARVEST PERIOD
Beans, snap	none	48–95	4 to 5 weeks
Beans lima	none	60–80	3 to 4 weeks
Broccoli	very good	60–80T	8 to 10 weeks
Cabbage	good	60–95T	4 to 6 weeks
Cabbage, Chinese	very good	80–90T	4 to 6 weeks
Carrots	good	65–76	6 to 8 weeks
Cucumbers	none	50–70	4 to 6 weeks
Eggplant	none	75–95T	until frost
Lettuce, leaf	some	45–60	4 to 6 weeks
Peas, green	some	55–85	1 to 2 weeks
Peas, snap	some	70	2 to 3 weeks
Peppers	none	60–75T	until frost
Tomatoes	none	52–80T	until frost

APPENDIX F
Vegetable Feeding and Watering Guide

Throughout this book, including the vegetable chapter, one spring application of a granular slow-release nitrogen fertilizer is recommended. This main meal is sufficient to produce healthy plants of all kinds over the whole season. This chart shows those vegetables which might appreciate a supplemental snack, either heavy or light. It also indicates which of the common vegetables are particularly heavy water users.

	FEEDING NEEDS	WATERING NEEDS
Beans, snap	*Light*	*Medium*
Beans lima	*Light*	*Heavy*
Broccoli	*Heavy*	*Medium to heavy*
Cabbage	*Heavy*	*Medium*
Cabbage, Chinese	*Medium*	*Medium*
Carrots	*Light*	*Medium*
Cucumbers	*Heavy*	*Heavy*
Eggplant	*Heavy*	*Heavy*
Lettuce, leaf	*Heavy*	*Light to medium*
Peas, green	*Light*	*Light to medium*
Peas, snap	*Light*	*Light to medium*
Peppers	*Medium*	*Medium to heavy*
Tomatoes	*Heavy*	*Heavy*

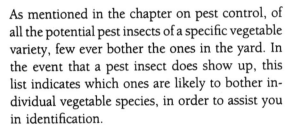

APPENDIX C
Common Pests That Might Turn Up in Your Vegetable Patch

As mentioned in the chapter on pest control, of all the potential pest insects of a specific vegetable variety, few ever bother the ones in the yard. In the event that a pest insect does show up, this list indicates which ones are likely to bother individual vegetable species, in order to assist you in identification.

BEANS, SNAP OR LIMA
Common—aphids, Japanese beetles, and especially Mexican bean beetles
Occasional—corn earworms, cucumber beetles, flea beetles, leaf miners, slugs, and whiteflies

BROCCOLI, CABBAGE, AND CHINESE CABBAGE
Common—aphids, cabbage loopers, cutworms, slugs, and especially the imported cabbage worm
Occasional—cabbage maggots, flea beetles, mites, and whiteflies

CARROTS
Common—carrot rust flies, carrot weevils, and parsleyworms
Occasional—leafhoppers and wireworms

CUCUMBERS
Common—aphids, slugs, and especially cucumber beetles
Occasional—squash bugs and squash vine borers

EGGPLANT
Common—aphids, Colorado potato beetles, and especially flea beetles
Occasional—cutworms, cucumber beetles, mites, and whiteflies

LETTUCE, LEAF
Common—aphids and especially slugs
Occasional—cabbage loopers, cutworms, leafhoppers, and wireworms

PEAS
Common—aphids are the most common
Occasional—cabbage maggots, cucumber beetles, weevils, and whiteflies. Songbirds, such as cardinals, love peas, especially snap peas.

PEPPERS
Common—aphids and tomato hornworms
Occasional—cutworms, European corn borers, flea beetles, and mites

TOMATOES
Common—aphids, tomato hornworms, whiteflies, and especially slugs
Occasional—Colorado potato beetles, corn earworms, cutworms, flea beetles, and mites

APPENDIX H
WHEN TO PICK VEGETABLE CROPS

When growing a vegetable for the first time, it is sometimes difficult to anticipate how soon it will be time to pick the crop. The paragraphs below provide some information on readiness for harvest.

Beans, green: Ready two to three weeks after first bloom when pods snap readily but the tips are still pliable. Pick before the seeds fill out pods. Wax (yellow) beans are slower than green beans to mature. Remember, bush beans give only one harvest, while pole beans, which ripen later in the season, provide beans for the rest of the season as long as the ripe ones are picked regularly.

Beans, lima: Pick when pods are well-filled and plump, but still bright-colored. The end of the pod should feel spongy when squeezed between your fingers.

Broccoli: Cut central head while buds are still compact and not showing any yellow color. Little yellow flowers indicate that the head is overripe and is preparing to make seed. Cut off the main head to encourage more side shoots to develop. Continue to harvest the smaller side shoots to encourage the plant to form more. It is not un-

common to eventually harvest more weight in side shoots than the weight of the original head.

Cabbage: Pick cabbage when its head grows obviously heavy for its size and is firm when squeezed. Heads that split have passed their prime.

Cabbage, Chinese: Cut types that form heads as soon as they reach usable size. Harvest leaf types a fewer outer leaves at a time, or cut the entire plant for a single harvest.

Carrots: Even though the sugar content is greater in mature carrots with big roots, pick them while they are small. The top that shows at the soil surface should be no more than 1 to 1½ inches in diameter. Roots should be firm but tender, and well-colored.

Cucumbers: They are at their best when dark green, firm, and of moderate size. Overripe fruit is yellow and tough. Regular picking stimulates continuous production.

Eggplant: Bigger is not better. Pick eggplants when the fruit reaches usable size, about three to five inches long. Look for shiny, deep purple skin. Dull skin and brown seeds are signs of overripe fruit.

Lettuce, leaf: Start harvesting a few outer leaves as soon as they reach usable size, about two inches long. Continue picking outer leaves for ongoing harvest until seed stalk appears.

Peas, green: Pods should be fairly well filled but still bright green. Raw peas should taste sweet. Harvest lower pods first. Regular picking stimulates continued production.

Peas, snap: The older, the sweeter—up to a point. Harvest before peas touch each other in the pod for the sweetest flavor and crunchiest texture.

Peppers, hot: Ready when fruit is shiny with uniformly colored skin. Peppers do not get hotter the longer they're left on the plant. They will usually turn red as they ripen but can be eaten in their green or yellow color, before the red appears.

Peppers, bell: Skin should be firm and shiny; fruit is green at first, but will turn red if left to mature on the plant. They are edible when either color. The bigger the pepper, the thicker its skin.

Tomatoes: Ripe fruit will have a rich color and feel firm. It will detach from its stem easily. The mature size of ripened tomatoes is governed by their variety. Tomatoes will ripen after picking, but vine-ripened fruit tastes the best.

APPENDIX I
Fresh Vegetable Storage Tips

To benefit from the value of fresh vegetables from the backyard or from the grocery store, it is important to store them properly. These tips assure maximum flavor and nutritional value.

Beans, snap: Can store in plastic bags for two to five days in the refrigerator.

Beans, lima: Can refrigerate unshelled lima beans for up to two weeks in plastic bags.

Broccoli: Always soak broccoli briefly in cold salted water to eliminate any pests that may be hiding in the dense head. Place the trimmed broccoli in a cup or glass of water and refrigerate. Alternatively, rinse and store in a clear plastic bag for ten to fourteen days.

Cabbage and Chinese cabbage: Can refrigerate cabbage heads in plastic bags for one to two weeks.

Carrots: Cut off the foliage tops and discard them, then wash. Can refrigerate carrots in plastic bags for two to four weeks.

Cucumbers: Cucumbers keep best in a cool, moist environment with temperatures ranging from 40° to 50°F and a humidity of 95 percent. Refrigerated in plastic bags or a hydrator drawer they will keep five to ten days.

Eggplant: Do not refrigerate eggplants. They are best stored in a cupboard at room temperature. They will last only three to five days.

Lettuce, leaf: Wash lettuce and store slightly wet in the refrigerator in a plastic bag or a container with a tight lid. It will keep for over a week.

Peas: Peas are best when used quickly after harvest. However, refrigerated in their pods in plastic bags, they will keep two to four days.

Peppers: Refrigerate peppers in plastic bags. They will keep one to two weeks.

Tomatoes: Keep unripened tomatoes at room temperature but out of the sun. When they ripen, refrigerate them. They will keep about a week. Store fully ripened tomatoes in the refrigerator if they are not to be used immediately. For best flavor, allow chilled tomatoes to reach room temperature before serving.

APPENDIX J
RESOURCES

GENERAL SOURCES FOR TOOLS AND SUPPLIES

The following mail order companies offer a comprehensive range of tools and supplies for caring for the yard and garden. Almost everything discussed in this book is sold by one of these companies. Order their catalogs and keep them on hand.

Alsto Company
P.O. Box 1267
Gatesburg, IL 61401
800–447–0048

Denman & Company
2913 Saturn Street
Suite G
Brea, CA 92621
714–524–0668

Gardener's Supply Company
128 Intervale Road
Burlington, VT 05401
802–863–1700

Kinsman Garden Company
River Road
Point Pleasant, PA 18950
215–297–5613

Natural Gardening Research Center
Highway 48
P.O. Box 149
Sunman, IN 47041
812–623–3800

Necessary Trading Company
New Castle, VA 24127
800–447–5354

Plow & Hearth
560 Main Street
Madison, VA 22727
800–627–1712

Ringer Corporation
9959 Valley View Road
Eden Prairie, MN 55344–3585
800-654-1047

SOURCES OF PLANTS AND SEEDS

The following companies offer numerous annual seeds, perennial seeds and seedlings, bulbs, shrubs, and trees. Some also include many basic tools and supplies.

Burpee Seed Company
300 Park Avenue
Warminster, PA 18974
215–674–9633

Gurney Seed & Nursery Company
Page Street
Yankton, SD 57079
605–665–4451

Johnny's Selected Seeds
Foss Hill Road
P.O. Box 2580
Albion, ME 04910
207–437–4301

Park Seed Company
P.O. Box 31
Greenwood, SC 29647
800–845–3369

Stokes Seed Company
Box 548
Buffalo, NY 14240
416–688–4300

Tomato Growers Supply Company
P.O. Box 2237
Fort Myers, FL 33902
813–768–1119

Wayside Gardens
1 Garden Lane
Hodges, SC 29695–0001
800–845–1124

Whiteflower Farm
Litchfield, CT 06759–0050
800–888–7756

Stark Bros. Nurseries
Louisiana, MO, 63353
800–325–4160

Musser Trees
P.O. Box S-91 M
Indiana, PA 15701
412–465–5685

Miller Nurseries
West Lake Road
Canandaigua, NY 14424
800–836–9630

INFORMATION RESOURCES

The most comprehensive and updated listing of sources for virtually everything a yardener might need is *Gardening by Mail—A Source Book*, by Barbara J. Barton (Houghton Mifflin Company, Boston, 1990, $16.95).

Further information on edible gardening is provided by *The Complete Book of Edible Landscaping*, by Rosalind Creasy, Sierra Club Books, 1982.

Designing and Maintaining Your Edible Landscape Naturally, by Robert Kourik, Metamorphic Press, 1986.

Another good souce of mail-order gardening products is a listing available for $1: "The Complete Guide to Gardening by Mail," published by the Mail Order Association of Nurseries, 8683 Doves Fly Way, Laurel, MD 20707 (301–490–9143).

The Lawn Institute, County Line Road, P.O. Box 108, Pleasant Hill, TN (615–277–3722) offers free information about lawn care.

Every county in the United States has a County Extension Service which offers information and advice on all aspects of gardening and yard care. They are often associated with the state university system. Consult the telephone book for the number of a nearby office.

SPECIALIZED SOURCES

The companies listed below offer products that are not necessarily available from the general merchandisers listed above. They sell products or items that are referenced at some point in this book.

Wildflower sod:
Applewood Seed Company
5380 Vivian Street
Arvada, CO 80002

Wildflower seed mixes in cans:
Clyde Robin Seed Company
25670 Nickel Place
Hayward, CA 94545

Porous drip irrigation:
Aquapore Moisture Systems
225 Larkin Drive
Suite 4
Wheeling, IL 60090

Emitter drip irrigation:
Raindrip, Inc.
14675 Titus Street
Panorama City, CA 91402

Compost tumblers and shredders:
Kemp Corporation
160 Koser Road
Lititz, PA 17543

Small suburban tiller:
Mantis Manufacturing Co.
1458 County Line Road
Huntingdon Valley, PA 19006

General purpose shredder:
Amerind Mackissic Inc.
P.O. Box 111
Parker Ford, PA 19457
215–495–7181

Tornado Products, Inc.
N114 W18605 Clinton Drive
Germantown, WI 53022
414–251–4600

Deer protectors for young trees:
Tubex
75 Bidwell Street
Suite 105
St. Paul, MN 55107
800–328–4826

APPENDIX K
USDA Plant Hardiness Map

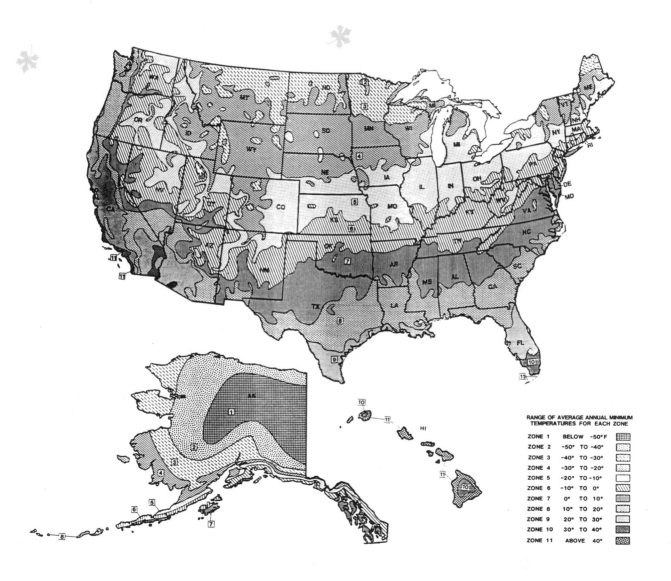

RANGE OF AVERAGE ANNUAL MINIMUM TEMPERATURES FOR EACH ZONE	
ZONE 1	BELOW −50°F
ZONE 2	−50° TO −40°
ZONE 3	−40° TO −30°
ZONE 4	−30° TO −20°
ZONE 5	−20° TO −10°
ZONE 6	−10° TO 0°
ZONE 7	0° TO 10°
ZONE 8	10° TO 20°
ZONE 9	20° TO 30°
ZONE 10	30° TO 40°
ZONE 11	ABOVE 40°

Index

Trees and shrubs (*cont.*)
on, 80; watering, 55–57, 75, 79; as windbreaks, 222, 223
Trellises, 138, *138*, 139–141

Utility areas, in home landscapes, 227–228

Vegetables, 119–146, 150; approximate yield from 12 sq. ft. bed, 249; beneficial insects attracted by, 178; birds attracted by, 180; boxed beds, 130–131, *136*, 137; choosing what to grow, 131–132; compost for, 172; containerized, 122, 127, 250–251; extended growing seasons, 141, 142–144, *144*, 145–146; fertilizing, 122, 123, 253; fresh, storage tips for, 257; growing guide, 252; grown for fun, 120–128; intensive planting, 132–133, *133*, 134; late fall garden, 145–146; light conditions, 121, 128; maintenance tasks, 134–137; mulching, 134–135, 143; pests and disease, 135, 138, 201, 204, 209, 254; planting seedlings, 122–123; raised beds, 129–130, *130*, 131, 133, *133*, *136*, 137; seed planting guide, 248; seeds vs. seedlings, 122–123; small beds of, 128–142; soil for, 121–122, 129–130, 132, 134–137,

143; temperature preferences, 132, 134, 142–146; times to pick crops, 255–256; trellises for, 138, *138*, 139–141; types of, 121, 123–128, 137–142; vertically grown, 137–138, *138*, 139–142; watering, 123, 135–136, *136*, 137, 253
Vertical growing, 137–138
Vinca, 3, 50, 79
Vines, 234; birds attracted by, 182; suitable for screens, 215; on trees, 80
Viral diseases, 188–189
Vitamins, 21, 52, 54–55

Waste, yard. *See* Yard waste management
Watering, 97, 178, 179, 213, 229, *230*, 233; drip irrigation, 135–136, *136*, 137, 230, *230*, 231; flowers, 97, 99, 113; lawns, 17, 19, 23–25, 27, 28; systems, 24–25, 229, 230, *230*, 231; trees and shrubs, 55–57, 75, 79; vegetables, 123, 135–136, *136*, 137, 253
Weeds, 50, 220, 234; beneficial insects attracted by, 178; birds attracted by, 183; for compost, 159; lawn, 18, 28, 30–31; mulch to control, 150; vegetable garden, 134
Weevils, 188, 208–209
Whiteflies, 186, 187, 188, 209–210

Wildflower ground covers, 218–220
Wildlife, plants for, 222–225
Windbreaks, trees as, 222, 223
Winter landscapes, plants for decoration in, 226
Winter protection of trees and shrubs, 62–64, 79
Woodchip(s): paths and driveways, 156, 228; used in yard waste management, 150, 153, 156, 160
Worms, 191; composting, 166–167, *167*, 168

Xeriscape landscape, 97

Yard cleanup, for pest control, 184
Yard waste management, 147–172; chopped leaves, 147, 149, 150, 151–154, *154*, 155, 156, 158, 159, *163*, 164–172; composting, 157–172; grass clippings, 7, *16*, 20, 21, 23, 27, 148–149, 153, 156, 158–159, 160, 164–172; kitchen waste (nonmeat), 149, 157, 158, 159–160, *163*, 167–168; mulching, 149–156; recycling, 148, 157–172; reducing, 147–149; reusing, 148, 149–156; tools for, 152–154, *154*, 155, 159, 162–163, *163*; woodchips, 150, 153, 156, 160

Zones, USDA Hardiness, 103

DESIGN YOUR OWN CUSTOMIZED YARDENING BOOK

Jeff and Liz Ball have an extensive collection of four- to six-page plant care tip sheets and related yardening guides covering over two hundred of the most common trees, shrubs, and other plants grown in the North. The list of tip sheets is organized by topic according to the chapters in this book. Select tip sheets for all the plants on your property and you'll have the most comprehensive yardening book you could possibly own; a book customized to your very own landscape.

CHAPTER ONE
LAWN CARE
_____(5001) Caring For Northern Lawns
_____(5016) Renovating Northern Lawns
_____(5002) Watering The Landscape
_____(5003) Fertilizing The Landscape
_____(5005) Vitamins For The Landscape

CHAPTER TWO
TAKING CARE OF TREES AND SHRUBS
_____(5006) Planting Trees & Shrubs
_____(5011) Winter Protection For Plants
_____(5033) Pruning Trees & Shrubs

SHRUBS
_____(1003) Andromeda, Japanese
_____(1005) Arborvitae, American
_____(1006) Arborvitae, Oriental
_____(1008) Azalea, Deciduous
_____(1009) Azalea, Evergreen
_____(1010) Barberry, Japanese
_____(1013) Boxwood, Common
_____(1014) Boxwood, Littleleaf
_____(1201) Butterfly Bush
_____(1202) Cherrylaurel
_____(1023) Cotoneaster, Tall
_____(1022) Cotoneaster, Spreading
_____(1216) Crape Myrtle
_____(1175) Daphen, Fragrant
_____(1174) Dogwood, Red Twig
_____(1030) Euonymnus, Evergreen
_____(1031) Euonymus, Winged
_____(1032) Euonymus, Wintercreeper
_____(1025) Falsecypress [Hinoki/Sawara]
_____(1034) Firethorn
_____(1035) Forsythia, Border
_____(1038) Hibiscus, Rose of Sharon
_____(1040) Holly, American
_____(1041) Holly, Chinese
_____(1042) Holly, English
_____(1043) Holly, Inkberry
_____(1044) Holly, Japanese
_____(1045) Holly, Meserve
_____(1046) Holly, Winterberry
_____(1181) Hydrangea, Bigleaf

____(1048) Hydrangea, Oakleaf
____(1183) Hydrangea, Panicle
____(1049) Hypericum, St. John's-wort
____(1050) Juniper, Chinese
____(1051) Juniper, Common
____(1178) Juniper, Creeping
____(1052) Juniper, Jap. Garden
____(1179) Juniper, Savin
____(1053) Juniper, Singleseed
____(1055) Laurel, Mountain
____(1056) Lilac, Common
____(1064) Mock Orange
____(1071) Peony, Tree
____(1176) Potentilla
____(1076) Privet, Northern
____(1078) Rhododendron
____(1079) Rose, Bush
____(1080) Rose, Climbing
____(1081) Rose, Miniature
____(1082) Spirea, Vanhoutte
____(1085) Viburnum, Doublefile
____(1086) Viburnum, Eur. Cranberry
____(1087) Viburnum, Judd
____(1208) Viburnum, Leatherleaf
____(1207) Weigela
____(1091) Witch Hazel
____(1093) Yew [English/Japanese]

TREES
____(1001) Acacia, Bailey
____(1002) Almond, Flowering
____(1004) Apple, Fruiting
____(1007) Ash [White/Green]
____(1065) Ash, Mountain
____(1011) Beech, American
____(1177) Beech, European
____(1012) Birch, White [River/Paper]
____(1015) Catalpa, Northern
____(1016) Cedar, Atlas
____(1197) Cedar, Deodar

____(1018) Cherry, Fruiting
____(1017) Cherry, Ornamental
____(1019) Cherry, Purple-leaved Sand
____(1170) Cherry, Weeping
____(1020) Chestnut, Chinese
____(1024) Crabapple, Flowering
____(1217) Cypress, Leyland
____(1184) Dogwood, Cornelian Cherry
____(1026) Dogwood, Flowering
____(1027) Dogwood, Japanese
____(1028) Douglas Fir
____(1029) Elm, Chinese [Lacebark]
____(1033) Fir, White
____(1036) Hawthorn
____(1037) Hemlock, Eastern
____(1039) Hickory, Shagbark
____(1047) Honeylocust
____(1077) Juniper, Eastern Redcedar
____(1054) Larch, American [Tamarack]
____(1198) Larch, European
____(1057) Linden, American [Basswood]
____(1185) Linden, Littleleaf
____(1058) Locust, Black
____(1059) Magnolia
____(1060) Maple, Japanese
____(1061) Maple, Norway
____(1062) Maple, Silver/Sugar
____(1190) Oak, Live
____(1067) Oak, Pin
____(1192) Oak, White
____(1193) Oak, Willow
____(1069) Peach, Fruiting
____(1270) Pear, Fruiting
____(1204) Pear, Ornamental [Bradford]
____(1194) Pine, Loblolly
____(1072) Pine, Mugo
____(1073) Pine, White
____(1199) Planetree, London
____(1074) Plum, Flowering
____(1075) Poplar, Eastern [Cottonwood]

CHAPTER THREE
FLOWERS IN THE LANDSCAPE

PERENNIALS

BULBS

CHAPTER SIX
DEALING WITH PESTS
____(5010) Spring Cleanup
____(5017) Controlling Weeds
____(5018) Basic Pest Medicine Kit
____(5019) Using Insecticidal Soap
____(5020) Controlling Grubs
____(5021) Contolling Borers
____(5022) Controlling Aphids
____(5023) Controlling Mites
____(5024) Controlling Slugs
____(5025) Controlling Poison Ivy
____(5026) Controlling Moles
____(5027) Controlling Deer
____(5028) Controlling Rabbits

____(5029) Controlling Squirrels
____(5039) Using Predatory Nematodes
____(5040) Using Dursban Insecticide
____(5041) Using Bacillus thuriengensis
____(5042) Using Horticultural Oils
____(5043) Using Pyrethrum Insecticide
____(5044) Using 2, 4–D Herbicide
____(5045) Using Roundup Herbicide
____(5046) Using Malathion Insecticide
____(5047) Using Carbaryl Insecticide

CHAPTER SEVEN
VALUE OF LANDSCAPING
____(5015) Thinking About Landscape Design
____(5048) Using Drip Irrigation
____(5049) Outdoor Lighting Systems

ORDER YOUR PLANT AND YARD CARE TIP SHEETS NOW!

Name_____

Street Address_____

City_____State_____Zip_____

If we need to call you about this order: Phone Number_____

_____Tip Sheets @ $1.00   _____

3-Ring Binder @ $5.00   _____

6% Sales Tax for PA residents   _____

Handling & Postage   _____$2.50_____

Total Enclosed   _____

Mail check and order form to:

New Response, Inc.
Box 338
Springfield, PA 19064